THEORIES OF
MANAGEMENT

McGRAW-HILL SERIES IN MANAGEMENT
Keith Davis, Consulting Editor

Allen Management and Organization
Allen The Management Profession
Argyris Management and Organizational Development: The Path from XA to YB
Beckett Management Dynamics: The New Synthesis
Benton Supervision and Management
Bergen and Haney Organizational Relations and Management Action
Blough International Business: Environment and Adaptation
Bowman Management: Organization and Planning
Brown Judgment in Administration
Campbell, Dunnette, Lawler, and Weick Managerial Behavior, Performance, and Effectiveness
Cleland and King Management: A Systems Approach
Cleland and King Systems Analysis and Project Management
Cleland and King Systems, Organizations, Analysis, Management: A Book of Readings
Dale Management: Theory and Practice
Dale Readings in Management: Landmarks and New Frontiers
Davis Human Behavior at Work: Human Relations and Organizational Behavior
Davis Organizational Behavior: A Book of Readings
Davis and Blomstrom Business and Society: Environment and Responsibility
DeGreene Systems Psychology
Dunn and Rachel Wage and Salary Administration: Total Compensation Systems
Dunn and Stephens Management of Personnel: Manpower Management and Organizational Behavior
Edmunds and Letey Environmental Administration
Fiedler A Theory of Leadership Effectiveness
Flippo Principles of Personnel Management
Glueck Business Policy: Strategy Formation and Management Action
Golembiewski Men, Management, and Morality
Hicks The Management of Organizations: A Systems and Human Resources Approach
Hicks and Gullett Modern Business Management: A Systems and Environmental Approach
Johnson, Kast, and Rosenzweig The Theory and Management of Systems
Kast and Rosenzweig Organization and Management: A Systems Approach
Knudson, Woodworth, and Bell Management: An Experiential Approach
Koontz Toward a Unified Theory of Management
Koontz and O'Donnell Essentials of Management
Koontz and O'Donnell Management: A Book of Readings
Koontz and O'Donnell Principles of Management: An Analysis of Managerial Functions
Levin, McLaughlin, Lamone, and Kottas Production/Operations Management: Contemporary Policy for Managing Operating Systems
Luthans Contemporary Readings in Organizational Behavior
Luthans Organizational Behavior
McNichols Policy Making and Executive Action
Maier Problem-solving Discussions and Conferences: Leadership Methods and Skills
Margulies and Raia Organizational Development: Values, Process, and Technology

Mayer   Production and Operations Management

Miles   Theories of Management: Implications for Organizational Behavior and Development

Mundel   A Conceptual Framework for the Management Sciences

Newstrom, Reif, and Monczka   A Contingency Approach to Management: Readings

Petit   The Moral Crisis in Management

Petrof, Carusone, and McDavid   Small Business Management: Concepts and Techniques for Improving Decisions

Pigors and Pigors   Case Method in Human Relations

Porter, Lawler, and Hackman   Behavior in Organizations

Prasow and Peters   Arbitration and Collective Bargaining: Conflict Resolution in Labor Relations

Ready   The Administrator's Job

Reddin   Managerial Effectiveness

Richman and Copen   International Management and Economic Development

Sartain and Baker   The Supervisor and His Job

Schrieber, Johnson, Meier, Fischer, and Newell   Cases in Manufacturing Management

Shore   Operations Management

Shull, Delbecq, and Cummings   Organizational Decision Making

Steiner   Managerial Long-Range Planning

Sutermeister   People and Productivity

Tannenbaum, Weschler, and Massarik   Leadership and Organization

Vance   Industrial Administration

THEORIES OF MANAGEMENT:
IMPLICATIONS FOR ORGANIZATIONAL BEHAVIOR AND DEVELOPMENT

Raymond E. Miles

Professor of Business Administration
Associate Director, Institute of Industrial Relations
University of California, Berkeley

McGraw-Hill Book Company
New York   St. Louis   San Francisco   Düsseldorf   Johannesburg
Kuala Lumpur   London   Mexico   Montreal   New Delhi   Panama
Paris   São Paulo   Singapore   Sydney   Tokyo   Toronto

THEORIES OF MANAGEMENT:
Implications for Organizational Behavior and Development

234567890KPKP798765

Library of Congress Cataloging in Publication Data

Miles, Raymond E
  Theories of management.

  (McGraw-Hill series in management)
  1. Management. 2. Organizational change.
3. Psychology, Industrial. I. Title.
HD38.M484   658.4   74-13529
ISBN 0-07-041927-2

This book was set in Times Roman by Black Dot, Inc. The
editors were Thomas H. Kothman, Sonia Sheldon, and Claudia
A. Hepburn; the designer was Pencils Portfolio, Inc.; the pro-
duction supervisor was Judi Frey. The drawings were done by
Vantage Art, Inc.
Kingsport Press, Inc., was printer and binder.

CONTENTS

Preface   xiii

Introduction   1

    Why a Book?   2
    Why This Particular Book?   3
        Management Theories 3
        Organization Dynamics 5
    From Whence These Views   5

Chapter 1   A General Conceptual Framework   8

    Some Characteristics of Organizations   9
    Organization Variables   9
        Goals   11
        Technology   13
        Structure   14
    Human Variables   15
        Capabilities   16
        Attitudes, Values, and Needs 17
        Demographic Characteristics 17

Chapter 2   The Role of Management   20

    Integrative Mechanisms   21
    Range of Alternatives   22
        Direction   22
        Organization and Job Design 23
        Selection and Training—Appraisal and
           Development 23
        Communications and Control 23
        Reward Systems   24

Linkages Across Mechanisms   24
Evidence of Consistency and Inconsistency   26
　　Example 1—Recruitment, Training, and Job
　　　Design   26
　　Example 2—Direction, Controls, and Rewards   27
　　Example 3—Policies, Job Design, and Controls   27
　　Example 4—Delegation and Controls   28
Determinants of a Managerial System   28
The Completed Model   29

Chapter 3   Managers' Theories of Management   **31**

Do Managers Have "Theories"?   32
　　Sources and Impact of Managers' Theories   33
　　Managers' Theories versus Scholars' Theories   34
Three Managerial Theories or Models   34
　　The Traditional Model   36
　　The Human Relations Model   39
　　The Human Resources Model   41
Implications for the Managerial Role   43
　　Which Theories Do Managers Actually Hold?   45
　　Which Theory Should Managers Hold?   47

Chapter 4   Job Design   **51**

Job Design under the Three Managerial Models   52
　　Job Design under the Traditional Model   53
　　Job Design under the Human Relations Model   54
　　Job Design under the Human Resources Model   55
The Impact of Technology and the Environment   57
　　Assumptions of Stability   57
　　Recognition of Variability   58
Some Examples of Job Design   59
　　Organization A—Stable Environment, Traditional
　　　Job Design   59
　　Organization B—Stable Environment, Traditional
　　　Job Design   60
　　Organization C—Stable Environment, Human
　　　Relations Job Design   61
　　Organization D—Stable Environment, Human
　　　Resources Job Design   63
　　Organization E—Turbulent Environment,
　　　Traditional Job Design   64

Organization F—Turbulent Environment, Human
    Resources Job Design   66
Concluding Remarks   67

Chapter 5   Organization Design   72

The Process of Organization Design   74
Traditional Organization Structure   75
    Relationship to Traditional Theory   75
    The Traditional Organization and Its
        Environment   80
Human Relations Organization Structure   81
    The Human Relations Organization and Its
        Environment   83
Human Resources Organizational Structure   84
    The Human Resources Organization and Its
        Environment   90
Concluding Remarks   92

Chapter 6   Communications and Control Systems   96

One View of Communications and Control Systems   97
    Example 1—The Line Supervisor   97
    Example 2—The New Cost Control Unit   98
Communications and Control under the Traditional
    Model   100
Communications and Control under the Human
    Relations Model   102
Communications and Control under the Human
    Resources Model   105
    Human Resources Concepts Applied—
        Management by Objectives   106
    Example 3—Jordon Press   107
    Example 4—Lectocom   107
Budgeting under the Three Managerial Models   108
Capital Expenditures and the Crisis Syndrome   110
Concluding Remarks   112

**Chapter 7   Leadership Styles and Subordinate
             Responses**   114

The Quality Aspect of Participative Management   116
    Manager's Attitudes and the Purposes of
        Participation   117

Subordinate Satisfaction under the Three Models   119
   Research Approach   119
   Findings   120
   Linking Findings to Theory   122
   Implications for Theory   123
Concluding Remarks   126

Chapter 8   Reward Systems   128

Reward Systems—A Broad Conceptualization   129
Reward Systems in Operation   130
   Example 1—Jo Ann Myers   130
   Example 2—Charlie Hutton   130
   Example 3—Centerville Community Hospital   132
   A Need-Path-Goal Model   134
   The Maslow Need Hierarchy   135
   The Expanded Need-Path-Goal Model   136
   The Expanded Model Applied   138
   The Porter-Lawler Model   140
Management Theory and Reward Systems   143
   Reward Systems under the Traditional Model   144
   Reward Systems under the Human Relations
     Model   145
   Reward Systems under the Human Resources
     Model   148
   Intrinsic and Extrinsic Rewards   155
Concluding Remarks   156

**Chapter 9   Development Concepts and Procedures:
An Introduction and Overview**   158

Development—Change by Design   158
   Goal or Target State   159
   Participation in Individual Development   162
   Participation in Organization Change and
     Development   164
The Total Process of Development   165

**Chapter 10   Individual Selection, Appraisal, Train-
ing, and Development**   167

Selection   168

Performance Appraisal   171
Performance Appraisal under the Traditional
    Model   171
Performance Appraisal under the Human
    Relations Model   172
Performance Appraisal under the Human
    Resources Model   172
Training   173
    Focus and Content   174
    Training Methods   176

Chapter 11   Emerging Concepts of Individual and
             Organization Development   180

Development Criteria and Environmental Demands   180
Turner Industries: A Case History Illustrating Trends in
    Selection, Training, and Development   182
Analysis of the Turner Industries Experience   189

Chapter 12   Organization Development: The State of
             the Art   191

Underlying Values and Concepts   192
Sources of Values and Concepts   193
The "Systems" Route to Organization Development   194
Some Examples of OD Today   197
    Organization A—A Limited Effort   197
    Analysis of OD Effort in Organization A   199
    Organization B—A Sustained, Low-Intensity
        Effort   200
    Analysis of the OD Effort in Organization B   203
    Organization C—A Small-Scale Success   204
    Analysis of the OD Effort in Organization C   207
    Organization D—A Limited Application of the
        Managerial Grid   208
    Analysis of the OD Effort in Organization D   209
    Organization E—Success and "Failure" with the
        Data Feedback Approach   210
    Analysis of the OD Effort in Organization E   213
A Critique of OD Today   214
    Objective Evidence   214
    A "Subjective" Appraisal of OD   216
    The Role of Top Management in OD Programs   218

A Final Criticism of OD   219

**Chapter 13   Organizational Adjustments to Environ-
                      mental Demands**   221

An Illustrative Model of Organizational Adjustment   222
OD Efforts and the Adjustment Model   224
OD Efforts, Major Structural Change, and Goal
   Realignments   226
The "Ultimate" Organizational Adjustment   227
Concluding Remarks   228

**Chapter 14   Some Concluding Comments and
                      Speculations**   230

The General Framework   230
   Managers' Theories   231
   Implications of Roles   232
   From Theory to Practice   233
Some Key Points Revisited and Expanded   233
   Human Relations Is Alive and Well and Living in
   Most Organizations   233
   An Unrecognized Complementarity   234
Contingency versus Universalism   236
   Contingency Model A   237
   Contingency Model B   237
The Future: Problems and Promises   238

PREFACE

A preface is in many ways a postscript. Even though it is placed at the beginning of the book, it is frequently written after the manuscript is completed and out of the author's hands. At such a point, it is tempting to use the Preface both to justify the way topics are treated in the book and to extend them by adding insights and information acquired after the printing process has begun. Having defined this temptation, the following paragraphs give evidence that I have succumbed to it, at least partially.

From my early experiences in a variety of educational, military, and work situations, I gained a hazy awareness of differences in organizational climates and managerial styles. This awareness began to take meaningful shape after I read two important books, Peter Drucker's *The Practice of Management* and Douglas McGregor's *Human Side of Enterprise.* The conceptual frameworks provided by these authors furnished a beginning perspective for my own experiences and stimulated a continuing search for the determinants and outcomes of managerial behavior. This effort became more sharply focused while I was studying at Stanford, when I had the opportunity to join Dale Yoder in some of the first survey research on managers' theories of management. My interests were further enhanced when we discovered through this research that managers' views did not fit neatly into existing frameworks.

After joining the faculty at Berkeley and integrating my research with that of Mason Haire, Edwin Ghiselli, and Lyman Porter, a new theoretical framework emerged which appeared to explain previously confusing elements in managers' views concerning their organizations, the people in them, and how they should be managed. This framework postulated three logically consistent models of management which I termed "traditional," "human relations," and "human resources." These models contained more or less explicit "theories" of motivation and leadership, along with implications for job and organization design, communications and control, reward systems, and approaches to managerial and organizational development—implications which I spent the next few years exploring and testing against the emerging literature in the field and against my own research and consulting experiences.

As these models and their implications took shape, their limitations also became apparent. What was needed was a framework which dealt simultaneously with managerial philosophies, their implications across various areas of organizational behavior, and the individual and situational differences which moderated their applicability. The general model explicated in Chapters 1 and 2 was developed to integrate this full range of variables, but no existing textbooks met its demands in terms of coverage. Moreover, it seemed that none was likely to appear—the framework was simply too broad to allow systematic treatment of all of its components in typical textbook format, and, thus, if I wished to utilize my conceptual framework, I would have to prepare my own material.

.   Having decided to write a book, I then had to choose between alternative approaches. It seemed clear to me that I could (1) develop an integrated treatment of the complete model, ignoring divergent themes and excluding consideration of many variables, or (2) attempt an encyclopedic treatment of a limited set of concepts and variables with little attempt at integration or synthesis. The choice was not difficult—I am a synthesizer by ability and antiencyclopedic by inclination.

The book emerged over a period of six years—my time frame was extended year after year as I sought to include only those topics which I felt I understood both through my research and reading in the field and through observation and experience in organizational settings. Further, I was attempting to cover these topics in a manner that would be appropriate both to the student and to the practicing manager. Thus, the chapters were used in mimeographed form in several university courses, ranging from the undergraduate to the doctoral level. I began to feel I might be on target when a student at another school used several chapters of the manuscript in a course and then sent them to his father, a successful manager. The father, in turn, wrote me to say that he was certain I had used his organization for many of my examples (I hadn't) and to inquire when and where he could buy the book.

The final product, as is always the case, is only as complete as the development of the field and my ability to interpret its advances allow. Nevertheless, while I am not fully satisfied with all aspects of the book, I believe that it generally accomplishes its objectives.

ACKNOWLEDGMENTS

My efforts were aided at various points by many colleagues and friends. George Strauss and Robert Biller of the Berkeley faculty read large portions of the manuscript and provided copious comments and criticisms, as did Charles Waters, President of Organization Dynamics, Inc., and Anthony Hite of the University of Michigan. Too often, however, I fear that I may have listened to their accolades and ignored their criticisms. I received encouragement and support along the way from Mason Haire, Dale Yoder, Rensis Likert, and many others. Roger Lamm, David Bowen, and others used the early versions of the manuscript in their classes and furnished useful feedback. Alan Meyer provided extensive editorial and graphic assistance. Charles Snow worked through the manuscript page by page making direct improvements in many sections and generally aiding in the search for consistency, continuity, and clarity. Barbara Porter not only brought crucial typing and editorial assistance to bear on this project but also pushed me (supportively) to meet deadlines. My sources for key ideas, particularly J. B. Ritchie, George Strauss, and Robert Biller, are acknowledged further in the introduction.

Finally, my family has not only been supportive in this venture but has contributed substantively to its development. My wife, Lucile, and my two older children, Laura and Grant, have followed my research and writings and have regularly used the concepts discussed in the book to analyze my own behavior. Pointed statements such as, "That's a pretty "traditional" way of responding," or "You're using "human relations" on me again," have aided greatly in my understanding of these concepts—so much so, in fact, that I may hide this book from my youngest child, Kenneth. However, I suppose he will have to see it to know that it is dedicated to him, to his brother and sister, and to his mother.

Raymond E. Miles

Introduction

Writing a book is a rather presumptuous act. It implies that I feel I have some things to say which are sufficiently worthwhile to warrant others spending the time to read about them. It also implies that I feel confident enough to run the risk that some may accept and be influenced by one or more of the points I have to make, and, given the importance of the subject I am addressing, this risk is not insignificant.

Recognizing these implications, it seems to me that I am obligated to explain as clearly and honestly as possible why I am writing this particular book and where I got the ideas I'm putting forth. I will elaborate upon these issues in the next few pages, and after that I will move forward in a somewhat more traditional, professorial style. Let me add that one or two of the points made in the following paragraphs are crucial to a full understanding of the concepts and notions covered in subsequent chapters. This rather blatant bit of manipulation is designed to assure at least a cursory reading of this introduction and thus to help me discharge the obligation expressed above.

WHY A BOOK?

My natural inclination is not to write a book (I'll leave this line as is, even though I recognize how tempting it will be for the reader, and particularly for some reviewers, to make comments on it). I am, in fact, much more inclined toward writing short pieces—my marginal rate of dedication and enthusiasm declines sharply after about twenty pages. Moreover, the typical short piece either covers a broad area so shallowly or else restricts itself to such a narrow topic that the risks of misleading readers are small. Nevertheless, having identified my usual inclination, let me explain why I am going against it.

I am violating my own norms first because I've become convinced that many controversial management issues remain controversial in part at least because they are usually raised and dealt with in isolation. Unless the full range of implications of a given concept is traced out and its linkages with other concepts and issues explored, the treatment is inevitably naïve. For example, the linkage between leadership style and the design of control systems is seldom explicitly examined and yet their interaction is a fact of organizational life. It is, to illustrate this linkage, troublesome for a manager to practice democratic or participative management when the data necessary for self-direction and control are collected in his unit but processed and retained elsewhere in the organization.

My recognition of the relationships among management concepts and practices is, of course, not unique. We are moving, fortunately, out of an era when managerial functions such as planning, directing, and controlling were dealt with as if they were entities and into a period in which the organization and its administration are viewed as a total system of interconnected parts and processes, open to the environment at both the input and output ends. The recognition of the need to explicitly spell out these linkages, however, forces those of us who would prefer to write articles to consider books.

More important than the simple act of tracing implications and exploring relationships among concepts and practices is the task of trying to pull out of the jumbled pile of writings on organization and management some consistent pattern, some broad overview notions, which will help us see more clearly where we are and where we are heading. Or, if pulling out a pattern is too difficult a task, one may take on the lesser chore of imposing his own pattern. In either instance a book-length treatment seems necessary.

At this point, I am convinced that a reasonably clear and consistent set of theories concerning management and organizations is emerging from the behavioral sciences. This convergence of thinking, if it actually exists, in no way suggests that we are at the point of creating a general theory of management and organizations—we still do not know nearly enough about most issues. In consulting with managers in a wide range of organizations and in working with them in executive development programs and research projects, I have learned, if nothing else, how truly complex organizations really are. The current call for more rigorous research focusing on "moderators," or situational factors, rather than for broad surveys aimed at uncovering basic causal relationships is clearly appropriate. In the meantime, however, organizations are operating and managers are running them according to their own understanding of the current state of knowledge. Thus, while it is always appropriate to proclaim honestly how little we know, it is also mandatory to proclaim what we do know, or at least what we think we know, in a clear and operational fashion. And it is in these summary statements of what we think we know that I perceive a convergence of key ideas.

In sum, the need which I believe exists to link together concepts and to deal with them consistently within a broad theoretical framework, acknowledging situational diversity but attempting to uncover sizable patterns of behavior, tends to force me to move beyond an article and into a book-length treatment.

WHY THIS PARTICULAR BOOK?

Management Theories

I am attempting to structure my synthesizing efforts around the central topic of theories of management because, in my view, that's where the action is. As mentioned above, for better or for worse, managers are managing, and they are doing so according to their own experiences, habits, rules of thumb, concepts, and theories.

One important aim of this book is to help managers (whatever their age or position) to examine what they think and do and to roughly assess the impact of their attitudes and behaviors on others. Clearly, the effort will be more successful with some attitudes and behaviors than with others. For example, much of what a manager does on any given day is obviously idiosyncratic and essentially undiagnosed. He attacks the work on his desk in a particular order, interacts with his secretary in a particular manner, and responds to a subordinate or superior in a given fashion—basically because that's the way he is. What's more, certainly no book, and more likely than not no short course or experience in or out of the organization, is apt to have much visible impact on his basic approach to life or his organizational role. Most changes here occur, when they do, as the result of the manager either being placed in new surroundings where new attitudes and behaviors are demanded, or through the process of conscious, supported experimentation over time with new approaches. Thus, although encouraging the manager to be a bit introspective about his own day-to-day behavior—and about the building of a conceptual framework to assist in this introspection—is one of the aims of this book, it is not the central one.

Rather, the key focus of this effort is one or two steps up the ladder of abstraction from routine behavior. As will be explained in much more detail later, this book is primarily addressed to those areas of managerial attitudes and behavior which are not day to day but which in fact have major, long-run impacts on the organization and its performance. For example, the way a manager interviews a prospect for a job is important, but perhaps far more important were the few moments' thought he gave (or did not give) to the way the job for which the prospect is applying was put together. Similarly, the way in which a manager responds, face to face, to a subordinate's request to know "what the hell is going on" is clearly important. Perhaps even more important, however, is the way in which the manager designs the total flow of information in his department.

Managers obviously have an impact on their organizations through their day-to-day, face-to-face interaction with other members at all levels. This impact is important, and it may help or hinder the performance of their unit and the organization. But managers are likely to make an even more profound impact on performance through their decisions concerning how tasks are grouped into positions, how positions in turn are grouped into departments and those departments related one to the other, how and by whom recruitment will be carried out, the relative emphasis to be placed on candidate selection as opposed to training, the methods by which individual performance will be appraised and individual development facilitated, the way in which communication and control systems will be structured, the nature, content, and use of the reward package, etc. It is in these broad decisions that his concepts of how organizations ought to be run—his theory of management, if you will— are most visible. On the assumption that these are the important issues, my aim in this book is to help the manager rethink the alternatives available to him in these areas and the reasons underlying the choices among these alternatives. In many instances my treatment is descriptive—stating alternatives or tracing out their logical implications. However, where I believe evidence of scholarly thinking dictates the choice among alternatives, the discussion becomes patently prescriptive. I will also try to illustrate how decisions made in these several areas link together more or less logically to produce an even more general and consistent expression of management theory.

I should make clear at this point that I am purposely excluding economic or entrepreneurial actions and decisions, although these may have an even greater effect, in the short run at least, on organizational performance than the ones suggested above. Product design, selling price, the size of the advertising budget, the make-or-buy and capital-investment decisions, expansions, mergers, acquisitions—all are crucial areas of concern with important, and in some instances life-or-death impact on the organization. In the main, however, they fall outside the scope of this book. Where they are relevant and where their impact on other decisions closer to the main theme of this effort is clear, they will be discussed. Otherwise, they will be treated as simply a fixed part of the environment in which all other managerial decisions are made.

Organization Dynamics

A closely related focus of this book is on the dynamics of organizational behavior. Organizations are always developing, or at least evolving, sometimes without apparent direction. I am concerned, however, with steps managers can take to improve the performance of their organization by restructuring, redirecting, or responding to their technical and human resources in a perhaps different manner. In addition, I would like to discuss some fairly recent and somewhat innovative approaches to planned change in organizations which have been and are being attempted and to point out some of their strengths and weaknesses. Finally, I would like to present a model of planned organization change (regularly referred to today as organization development) which is generally consistent with the main theoretical foundations of this book.

The conceptual linkage which I draw between theories of management and approaches to organizational improvement should not be surprising. Organization development is in large measure centered around the choice of new alternatives in the areas of organization and job design, communications and control, etc. In addition, it clearly involves how the choice of new alternatives is made and how these alternatives are implemented. A manager's concepts or theories will obviously affect which alternatives are considered and how they are chosen and put into practice.

FROM WHENCE THESE VIEWS

As I have indicated, this book is aimed at synthesizing some mainstream concepts in the area of management theory and their implications for organizational behavior and development. It is appropriate, therefore, that I acknowledge the key sources of my ideas. The list here is not inclusive, for at least three reasons. First, I have been selective not by default but by explicit intent. This book is, as described above, an effort to highlight the convergence among a variety of viewpoints. It will, hopefully, pull together some viewpoints whose linkages have not been noted and which may not be completely obvious, and it will acknowledge and in some measure attempt to explain some of the more interesting and important areas of divergence. Nevertheless, it is a *synthesis*, and primary attention will be given to those sources whose concepts appear to be related in such a way that a meaningful and operational pattern emerges. Second, neither the discussion here nor in later chapters will include all those who have been or are making significant contributions on these topics. To include them all would be impossible. No single scholar can keep pace with all the disciplines which deal with organizations. Finally, not all the key sources of the ideas included will be discussed here because I am not at present aware of them. My thinking has been influenced by innumerable books, articles, conversations, and observations that have now slipped below the point of easy recall. These have gradually blended together and become an indistinguishable part of "my" ideas.

The general conceptual framework presented in Chapter 2 was developed several years ago with the aid of Professor George W. England of the University of Minnesota. This framework was designed to help identify (1) the role of a manager, (2) some of the factors which influence his behavior, and (3) the key areas in which managers' attitudes and behavior are expressed. The central role which managers' theories (discussed in Chapter 3) play in this model was influenced by the writings of the late Douglas McGregor and his colleague, Warren Bennis; by Dale Yoder, with whom I worked on some of the first empirical surveys of managers' concepts, philosophies, and theories; and by Edwin Ghiselli and Mason Haire, who helped me formulate some of my early studies of managers' theories and interpret their results.

Chapter 4 draws together concepts and ideas on job design from Professors Louis Davis and Frederick Herzberg and from Robert Ford at American Telephone and Telegraph. Chapter 5 synthesizes and, hopefully, additionally clarifies ideas on organizational structure and design from Rensis Likert, Victor Thompson, the late James Thompson, the late Joan Woodward, and others at the Tavistock Institute of Human Relations. It also owes a handsome debt to my friend and colleague, Robert Biller.

Chapter 6 on communications and control systems borrows heavily from the work of Arnold Tannenbaum and others at the University of

Michigan. It also draws on the pioneering work in the area of the impact of measurement on individual behavior by Chris Argyris and Peter Blau. In addition, this chapter, as do most recent materials concerning communication and control, owes a substantial debt to Peter Drucker and his perceptive prescriptions for management by objectives.

Chapter 7, which deals with superior-subordinate relationships, owes its largest debt to McGregor, Likert, and Argyris, although it also co-opts some concepts from one of their more perceptive critics, my own colleague at Berkeley, George Strauss, and a former colleague now at Tavistock, Frank Heller. As the specific credits in the chapter will show, it has also been strongly influenced by the thinking of a research and writing partner of long standing, J. B. Ritchie, who is now at Brigham Young University.

The concepts on reward systems covered in Chapter 8 largely reflect the writings of Lyman W. Porter, Edward E. Lawler III, and Victor Vroom. Once again Drucker's views are heavily represented, along with those of Herzberg. The material on appraisal and development may be recognized as essentially a synthesis of ideas developed by McGregor and by Norman R. F. Maier.

My ideas on organization development, presented in Chapters 9 through 13, have been heavily influenced by the work of my friends and colleagues at the University of Michigan: Floyd Mann, Stanley Seashore, David Bowers, and Charles Waters, now head of Organization Dynamics, Inc. In addition, the ideas of Warren Bennis and Edgar Schein are clearly visible, at least to me, as again are those of Robert Biller. The final chapter, Chapter 14, is a sort of synthesis on top of a synthesis and thus borrows a bit from all the sources mentioned above.

With each chapter, I will include a brief bibliography listing some of the most direct sources of ideas and concepts. Beyond that, with the exception of references for specific quotes and ideas borrowed directly, I will make no further payments to those to whom I am in debt for concepts and inspirations. I will make my apologies now to those from whom I have borrowed without acknowledgment and to those who, because of the way I have handled their ideas, would have preferred to have gone unacknowledged.

Chapter 1

A General Conceptual Framework

Imagine that we are looking over the shoulder of a hypothetical manager. He is thirty-seven years old and chief of a major division within a medium-sized organization. He is slowly scratching his head as he examines the materials before him. He is about to make a decision, to take action on what seems to be a weighty issue. What factors will he take into account? What decision will he make? Will it make any difference in his division's performance?

The purpose of this chapter is to put into perspective this manager and his activities, along with the actions of his colleagues throughout the organizational hierarchy. We will attempt to put together, piece by piece, a simple descriptive model which will highlight the manager's role in modern organizations. The pieces of this model will include factors which influence managerial attitudes and behavior and which, in turn, are influenced by them. The model is expanded in Chapter 2, where we broadly specify some of the mechanisms by which managers' actions affect their organizations and the people within them, and examine some of the logical relationships among these mechanisms. In subsequent chapters, we continue this examination of the general model, both extending the list of structural and human characteristics under consideration and increasing the specificity and depth. with which they are discussed.

SOME CHARACTERISTICS OF ORGANIZATIONS

While in-the-flesh organizations tend to be more or less complex, in the abstract they can be made to appear rather simple. It is, in fact, true that an organization is nothing more than a collection of people grouped together around a technology which is operated to transform inputs from its environment into marketable goods or services. The oversimplified model illustrated in Figure 1-1 highlights a crucial point which will be made repeatedly in this and subsequent chapters—organizations inseparably intertwine people and processes into what is currently referred to as a "sociotechnical" system. People in organizations operate the technology, they run the process. But they in turn, as part of the process, have much of their behavior determined by the system they operate.

To answer the questions with which we began this chapter, we must move down the abstraction ladder a rung or two and build a model that identifies more explicitly some of the variables subsumed in and around the box in Figure 1-1. In doing so, we will for the moment break apart the sociotechnical system referred to above and deal separately with one set of factors, or variables, which we tend to associate with the organization itself, and with another set of variables which we tend to associate with the people in the organization.

ORGANIZATION VARIABLES

When we discuss organizations we frequently feel the need to differentiate among them or to group them together along certain dimensions. Several such dimensions have been used, among the more prominent of which are goals, technology, and structure.

Organizations can be classified according to their *goals*, or purposes,

Figure 1-1 An abstract model of an organization

and we readily so classify them, even in casual conversations. For example, we differentiate between profit and nonprofit organizations, public and private ones, sectarian and nonsectarian, etc. More often than not we move beyond this level of goal differentiation and discuss organizations in terms of their specific product, or *output*; for example, important differences appear to exist between a steel firm and a stock brokerage house (although in this age of the conglomerate such differences seem to be disappearing), and we imply that a substantial gap does or should exist between religious and educational organizations, though each may feel that it is engaged in the determining and disseminating of truth.

Similarly, we differentiate among organizations according to their *technology*, or the methods they use to get things done. A housewife concerned about zoning regulations has a mental picture of the characteristics of light versus heavy industry, and most of us, from observation or imagination, can discuss such differences and some of their more dramatic implications—as, say, between an assembly plant and a research and development organization.

Finally, we regularly refer to or distinguish between organizations in accordance with characteristics related to their *structure*. We separate, and have feelings about, large and small organizations, and we differentiate impersonal, nationally owned and operated firms from locally controlled ones, frequently stating or implying a value judgment as we do.

The scholar's concern with these organizational dimensions reflects and extends the layman's discussions and observations. The scholar is concerned with how these variables—goals, technology, and structure—relate to each other and how they may serve, individually or jointly, as determinants of managerial behavior and organizational performance. He is concerned with more precise differentiation than that required by casual conversations and is aware, for example, that size is only one aspect of structure. Moreover, he is alert to the fact that these variables must ultimately be linked with human variables if differences in their effects are to be fully acknowledged and explained. Nevertheless, on occasion he finds it convenient to make use of just those dimensions which are characteristics of organizations as such, and not of the people within them, so that he can examine a number of important hypotheses which are frequently different only in their wording and precision from the everyday observations of the layman.

We are concerned, for the next few pages, with only a narrow segment of all the possible scholarly issues surrounding these organizational variables—the broad impact of organization goals, technology, and structure on *managerial* attitudes and behavior.

Goals

The goals of organizations, in theory and in fact (though the fact is sometimes difficult to describe), result from interactions with the environment. In the public domain, the idealized process occurs as follows: society has a visible need, constituents demand that it be filled, legislators vote into existence an organization to meet this need. Of course, examples can be pointed out where the process appears to have been reversed, or begun in the middle, but generally this procedure tends to hold. In the private domain, the process, though somewhat less visible, is similar. Whatever his personal motives, the entrepreneur moves to provide a product or service which the public will purchase, with the purchase demonstrating a real or presumed need. This process is sanctioned directly by the granting of a corporate charter or business license, and indirectly by our total economic-political system, which promotes privately controlled production of goods and services. Again, constituents (consumers) presumably regulate the process, expressing their needs and their degree of satisfaction with the way these needs are met by "voting" their dollars in the market place among competing products.

Within the process, in both the public and the private domains, managers at the top and at points on the periphery where the environment and the organization interact, either find themselves in—or set for themselves—the role of mediators between the organization's needs and those of its constituents. Where the managers have sufficient leverage, a factor frequently associated with organization size, they may try to remove all or some of the controls which environmental elements exercise over the goals of their organization—or, more simply, to ignore certain demands of some constituents and fill or promote others in the course of serving what they believe to be the best interests of the organization (or of themselves personally). Where such leverage does not exist, managers at the periphery may find their primary task that of attempting to cope with changing environmental demands, adjusting organizational goals as rapidly as possible in order to keep them aligned with the wishes of powerful constituents. Of course, even where the organization is large and powerful, it generally finds it difficult to influence or maintain control over the demands of its environment completely and/or indefinitely. The most prestigious firms and governmental agencies have proved vulnerable to private and public muckrakers, and pressure groups lie in wait to ambush the organization's efforts to protect itself from environmental demands.

Whether organizations are becoming more vulnerable to environmental demands and must, therefore, be more adaptive to them is difficult to prove. There appears to be a growing consensus, however, that this is the case and that the need for managerial skill in adjusting rapidly to, or controlling, environmental demands is becoming increasingly evident. Of course, some managerial activities, and many managerial positions, seem to be effectively shielded from direct environmental influences. Nevertheless, even for those entombed deep within the organizational pyramid, the environment is frequently being brought into the organization in the form of demands by various members for revised status and opportunity.

As implied earlier, the ultimate goals of organizations may not be identical with their output. The ultimate goal of a business firm may be to "maximize the dollar value of its common stock," and the fact that it is engaged in trying to make and sell widgets at a profit is merely a means to that end. Nevertheless, to many if not most people in the organization, the production and sale of widgets *is* the goal of the organization and the diversion of resources from this activity, no matter how cleverly they are diverted, may present substantial problems for the individual manager. Management's continuing task of interpreting and making the organization's goals relevant and operational at all levels is obviously made easier when product and purpose are closely linked and the contribution of various activities to these throughout the organization is clearly visible.

Similarly, a public health organization, broadly charged to "improve and maintain the public's physical and mental well-being," may discover that in some areas it is achieving this goal more effectively by serving as a source of employment opportunities than by giving innoculations and providing information on nutrition. It is, under these circumstances, frequently difficult for anyone except top management to understand and make clear what the organization is accomplishing and how it is going about it.

Despite the dynamic nature of goals implicit in these remarks (I recently attended a meeting in which the management of a firm was developing its third "corporate image" in as many years), the manager's task at any point is to take all or part of the organization's stated goal and to try to devise means of achieving it. He does this partly by creating or modifying a technology to fit specific objectives derived from such goals. Obviously, this process can and does become circular; technology may well dictate goals. Organizations, as people, look for new areas in which to invest their know-how, for new goals which can use their technology. Nevertheless, logically speaking, a means is created to achieve an end—technology is designed to achieve organizational goals—and it is with this sequencing in mind that we move to a brief discussion of technology and its impact on managerial roles.

Technology

The technology of an organization includes not only the visible machinery, tools, and equipment used in turning out its product or service but also the specific human skills, knowledge, and procedures used to operate these devices. It is, therefore, difficult to maintain our temporary separation of organization and human variables. For the moment, however, let us imagine that the possessors of such skills, knowledge, etc., are simply standardized extensions of the physical processes they operate—that is, let us focus on the idiosyncrasies of the locomotive and its operation, not on those of the engineer, even though we know that in fact the two are in large part inseparable.

Given this focus, we can imagine various sets of continua on which we might classify and differentiate technologies. For example, we might array them from those built around simple, multipurpose hand tools to those that are highly specialized and almost completely automated. Or, we might focus on the input and output ends of the process and arrange technologies in terms of the variability of the materials feeding in and the complexity or the diversity of the products or services coming out. Moreover, with a bit of imagination, we could arrive at various cross-classification schemes which would allow us to categorize technologies more accurately.

Assuming we were able to derive a meaningful classification scheme that captured and highlighted the key variables among different technologies, we could then examine the impact of each class or category on management—on its role, attitudes, and behavior. Such efforts have been made and are under way in several disciplines and most of the results to date are not too surprising. The manager in a research lab, for example, cannot respond to the sociotechnical system of which he is part in the same manner as the manager in the assembly plant, or at least if he does the results are often disastrous. On the other hand, it is interesting to recognize that technological characteristics may be quite similar even though the output—the goods or services produced—is quite different. For example, an oil refinery and an automated cookie plant have technologies which are in many ways surprisingly similar and thus may produce similar impacts on management.

A manager, of course, is not controlled by the organization's technology, but its characteristics restrict the range of alternatives open to him at any given moment. One of his key tasks is, of course, to operate a technology as effectively and as efficiently as possible, but an increasingly important requirement is that he be able to cope with change—to recognize the need for and to make adjustments in the technology to keep it aligned with organizational needs and environmental influences, and at the same time to adjust his own role and behaviors to match the changes in technology.

Concurrently, as a manager makes adjustments in the technology, he regularly discovers the need to restructure and realign affected portions of the organization. The maxim that form follows purpose (or process) is not precisely accurate, as is the case with all such rubrics, but it contains at least a germ of truth. Departments, and positions within them, can be structured in many ways around almost any given technology, but some ways seem clearly superior to others. Thus, while technology does not fully determine organizational structure, it does restrict choices among various ways of organizing.

Structure

The concept of structure employed here refers to the way in which departments or units are arranged within a system, the linkages established among these, and the ways in which positions are arranged within them. First, management establishes and modifies structure by the way in which it groups tasks into units. It may, for example, pull together related tasks into functional departments, or, alternatively, it may cluster complementary tasks around a given product or stage in the process. Second, management establishes structure by binding units or departments together with lines of authority, responsibility, communication, and control. The choices made in each of these areas clearly affect the role and task of the manager. Thus, the behavior of a manager who is part of a project team incorporating diverse individuals and skills and charged with bringing a new part of a *product* from the drawing board all the way to the assembly line is influenced by a very different set of requirements than is the manager of a group of specialists who work on only a given piece or *function* of a larger task. Further, each subordinate manager's role and behavior are strongly affected by the manner in which his unit is tied to those with whom it must interact. The way in which information flows between or among such units, the individuals within the organization to whom these units report, the manner in which their outputs are evaluated, etc., all influence managerial behavior. Once again, the manager is not entirely controlled by the structure in which he operates, but he is at least constrained by it.

As indicated above, this chapter is intended to provide only an overview of the manner in which certain key organizational variables determine, or at least place limits on, the manager's role and behavior. For the moment, it is sufficient that we recognize that key organizational characteristics are influenced by their environment (and vice versa) and by one another, and that they in turn are major factors influencing the role of management. This influence process (illustrated in Figure 1-2) is, of course, not unidirectional. Managers can and do influence these variables, but at any given time these variables tend to be more or less fixed factors which must be taken into account as choices are made among alternative courses of action.

HUMAN VARIABLES

Just as the manager's role and behavior are influenced by characteristics associated with the organization itself, they are also strongly affected by the characteristics of the people within the organization. And, just as we have ideas concerning the influences of various organizational variables most of us have ideas concerning how people in work settings differ and how these differences affect managerial behavior and organizational performance. Moreover, our observations are usually clustered around a set of easily recognizable dimensions. For example, we regularly classify people in organizations in accordance with their capabilities. We separate the highly trained from the less skilled, the educated from the uneducated, the experienced from the inexperienced, etc. Similarly, we differentiate among people in organizations according to their attitudes and values. We categorize in this area in terms of motivation, loyalty, trustworthiness, etc. Finally, we tend to differentiate on a host of demographic dimensions. Age, for example, is a commonly used classification device with a cluster of opinions and judgments attached—e.g., "You can't teach an old dog new tricks," but, on the other hand, "Experience counts." Similarly, although restrained by ethic and law, we regularly differentiate on the basis of sex and race.

In each of these areas, the scholar is trying to supplant axioms with precise hypotheses and to test these empirically. We will not attempt here to survey this research but will merely make a few comments about the

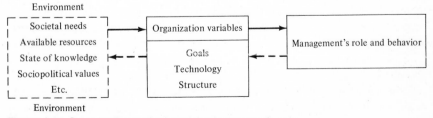

Figure 1-2 Organization variables and management's role

dimensions suggested above in order to obtain a general feeling for the way in which a manager's role is affected by the characteristics of those he manages.

Capabilities

We observe a hospital administrator varying his behavior as he moves from a meeting with his medical staff to a discussion with his new secretary concerning the routing of interoffice communications. He varies his behavior not only because of differences in the issues involved but because of the differences in the capabilities and status of the persons involved. The training and experience of the medical staff are such that usually they prescribe their own course of action and the administrator merely coordinates schedules and facilitates the performance of their duties. The beginning secretary, however, wants and needs a more directive set of behaviors from the administrator. As she grows more knowledgeable she will be able to exercise a growing amount of discretion on her own. After many years on the job, she may well behave with a good deal of autonomy—which, if carefully documented, might prove surprising even to her.

This example is obviously broadly drawn, but it indicates how the manager's role and his behavior may vary with actual and perceived differences in capabilities between individuals, groups of individuals, and even different times in the work life of a single individual. A closer look suggests that the total relationship between the person and the organization is strongly affected by which rung he occupies on the ladder of relevant skills, experience, and training. As he moves up the ladder, we discover that the organization expects more from him, but he in turn can demand more from it. The tasks assigned become more important and more demanding, but the system becomes more accommodating.

We used the term "relevant" to modify skills, experience, and training for obvious reasons. The individual may possess a range of capabilities which cannot be, or are not, used in his particular position. Under these circumstances, he may discover that the organization tends to respond to him in relationship to the skill, experience, and training requirements of his job and not in terms of his actual inventory of capabilities. Such individuals, as we will discuss in more detail later, may make even greater demands on the manager's role and behavior than those whose capabilities fall below those required in their position. At this point, it is sufficient to acknowledge a fairly obvious fact—a major and continuing task of management is that of matching organizational requirements to the varying capabilities of individuals and groups, adjusting its own role and behavior to assist this merging process.

Attitudes, Values, and Needs

In the thirties and forties it was popular to remind managers that individuals bring with them to their jobs each day an accumulation of values, attitudes, and feelings which are only partly the direct products of their work environment. Most managements today, in their policy statements at least, would appear to be bearing this in mind, seeking, perhaps somewhat sporadically, to respond to "the whole man" and to minimize any appearance of treatment of individuals as "just another number" or "another cog in the machine."

When management does, in fact, take explicit action in an effort to affect the attitudes of organization members, whether this action is aimed broadly at "increasing loyalty, trust, and confidence, and improving morale and motivation," or focused narrowly on, for example, "putting out the fire down in the Receiving Department," it is acknowledging another influence on its role, another factor which constrains its choices among available behaviors. Similarly, the individual manager, if he is at all alert, is aware of attitudinal differences among those in his own unit and adjusts his behavior, where possible, to accommodate these differences. The extent to which organizations and individual managers tend to recognize and respond to attitudinal factors, and the nature and impact of the various responses they may make, is a subject for closer analysis in later chapters. Again, at the moment, it is enough to acknowledge that this factor can, or perhaps should, be influential in shaping a manager's role and behavior.

Demographic Characteristics

As indicated earlier, a broad set of variables on which people tend to be classified is subsumed under this heading. Organizational policies, written and unwritten, have established varying responses to individuals according to their age, sex, race, religion, family background, geographic origin, etc. Moreover, individual managers have adjusted, or at least have believed they should adjust, their roles and behaviors in accordance with variations on these dimensions.

While unfairly discriminatory policies and practices in this area are under growing moral and legal indictment, it seems clear that they still do exist. However, new responses, involving in some instances not only removal, but in fact reversal of previous postures are developing. The individual manager is influenced by these characteristics not only when he specifically differentiates on the basis of them but also when he recognizes differences and then either explicitly or implicitly ignores them.

Here, as before, our purpose is not to attempt to pinpoint precisely

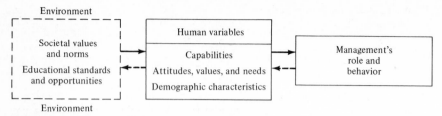

Figure 1-3 Human variables and management's role

how managers' roles and behaviors are influenced by these differences but merely to acknowledge that they are. This pattern of influence is illustrated in Figure 1-3, which shows individual characteristics, drawn in large measure from the environment, interacting and influencing one another and affecting the manager's role and behavior. Again, and as illustrated, the influence arrows go in both directions—the manager also influences human characteristics. He can, in time, help individuals to increase their capabilities, influence their attitudes, and cooperate with them in removing barriers imposed by race, creed, sex, etc. Nevertheless, at any given moment, the characteristics of individuals and groups tend to exercise some constraining influence on his choices among alternative behaviors. In the following chapter we will examine in more detail how organizational and human characteristics shape the role and behavior of management and the mechanisms managers use in integrating these variables.

BIBLIOGRAPHY

Organizational Goals

Cyert, Richard M. and James G. March, "Organizational Goals" (abridged from Cyert and March, *A Behavioral Theory of the Firm*), in B. L. Hinton and J. J. Reitz, *Groups and Organizations: Integrated Readings in the Analysis of Social Behavior* (Belmont, Calif.: Wadsworth, 1971), pp. 404–411.

Perrow, Charles, "Organizational Goals," in David L. Sills (ed.), *International Encyclopedia of the Social Sciences*, vol. 11 (New York: Macmillan, 1968), pp. 305–310.

Thompson, James D. and William J. McEwen, "Organizational Goals and Environment: Goal-Setting as an Interaction Process," *American Sociological Review*, vol. 23, pp. 23–31 (February 1958).

Technology

Thompson, James D., *Organizations in Action* (New York: McGraw-Hill, 1967), chaps. 5 and 6.

Woodward, Joan (as presented by J. J. Rackham), "Automation and Technical Change—The Implications for the Management Process," in Gene W. Dalton and Paul R. Lawrence, *Organizational Structure and Design* (Homewood, Ill.: Irwin, 1970), pp. 297–309.

Structure

Burns, Tom and G. M. Stalker, "Mechanistic and Organic Systems" (abridged from *The Management of Innovation*), in J. Litterer, *Organizations: Systems, Control, and Adaptation* (New York: Wiley, 1969), pp. 345–348.

Chandler, Alfred D., Jr., *Strategy and Structure* (Cambridge, Mass.: M.I.T., 1962), chap. 8.

Pugh, D. S., "The Measurement of Organization Structures: Does Context Determine Form?" *Organizational Dynamics*, vol. 1, pp. 19–34 (Spring 1973).

Human Variables

Leavitt, Harold J., *Managerial Psychology*, 3d ed. (Chicago: University of Chicago Press, 1972), chaps. 1–9.

Schein, Edgar H., *Organizational Psychology* (Englewood Cliffs, N.J.: Prentice-Hall, 1965), chaps. 3 and 4.

Tiffin, Joseph and Ernest J. McCormick, *Industrial Psychology* (Englewood Cliffs, N.J.: Prentice-Hall, 1965), chap. 2.

Chapter 2

The Role
of Management

The basic concept of management and its role in modern organizations found here is implicit in the discussion in the previous chapter. The manager's chief task, as we perceive it, is that of integrating organizational and human variables into an effective and efficient sociotechnical system. On occasion, he carries out this task rationally and before the fact, attempting to blend an appropriate mix of these variables. More often, he finds that someone has already provided him with a recipe and that one of the sets of variables, organizational or human, is more or less fixed and he must adjust the other set to it. Typical here is the situation where goals and technology are set and the manager's task is that of fitting persons with an appropriate set of characteristics to them. On occasion, however, the opposite occurs—the manager has before him a group of people with given characteristics for whom he must design appropriate objectives and a structure through which these can be accomplished.

Most often, the manager finds himself in the midst of an ongoing

Figure 2-1 Management's role: Integration of human and organizational variables

sociotechnical system, with concurrent—and frequently conflicting—requirements for adjustments of both organizational and human needs and characteristics. The manager's position and his task can be illustrated by pulling together our earlier diagrams to make Figure 2-1. The manager is pictured as being influenced and/or constrained by both organization and human variables and, in turn, as having an impact on them, modifying and adjusting them in the interest of organizational performance.

What is missing from Figure 2-1 is the mechanism, or set of mechanisms, by which managers make these adjustments. It is to these integrative tools, devices, or mechanisms that we now turn our attention.

INTEGRATIVE MECHANISMS

The manager attempts to blend human attitudes and energies to achieve organizational objectives through the mechanism of *direction*. He explains these objectives, plans how they can be attained, issues instructions concerning how, when, and by whom these plans will be carried out, and, in person or through reports, oversees their progress. He attempts to merge people and technology into a smoothly functioning system by structuring and restructuring organizational units and the jobs which make up these units—the process of *organization and job design*. On an ongoing basis he uses *selection and training* devices to find and hire people with characteristics appropriate to organizational needs, and, once the individuals are in the organization, he uses *appraisal and development* mechanisms to maintain and enhance these characteristics. He builds linkages between the technical system and its human element and between segments of the sociotechnical system through *communications and control* systems. Finally, he uses a *reward system* to attract individuals to the organization, maintain them within the system, and, hopefully, increase their performance level and contribution to the organization.

These mechanisms (shown in Figure 2-2) are some of the more important means by which managers carry out their integrative task. Clearly, the set of mechanisms shown here is not the only possible one that could be constructed. The list could be shortened by pulling activities

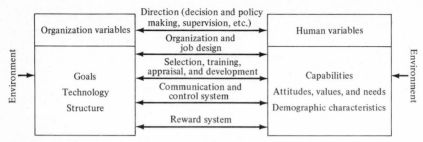

Figure 2-2   Integrative mechanisms employed by management

together or lengthened by spelling out more precisely the separate steps
involved in each. Nevertheless, this list is both descriptive of some of the
more visible and crucial means by which managers have an impact on
their organization and the people within them and operational as a means
of structuring our discussion.

We should acknowledge that while we have described and listed
these mechanisms separately, they are in fact and in practice closely
intertwined. They are all in operation, manifestly or latently, at the same
time and what the manager does with regard to one of them affects what
can and will be done with another. Unfortunately, many managers behave
as if these mechanisms were separate and distinct and therefore fail,
apparently, to recognize that what the one hand is accomplishing with
adjustments to one mechanism, the other hand may be undoing with its
adjustments to another. Thus, a few paragraphs here on (1) the range of
alternatives open to management with regard to each of these mechanisms and (2) the ways in which the mechanisms may interact will help
us complete our theoretical framework and lay the foundation for more
detailed discussion in later chapters.

RANGE OF ALTERNATIVES

Managers, in one manner or another, exercise direction. Similarly,
according to one scheme or another, they structure organizations, design
jobs, select and train employees, communicate and control, etc. In each of
these areas, various continua of alternative behaviors or approaches can
be constructed. Some examples of these, with detailed presentations and
analyses reserved for later chapters, are as follows:

Direction

With regard to direction, managerial behavior might range

1   from unilateral determination of plans, policies, and objectives to joint determination with those individuals affected.

2   from close and direct supervision (either in person or through detailed procedures and reports) to general, supportive supervision which allows broad self-direction and self-control to be exercised in the pursuit of agreed-upon objectives.

Organization and Job Design

Alternatives available in utilizing these mechanisms might range

1   from structures which arrange groups of functional specialists in traditional hierarchical layers to more loosely linked, self-paced teams with heterogeneous skills grouped around a product, part, or integrated stage of the process.

2   from job designs emphasizing highly specialized and segmented collections of tasks to designs which attempt to encompass a meaningful range of activities into self-paced, self-evaluated operations.

Selection and Training—Appraisal and Development

For these mechanisms, alternatives might range

1   from selection and training processes which focus on presumed traits and abilities associated with immediate job requirements to more flexible systems which attempt to balance the long-run needs of the organization and the individual.

2   from superior-conducted appraisal based on standard characteristics and behaviors to joint appraisal (superior/subordinates) focused on progress toward previously agreed upon job targets or objectives.

3   from unilaterally planned and directed development programs to flexible procedures where organization members are included in the process of setting their own development goals and choosing the means of achieving them.

Communications and Control

Here, alternatives might range

1   from communication systems which primarily provide for downward flows of orders and instructions and upward flows of reports to information systems designed to provide operating units with access to all the data they feel are necessary to their performance.

2   from control systems which collect progress information from operating units for transmission to distant evaluation points to short

feedback loop designs which allow operating units to immediately appraise and adjust their own performance.

Reward Systems

Within reward systems, alternatives might range

1   from systems built exclusively around *either* longevity or merit alone to more flexible systems which acknowledge *both* loyalty and performance.
2   from unilateral determination of rewards and the method of their attainment to systems in which organization members have a voice in determining the nature of rewards and the paths by which these can be achieved.

LINKAGES ACROSS MECHANISMS

The reader may have noticed by now a rather close relationship between some of the continua of alternatives suggested above and a more detailed listing of managerial systems provided by Rensis Likert. The similarity is intentional, as are the differences. Likert has specified alternative managerial behaviors in each of seven areas (e.g., motivation, communication, decision making, goal setting), thereby defining four distinct "systems" of management. We have both compressed his list into three or four of our categories and added mechanisms which he does not explicitly cover, such as organization and job design. In later chapters, we will use his detailed specifications, adding a critical comment or two in the process, but our need at the moment is not for additional sets of behaviors but for a recognition of how such behaviors interact with each other.

Here again, Likert offers us guidance. As indicated, he has arranged each of the alternative managerial behaviors across the seven areas to produce four systems of management. Some aspects of these four systems are shown in abridged form in Figure 2-3. The logical linkages among alternatives in Likert's systems seem clear enough. For example, system I links limited communication flowing primarily downward to decision making carried out primarily at the top of the organization, whereas system IV ties free-flowing vertical, horizontal, and diagonal information channels to decision making which is highly decentralized.

Moving back to the continua we have suggested here, one can imagine similar "systematic" linkages occurring across direction, organization and job design, communications and controls, rewards, etc. For example, job designs featuring narrowly structured, segmented, routinized tasks appear to fit with detailed supervision (by person or

	System I	System II	System III	System IV
Character of motivational forces				
a. Underlying motives tapped	Physical security, economic security, and some use of the desire for status	Economic and occasionally ego motives, e.g., the desire for status	Economic, ego, and other major motives, e.g., desire for new experience	Full use of economic, ego, and other major motives, e.g., motivational forces arising from group processes
b. Manner in which motives used	Fear, threats, punishment, and occasional rewards	Rewards and some actual or potential punishment	Rewards, occasional punishment, and some involvement	Economic rewards based on compensation system developed through participation
Character of communication process				
a. Amount of interaction and communication aimed at achieving organization's objectives	Very little	Little	Quite a bit	Much with both individuals and groups
b. Direction of information flow	Downward	Mostly downward	Down and up	Down, up, and with peers
Character of decision–making process				
a. At what level in organization are decisions formally made?	Bulk of decision at top of organization	Policy at top, many decisions within prescribed framework made at lower levels	Broad policy and general decisions at top, more specific decisions at lower levels	Decision making widely done throughout organization, although well integrated through linking process provided by overlapping groups
b. How adequate and accurate is the information available for decision making at the place where the decisions are made?	Partial and often inaccurate information only is available	Moderately adequate and accurate information available	Reasonably adequate and accurate information available	Relatively complete and accurate information available based both on measurements and efficient flow of information in organization

Figure 2-3 Some illustrative dimensions of Likert's four systems of management [Adapted from Rensis Likert, *The Human Organization* (New York: McGraw-Hill, 1967), table 3-1]

process), and these in turn link closely with downward communications flows and externally operated control systems.

EVIDENCE OF CONSISTENCY AND INCONSISTENCY

In a continuing series of studies, Likert and his associates have asked members of numerous organizations to evaluate the systems of management under which they operate, using his seven dimensions mentioned above. His findings suggest that although individual members may differ widely in their assessments of the alternative behaviors they perceive in the several areas, a profile of their responses does indicate the existence of a "system" of management. Moreover, measurements taken in the same organization over time indicate that this profile can change— members perceive that they are operating under a different system of management—thus illustrating the logical linkages among alternative behaviors described above.

My own experiences tend to support Likert's findings. Far more often than not, for example, what management appeared to be doing in terms of job design seemed to link logically to their general approach to or personal theory of direction and supervision, and communications and control systems seemed designed to complement the manner in which rewards were given. In fact, where behaviors in these several areas did not appear to fit, where inconsistencies were visible, they tended to be associated with currently recognized, but not always diagnosed, problems. Here, as is frequently the case, the exception best demonstrates the rule, and a brief look at a few of the inconsistencies I have encountered in managerial applications of these systems may serve as the best means of getting a feeling for how integrative mechanisms do link together logically.

EXAMPLE 1—(Recruitment, Training, and Job Design) In the area of *recruitment and selection* of managerial personnel, firm A follows an apparently laudable model. It selects only the top graduates from the more prestigious colleges and universities and *rewards* them with initial salaries in keeping with the market and with their academic achievement. Further, its *training* program is innovative and geared to the expectations of its recruits, incorporating rotation and the opportunity to work on challenging problems as individuals or in teams. The inconsistency in this system occurs in the area of *job design*. Once through the training program, young managers are placed in operating departments and into jobs which have frequently not been tailored to their capabilities or to their expectations. Dropped into routine assignments which are easily mastered, many of these young managers become disenchanted and leave. Top management in this organization has been somewhat baffled by the high turnover rate among their young managers, given their more than adequate salary and benefit schedule. If top management of firm A is aware of the inconsistency which exists between its selection, training, and reward procedures and its approach to job design, it has not acknowledged it, and no action has been taken to correct it.

EXAMPLE 2—(Direction, Controls, and Rewards)   A quick tour through a second organization highlights another example of inconsistency in the application of management's integrative mechanisms, accompanied again by a persistent problem. This organization produces a number of products, which, although different in final form and market, have a similar basic technology. The organization has a central research and development group at corporate headquarters, highly skilled in the basic technology, and smaller R&D units in each of the divisions. In the area of *direction*, top management has, for the last several years, attempted through policy statements, persuasion—individual and group—and even through explicit directives, to promote (1) greater use of the central R&D staff by the operating divisions and (2) greater sharing among the divisions of basic and applied advances (directly, or through central R&D) in the common technology. For the most part, however, their efforts appear to have failed. Advances uncovered in the central R&D staff tend to be ignored at the operating level, and the central staff group is seldom called in to assist with division problems. Moreover, discoveries made within the operating divisions are frequently not brought to the attention of the central R&D group until it is too late to incorporate them into product or process designs in other divisions.

Surprisingly, top management, in its search for a solution to this problem, had apparently failed to examine its *control and reward systems*. Operating divisions work on an extremely tight R&D budget, and when central staff R&D personnel are called in either to solve problems at the division level or to assist in installing new ideas developed in the central research laboratory, their costs are charged to the division budget. Thus, divisions are told to make use of the central R&D unit but then are penalized for doing so. Moreover, while top management pleads for the sharing of new developments among divisions, its *reward system* is based on competitive evaluation of division performance. As performance is frequently tied to being first with new developments in technology, and as no reward for sharing these developments is provided, division managers behave rationally when they are slow to bring technological innovations to the attention of other divisions or to the central R&D group.

EXAMPLE 3—(Policies, Job Design, and Controls)   Another rather glaring illustration of inconsistency can be observed by following a group of head nurses through a normal duty shift. In this particular hospital, management, in directives and in monthly meetings with the nurses, stresses two key responsibilities of the head nurse: (1) assuring a high level of patient care by working closely with nurses and aides and by using her own presumably superior talents with as many patients as possible, and (2) training and developing the nurses and aides in her unit in the best possible patient care procedures.

Given this emphasis in the area of *direction*, a few hours observing the typical head nurse at work in this hospital is likely to prove confusing. The bulk of her time appears to be taken up in such tasks as maintaining an inventory of supplies, for which she alone is responsible, and making out forms and reports required by the head office. She is, of course, available for emergency assistance to other members of her group but returns then, distracted, to the more pressing demands of her job. Thus, the basic *design of her job* and the *control system* imposed on her appear to be in direct contradiction to management's *directives* concerning her key goals and responsibilities.

EXAMPLE 4—(Delegation and Controls)   A final example of inconsistency in the application of integrative mechanisms requires us to look only at the top of the desk of one manager. Side by side on the blotter lie (1) a page of scrawled notes used in a brief talk given to his unit managers in their regular weekly meeting, and (2) a monthly production chart from one of these units indicating quantity and quality levels achieved along with the targeted objectives in each area. The key idea expressed in the scrawled notes of the talk he gave to his group is "initiative." The term is underlined several times on the page and one key phrase is intelligible: "Solve your own problems as they emerge. It's your unit, run it like you want to as long as you produce." On the production chart it is clear that while quality levels appear to be going up, quantity levels are not on target. One product is running slightly ahead of schedule while another is clearly running behind. Across the face of the chart the manager has scrawled a simple and direct instruction, *Explain this.*

DETERMINANTS OF A MANAGERIAL SYSTEM

In each of the examples above, managers appeared to be behaving inconsistently because their method of operation with regard to one integrative mechanism did not fit with the alternative chosen in another area. In Likert's terminology, they appear to be operating under one system of management in one area and under another in a second area. These inconsistencies, and the problems which appear to result from them, are interesting in their own right, and a similar search for such contradictions might prove valuable in most organizations. Nevertheless, they are even more important because they serve, as suggested earlier, to demonstrate the logical "fit" which appears to exist across the integrative mechanisms shown in Figure 2-2. The fact that these examples are so glaring in their illogic suggests that behaviors in each of these areas are, or at least should be, tied together into a consistent pattern.

Consistency, however, is only a necessary and not a sufficient characteristic of good management. Organizational performance is affected not only by whether management behaves consistently across all these areas but also by which consistent pattern of behavior management chooses to follow. To complete our theoretical framework, we need to suggest the full range of factors which influence the system of management followed in a given organization or unit.

We have already suggested that managerial behavior is affected by the set of organization variables (goals, technology, structure, etc.) with which it interacts and by the set of human variables (capabilities, attitudes, etc.) present. Casting this in larger terms, we can argue that the system of management which is chosen must be not only internally consistent but also consistent with both organization and human variables and with environmental demands. Returning to an earlier example, it is clear that the "system" of management usually associated with assembly line operations, including the way in which jobs are designed, controls applied, and rewards distributed, is unlikely to be as successful, even if consistent, when transposed into a research laboratory. (Whether the reverse is true, we leave for later discussion.) The transposition of an assembly line system of management to a research laboratory might not result in a total loss of output, but few would argue that such a system was being most appropriately applied.

Usually, however, the applicability of various systems of management to given organizational situations is not as clear-cut as it is in this example. In many, if not most instances, a number of systems of management may well work. While management is nudged a bit in one direction or another by organization and human variables, its choice of alternative behaviors with regard to each integrative mechanism, and its choice of a given system of management, is not dictated.

In these situations, managers are influenced by a third set of variables not yet incorporated into our model. They are influenced by their own concepts and philosophies concerning people and processes, their own theories of how and why people in organizations behave as they do and, thus, how and why they as managers ought to behave in a particular way.

THE COMPLETED MODEL

We can now complete our conceptual model by adding to Figure 2-2 the variable of managers' own theories of management as a partial determinant of the system of management chosen in a given organization or unit and by adding also two broad "outcomes" variables, effectiveness and efficiency. Within the block assigned to managers' own "theories," as shown in Figure 2-4, we have specified only three, the *traditional, human*

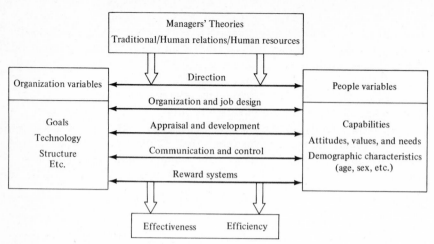

Figure 2-4   Managers' theories as a factor influencing choice of integrative mechanisms

relations, and human resources. While in fact every manager has his own theory of management, his own set of concepts which in part guides his behavior and his choice among alternatives in the areas described, we believe most managers' views can be clustered around one of the three sets of assumptions, policies, and explanations we have labeled as traditional, human relations, or human resources.

In the following chapter, we will examine these three theories of management, tracing their origins, exploring their logic, and indicating the extent to which they appear to be descriptive of the actual views managers tend to hold.

BIBLIOGRAPHY

Likert, Rensis, *The Human Organization* (New York: McGraw-Hill, 1967), chaps. 1, 2, 3, and 7.

Chapter 3

Managers' Theories
of Management

In the last chapter, we argued that managers' roles and behaviors are influenced not only by the sociotechnical system of which they are a part—the human and organization variables with which they interact—but also by their own theories of management. Moreover, we claimed that most managers' theories, with perhaps some pushing and molding, could be grouped under three general headings: (1) traditional, (2) human relations, and (3) human resources. Our task now is threefold. First, we must make clear what we mean when we refer to "theories" of managers and how they relate to management theories developed by scholars. Second, we must describe and briefly discuss the three theories. Finally, we must examine the extent to which managers actually hold or tend to hold to one of these three theories. In our closing comments, we will raise, but not attempt to answer, the general question of which theory managers *ought* to hold.

31

DO MANAGERS HAVE "THEORIES"?

Does the typical manager actually have a "theory" of management as such? The answer to this question is the standard equivocation—yes and no. A relatively small number of managers—Lyndall Urwick, Chester Barnard, and Alfred Sloan are notable examples—have at some point in their careers drawn back from day-to-day affairs and prepared detailed statements of their own theories of management. Most managers, however, have never attempted to develop a carefully worked through, "logical" description of why they manage in a given fashion.

Nevertheless, even though he may never have put them on paper, or perhaps even been aware that he was using them, the typical manager has a set of views and concepts which influence his behavior and affect his decisions. These may be held in the form of folksy axioms, such as:

If you give a subordinate an inch, he'll take a mile.
When the boss is away, the workers will play.
If you want a job done right, do it yourself.
An ounce of recognition is worth a pound of pay.
Look after your men and they'll look after you.

Or, if these axiomatic examples of managers' views appear a bit too primitive, we can consider some slightly more sophisticated statements:

Where coordination is everyone's business, it is no one's business.
When quality control is placed within a line department, it inevitably breaks down under the pressure of production schedules.
Centralized decision making results in better decisions—decentralized decision making results in improved implementation.

It is, of course, difficult to defend any of these axioms or statements as representing theories of management. Nevertheless, each has within it the basic components of a theory. A theory, as defined here at least, is simply a more or less complete explanation of how and why someone or something behaves, occurs, or responds as he or it does under a given set of circumstances. A theory usually begins with a set of assumptions, then describes or prescribes a set of actions possible under the assumed conditions, and finally predicts and explains the causal linkages determining a set of results. For example, the statement that workers play when the boss is away implies a set of beliefs about employees' attitudes toward work and their predispositions toward organization and department goals. Given these assumptions, it indicates what will happen (workers will play) if the boss does not behave in a given manner (supervise them closely). Similarly, the statement that quality control exercised by a line department breaks down under production pressure implies a set of beliefs concerning the interaction of human attitudes and behaviors and a particular set of structural and technological conditions. It predicts one result (breakdown) under one set of actions and implies another result (better control) under a second set of conditions.

Our point is that the typical manager does have a set of beliefs, whatever the degree of sophistication, which, taken as a set, could be described as his theory of management. It is likely that he has never tried to think these through or put them down systematically, and there is some evidence that his views may well be inconsistent somewhere—one axiom, statement, or belief unrecognized as being in conflict with another. However, even though it is frequently unspoken and occasionally inconsistent, his theory of management nevertheless influences his actions and decisions.

Sources and Impact of Managers' Theories

Recognizing that the path leads toward a psychological morass, we should attempt to differentiate a manager's theories from his basic life values and from the habits, attitudes, and behaviors which combine to form his personality. What we are calling management theories are those concepts and views which the manager has acquired through reading, training, and observation and which he feels are rationally structured and for which he feels supporting evidence is available or could be collected. They may or may not be influenced by his basic life values. For example, a manager may have strong egalitarian values while at the same time he holds to the concept that most women are emotionally unsuited for high-level executive positions.

Similarly, as suggested in Chapter 1, the concepts a manager holds may or may not be reflected in his daily activities. For example, even though he responds warmly in contacts with his peers and subordinates, he may hold the view that good job design minimizes interpersonal dependencies. Thus, while his daily behavior may be closely tied to his theory of management, it is also possible that his concepts of how people ought to be motivated, controlled, and rewarded may show up in his policy statements and directives but not in his one-to-one, face-to-face interaction with his subordinates.

Fortunately, our treatment of managers' theories of managing does not force us to defend either their consistency or inconsistency with life values and daily behavior. We *are* interested in the manager's general "style" of behavior with those around him because we believe it has an impact on organizational performance. We have an even greater interest, however, in the way his concepts of management influence his decisions in the areas of job design, communications and control systems, systems of rewards, etc., because we believe these are more important in determining unit and organization performance.

Managers' Theories versus Scholars' Theories

As managers, with some exceptions, do not regularly and systematically attempt to set forth their theories, scholars are forced to piece together from statements, policies, decisions, and practices, the theories of management which appear to prevail. Such theories, thus constructed, do not reflect precisely the views of any single manager—each one, as indicated earlier, has his own set of concepts. Nevertheless, such efforts on the part of scholars may capture the main thrust of key concepts previously or currently held by a large segment of the managerial population.

Moreover, many scholars tend not only to be descriptive but also prescriptive. On the basis of their own research, readings, and experiences, they may well indicate not only what they believe managers' theories are but also what they feel they should be. The process, of course, is circular. As scholars define systematically the theories which they believe managers hold and describe these in publications, from the conference podium, and in the classroom, they tend to influence the views of managers and future managers. This occurs when they simply describe existing theories; it is clearly intended when they prescribe alternative views.

In the following pages we will describe and discuss three theories which scholars have been presenting as representing the main components, or core, of alternative views actually held by practicing managers. Inevitably, however, they are also to some extent prescriptive—they reflect the beliefs and attitudes of their creators. In a later section, we will present some evidence of the extent to which managers actually claim allegiance to one of these three models. The reader, however, is encouraged to collect additional evidence by comparing his own views and the views of managers he knows with each of the three models presented here.

THREE MANAGERIAL THEORIES OR MODELS

The traditional, human relations, and human resources theories of management are presented in outline form in Figure 3-1. Note that each of the theories follows the format described earlier. Each begins with a set of assumptions about human attitudes and behaviors. Based on these assumptions it then describes appropriate managerial actions. Finally,

Traditional model	Human relations model	Human resources model
Assumptions	Assumptions	Assumptions
1. Work is inherently distasteful to most people	1. People want to feel useful and important	1. Work is not inherently distasteful. People want to contribute to meaningful goals which they have helped establish
2. What workers do is less important than what they earn for doing it	2. People desire to belong and to be recognized as individuals	
3. Few want or can handle work which requires creativity, self–direction, or self–control	3. These needs are more important than money in motivating people to work	2. Most people can exercise far more creative, responsible self–direction and self–control than their present jobs demand
Policies	Policies	Policies
1. The manager's basic task is to closely supervise and control his subordinates	1. The manager's basic task is to make each worker feel useful and important	1. The manager's basic task is to make use of his "untapped" human resources
2. He must break tasks down into simple, repetitive, easily learned operations	2. He should keep his subordinates informed and listen to their objections to his plans	2. He must create an environment in which all members may contribute to the limits of their ability
3. He must establish detailed work routines and procedures and enforce these firmly but fairly	3. The manager should allow his subordinates to exercise some self–direction and self–control on routine matters	3. He must encourage full participation on important matters, continually broadening subordinate self–direction and control
Expectations	Expectations	Expectations
1. People can tolerate work if the pay is decent and the boss is fair	1. Sharing information with subordinates and involving them in routine decisions will satisfy their basic needs to belong and to feel important	1. Expanding subordinate influence, self–direction, and self–control will lead to direct improvements in operating efficiency
2. If tasks are simple enough and people are closely controlled, they will produce up to standard	2. Satisfying these needs will improve morale and reduce resistance to formal authority—subordinates will "willingly cooperate"	2. Work satisfaction may improve as a "by–product" of subordinates making full use of their resources

Figure 3-1 Alternative theories of management

each theory predicts results which are likely to follow if managers behave as suggested. Rather obviously, only the basic tenets of each of these theories are shown in Figure 3-1, and our discussion in this chapter will expand these core concepts only slightly. The full range of implications of each theory for the integrative mechanisms of management—direction, communication, control, appraisal, rewards, etc.—will be developed in later chapters.

Even recognizing the incompleteness of these theories, the reader is nevertheless urged to spend a few moments looking carefully at them as they are outlined in Figure 3-1, examining not only the similarities and differences among the three models (and their relationship to his own views) but also testing their internal consistency. Do the policies suggested in the traditional model, for example, flow logically from the assumptions it makes about human attitudes and behavior (whether or not the reader agrees with these assumptions)? Do the expectations of the human relations model seem reasonable in light of the policies it suggests managers should follow? And so on.

With the basic properties and logic of these three theories in mind, we can proceed to a brief analysis and discussion of each.

The Traditional Model

This model is drawn from several sources and could easily be broken down into at least three more distinct, though related, theories. It draws, first of all, on the writings of nineteenth-century philosophers and their popular interpreters. The Social Darwinists, particularly Herbert Spencer, argued strongly that with man, as with other species, not only do the fittest survive but that they *should* survive, as they can and do contribute disproportionately to their numbers. Conversely, efforts made to preserve and improve the lot of the inept are not only expensive but are potentially damaging to the natural evolutionary progress of mankind. The popularizers of this philosophy, supported by many Protestant theologians of this period, tended to accept the American business hero and his rise to prominence, prosperity, and power as evidence that man could serve both himself and his society through the energetic application of his own natural capabilities. On the other hand, those who failed to succeed gave evidence either of their basic lack of ability or their unwillingness to apply it vigorously. Transferred into an organizational arena, this view suggests that those relatively few persons who, because of their superior capabilities, achieve high positions must, in the interest of progress and efficiency, use their talents to guide firmly—but fairly—those of lesser ability.

Similarly, the writings of classical economists contribute to the traditional theory. Borrowing generally from our Judeo-Christian heritage, and specifically from Biblical stories of the creation, classical economists defined leisure as man's desired state and work as his required state. Man is drawn out of leisure and into work by the payment of money which he requires to meet his needs, and the substitution of money for leisure will continue up to some point of marginal satisfaction. Although classical economists recognized that many factors other than money were considered by the employee in choosing to take or remain on a job, they tended to focus on money as the sole reason for work, holding other issues constant for the sake of analytical purity. Further, building on the early observations of Adam Smith, classical economists accepted task specialization as the prime building block of productive efficiency. Although task specialization was seldom dealt with explicitly, its positive contribution was assumed and no dysfunctional consequences resulting from it were incorporated into their theories. Restricting ourselves to just these sources, we could structure a "natural law" theory of management which would be similar to but not quite the same as the traditional model illustrated in Figure 3-1.

A second set of views to which the traditional model is closely linked is that put forth by Frederick Taylor and other leaders of the scientific management movement. Writing from around the turn of this century to the midtwenties, Taylor, Frank and Lillian Gilbreth, Henry L. Gantt, and others had and continue to have a significant impact on managerial thinking in America and in England. Based on shop-floor observations, this group claimed that most departments and jobs were inefficiently structured and that most workers were poorly trained. They argued that even presumably skilled craftsmen used wasteful methods and that these inefficiencies, along with widespread "soldiering" on the job, could be attributed not only to worker attitudes and abilities but also to poor management and inadequate reward systems.

Using a variety of related analytical techniques, this group studied and redesigned processes and jobs around developing principles of time and motion economy, controlled pacing and rest, and task specialization and grouping. Standard methods—the "one best way" to carry out an operation—were sought and then, under careful and detailed supervision, workers were trained to follow these methods. Taylor and others coupled their efforts to fit the "right" man to the job, and to supply him with standardized methods and equipment, with attempts to build effective incentive pay plans. They were frequently able to illustrate that a "first class worker," in Taylor's terms, could earn "first class wages" if he would carefully follow the detailed instructions for carrying out his task.

Just as he felt that the task of discovering and applying efficient job methods was beyond the capabilities of the typical worker, Taylor also felt that the typical shop manager was unable to carry out the full range of duties required by his job. He suggested a system of "functional" foremen, one in charge of training, another in charge of scheduling, another in charge of discipline, etc., to replace the traditional shop manager. (Although Taylor's ideas in this area were never widely accepted, it should be noted that modern staff departments have been built around these and other functions to assist the shop manager.)

Similarly, Gantt focused on inadequate managerial skills in the areas of planning and work flow coordination, and modified versions of his simple scheduling and control charts are widely used today.

Much of modern industrial engineering is founded on the basic tenets of scientific management—current concepts of job design, methods analysis, and work scheduling, although more sophisticated, have their roots in the work of Taylor and his colleagues. Once again, a full-blown theory of management could be drawn out of the writings of the leaders of scientific management, a model which would differ to some degree from the traditional model pictured in Figure 3-1 but which would resemble it in most of its basic tenets.

In addition to these two key sources of concepts, the traditional model is also drawn from or can be related to the ideas of Max Weber, a German sociologist. Writing at about the same time as Taylor (though each was probably unaware of the other's work), Weber lifted the notion of task specialization upward from the shop floor and applied it to the middle and upper levels of large-scale public and private organizations. Weber described—and, in the process, prescribed—bureaucracy, a system of interlinked offices (bureaus), each designed around a specific segment of knowledge, skill, and expertise. Hierarchically arranged, these offices provided a stable structure through which the individual could move, on the basis of merit, as his career progressed. Authority and responsibility would thus be rooted in the office and not in the man currently occupying it—the basic methods and procedures associated with a given office would remain essentially constant, undisturbed by the transfer of position holders.

Common Features   Glancing back through this brief survey, it can be seen that two concepts central to the traditional model—(1) orderliness and stability and (2) authority based on capability—are also central to each of its diverse sources. The "natural law" theorists see order and stability as flowing from the firm but equitable direction of those whose superior capabilities clearly entitle them to the exercise of power. The scientific management theorists see order and stability as the necessary and logical outgrowths of method standardization. Authority, in Taylor's mind, had only one legitimate basis—science. If jobs were designed scientifically, if methods, equipment, and working conditions were determined scientifically, and, most important, if scientific measurement were the basis of pay rates, then the orderliness he sought in the work process should, he felt, carry over into the interpersonal relationships among managers and their subordinates. Thus Taylor argued that in a science-based, democratic society, management could exercise direction only on the basis of its superior scientific knowledge and its willingness to rely on scientific analysis as the arbitrator of disputes. Finally, Weber closely parallels Taylor in his defense of "rational" authority based on expertise and its appropriateness in democratic cultures. The orderliness and stability in his structure were not only necessary for day-to-day operations, but they allowed persons to train for established positions (offices or bureaus) and to achieve these through merit. Authority and responsibility, therefore, could be rooted in positions and position holders appointed solely as a result of merit.

The Human Relations Model

The human relations model in many ways merely incorporates and extends the traditional model, although it has one or two basic differences. Many of its concepts emerged as managers and scholars pointed out what they believed were problems arising from some of the ways in which the traditional model was being interpreted and applied.

As early as the 1920s, business spokesmen began to point out the harmful effects of trying to standardize men as well as jobs. Although they did not challenge the basic tenets of task specialization, orderliness, stability, and control that were central to the traditional model, they criticized sharply those they felt were treating employees as mere appendages to machines. Management might seek standard skills and standard methods, but it could not, they argued, expect perfectly standard, emotionless behavior from employees. Management must deal with the "whole man" rather than just his skills and aptitudes, for people want to be treated as human beings, with at least some recognition given to their individual needs, wants, and desires. Further, they felt that management must help people to satisfy their natural desires to belong, to feel an important part of the unit and organization of which they were members.

Although moralistic in some of their overtones, these arguments were usually tied to criteria of effectiveness and efficiency. Unless management responded with greater warmth and consideration to employees' feelings and needs, these critics claimed, it could rightfully expect nothing more than resistance to authority along with lagging, poorly motivated performance. Moreover, management could not reward simply with money. Some argued, in fact, that most people were willing to take part of their reward in the form of personal attention, humane treatment, and the chance to feel important, providing, of course, that they were receiving a reasonable salary anyway.

This demand that management recognize that people expect more than money from their jobs was given additional weight by problems which developed over incentive pay schemes before and during the 1920s. Managers in many organizations, quite contrary to the philosophies of Taylor, Gantt, and others, had tended either to cut pay rates sharply or to raise standards of performance as workers had begun to earn substantially more money as the result of increased output. Moreover, workers and their union spokesmen reacted angrily to so-called efficiency experts who, they claimed, sought to raise performance without raising pay. In the myriad incentive pay plans developed during this period, workers discovered many that were in their view either exploitative or else so complex in their determination that they could not tell whether they were exploitative. Given these concerns, some firms moved away from incentive systems and others stopped their movement toward them, so that in the twenties, as today, most workers were paid according to hourly or other rates rather than through incentive plans.

In sum, these early spokesmen, most of whom were in fact practicing managers, argued that whereas the organization could appropriately be described as a machine, its human parts, as well as its equipment, needed regular lubrication. Poor morale, resistance to authority, and, ultimately, inefficient production would result from the failure of management to satisfy people's basic human needs. On the other hand, if management would simply treat people as human beings, acknowledge their needs to belong and to feel important by listening to and heeding their complaints where possible and by involving them in certain decisions concerning working conditions and other matters, then morale would surely improve and workers would cooperate with management in achieving good production.

Hawthorne Experiments   Major support for the concepts put forth by these early spokesmen was provided by the first major social science studies in industry, the famous experiments conducted at the Hawthorne, Illinois plant of the Western Electric Company. Beginning in the late twenties, these studies documented employee resistance to certain types of managerial controls and the efforts of employees to regulate incentive pay levels. In addition, the researchers claimed to have demonstrated that people respond not so much to actual levels of pay and conditions as they do to the manner in which these are determined and implemented. They pointed to evidence that employees in a congenial work group, interacting and involved with supportive supervisors, either increased their output or maintained it at high levels throughout an experiment ostensibly designed to improve working conditions, and during which the intensity of lighting was raised, returned to its initial level, lowered to substandard levels, and then raised again. These results, they felt, could only be explained by the fact that the employees were made to feel important through receiving supportive and concerned treatment that in turn made them feel that their opinions and feelings were given full consideration.

As these studies began to receive attention and as they were popularized by numerous interpreters, questions which might have been raised concerning research methods and a host of less spectacular but important findings were submerged in the wake of the dramatic support which many managers felt was provided for the basic concepts illustrated in the human relations model. For many, these studies gave welcome evidence that the manager need not—in fact, could not—run his organization as an impersonalized and coldly efficient machine. Rather, he should acknowledge that the parts in this machine were people with whom he could appropriately interact to provide satisfaction for their needs and receive in return not only the respect due his position but also their warm regard and cooperation.

The Human Resources Model

Just as the human relations model subsumed, implicitly at least, many tenets of the traditional model, the human resources model accepted and extended the assumptions about people made in the human relations model. It recognized that people have needs for acceptance, status, and recognition. It went beyond this, however, and argued that many people want opportunities to develop and apply their full range of abilities and to gain satisfaction from achieving demanding, worthwhile objectives.

The human resources model draws its assumptions about people first of all from theories of human needs and their development which originated in the late thirties and early forties and which began to be popularized following World War II. Most prominent among these is the theory of needs proposed by the late psychologist Abraham Maslow. He argued that man has a number of wants and needs arrayed in ascending order from the most basic physical needs for food, shelter, and clothing to the most intangible needs for self-actualization, or fulfillment. In between are the need for safety and security, the need to belong—to be wanted and loved—and the need for achievement, status, and self-esteem.

Maslow's theory is developmental. He argues that as each lower level of need is at least minimally satisfied, a higher-level need becomes operative. To support this logic, one may point out that in infancy most of our concerns are centered on physiological and safety needs. Through later childhood and adolescence our needs for belonging may come to the fore, followed by our needs to establish our own identity and to begin to make our mark in the world. Ultimately, we may reach a state in which external recognition is secondary to inner satisfaction achieved by reaching self-set goals of growth, accomplishment, and service.

Numerous exceptions to this general pattern of development can be quickly found. The artist starving while he paints appears to violate Maslow's need hierarchy, as does the person who sacrifices his own security for the sake of another. Moreover, most human behavior, as Maslow recognized, is complex enough for us to suspect that several needs may be at the root of most actions. Finally, solid empirical support for the Maslow theory has not yet been produced, and competing, though frequently related, theories are available.

Whether Maslow's theory is precisely accurate, its basic tenets are widely known and are regularly used to explain human behavior. Its supporters claim that many organization members are not motivated to perform at high levels because their basic needs are already satisfied and there is no opportunity for them to achieve satisfaction of higher-level needs in their work setting. Management, they argue, must go beyond simply providing fair pay and treatment and trying to make members feel important. In the interest of organizational performance, management must design jobs, structures, and processes in which individuals can fulfill their needs to develop and expand their abilities. Thus, they argue that work is not inherently distasteful; what is distasteful is a set of tasks so limited as to inhibit growth and development and a job environment which restricts satisfaction of the individual's needs to move toward increasingly mature, self-directing, self-controlling behavior.

Support for the assumption that many if not most organization members not only *wish to* but *can* contribute more than their present jobs demand or allow is pieced together from many sources. Most often pointed to by advocates of this theory is the dramatic and continuing upward trend in the training and education of our work force. Extending this, they argue that we have not yet begun to recognize the potential for growth in most people, and they present evidence of sizable gains in ability made by individuals previously thought to be inherently deficient in ability.

Thus, the main thrust of the assumptions of the human resources model is an emphasis on abundance rather than scarcity in the area of human capabilities, which in turn indicates that the manager's role is not so much one of controlling organization members as it is of facilitating their performance. If, as suggested, most people, whatever their level of current ability, have untapped resources, the manager's task becomes that of tapping these in the interest of organizational effectiveness and efficiency.

This logic is carried over into the expectations of the human resources model. As shown in Figure 3-1, this theory holds that the purpose of allowing organization members to participate in decisions related to their work (and, concomitantly, to exercise self-direction and self-control in carrying out their tasks) is to achieve direct improvements in organizational performance. It is expected that members will derive satisfaction from creative task accomplishments, but this is treated as the by-product, not the purpose, of allowing them broader participation in the affairs of their unit.

These expectations can be contrasted with those of the human relations model, in which managers' efforts to give recognition and support to their subordinates and to allow them some participation in unit decisions are viewed primarily as a means of increasing morale. Thus, in the human relations model, the manager is encouraged to allow his subordinates greater involvement so that they will be more satisfied with him and with their jobs and, thus, more willing to cooperate in carrying out his directives. Similarly, the human relations and human resources models can be compared in the area of prescribed policies for managerial action. Both, as shown in Figure 3-1 and as discussed above, advocate subordinate participation in departmental decision making. The human relations model, however, because it is using participation primarily as a means of promoting *feelings* of belonging and importance, suggests that involvement be limited to issues of concern to department members but not necessarily central to actual work tasks. For example, involvement under the human relations model might be focused on working conditions, routine scheduling problems, the location and use of secondary equipment, etc. The human resources model, on the other hand, advocates involvement not only on matters pertaining to the context of the job but on important issues concerning how and by whom departmental tasks will be done. In fact, the human resources model implies that the more important the issue is to departmental performance, the greater should be the manager's effort to tap the full range of resources of his subordinates.

IMPLICATIONS FOR THE MANAGERIAL ROLE

Each of these models—traditional, human relations, and human re-sources—contains a clear concept of the basic role of the manager. These role concepts specify his relationship and obligation to the technical and human systems of the organization and guide his choices of behaviors along each of the integrative mechanisms continua (i.e., his style of leadership, approach to organization and job design, communications and control, reward design and allocation, etc.). Although, as suggested, these role concepts are clearly implied in the model, it is worth taking a moment or two here to make them explicit.

Under the traditional model, the manager's role is essentially that of a controller. His basic obligation is to the needs of the technical system. People are viewed as necessary components of the technical system, and, therefore, the manager is responsible for directing and controlling their behavior in line with the system's needs. It is assumed that the system's goals are known and are relatively stable and that tasks and procedures can be rationally designed. Further, it is assumed that if the manager specifies tasks and procedures clearly, selects and/or trains members properly, treats them fairly, and pays them equitably, he should be able to expect their full compliance with the system's needs. Obviously, as a controller, he is expected to take corrective action if compliance is not forthcoming, but no other relationship with or obligation to members is specified.

Under the human relations model, the role of the manager is modified to include responsibility for maintenance of the human system. That is, this model recognizes human social and egoistic needs which may not be satisfied fully through simple fair treatment and equitable pay, and whose frustration may lead to resistance to the demands of the technical system. Thus, while the manager is still viewed as essentially a controller with prime responsibility to the system, he is expected to take preventive steps to keep his people cooperative and compliant. Such behaviors as praising performance and consulting with members on routine issues are recommended as means of satisfying employee needs and assuring cooperation. Note that under the traditional model, the technical system and human system were viewed as basically compatible, and thus poor performance could result only from incompetence or perversity, either of which represents appropriate grounds for removing the noncompliant member. Under the human relations model, some possible incompatibility was reluctantly recognized, and, therefore, dismissal as a correction for noncompliance was less easily justified. Further, although the goals of the technical system were still viewed as stable and/or predictable, the value of system-specific training was recognized, along with the costs of replacing human components, thereby providing an additional rationale for trying to prevent uncooperative behavior through the satisfying of human needs.

Under the human resources model, the manager's basic role is rather dramatically redefined. No longer is he viewed as a controller but rather as a developer and facilitator of the performance of the sociotechnical system to which he is assigned. He is presumed to be working with his superiors and peers in the continuing process of goal setting for the organization and with his subordinates in the definition of unit objectives and procedures. Once-and-for-all designs of technical systems and/or member requirements are viewed as inappropriate in that technical demands are likely to change and member capabilities are expected to grow with time. Numerous possible causes of poor performance are recognized, some rooted in the organization, some in the design and operation of the technical system, and others in the members themselves and their relationship with one another and with the manager. The manager's facilitative-developmental role carries the obligation of concern for all these barriers to performance—a series of new and recurring dilemmas. Basic compatibility between member and system needs is not assumed, but certain approaches to leadership, job design, control, and rewards (to be illustrated in later chapters) are viewed as more likely than others to enhance member development and contribution. However, the assumption of widespread capability for self-direction and self-control and the desire to contribute meaningfully minimizes, but does not remove, the controller–preventive-maintenance aspects of the managerial role, and it maximizes the obligation to remove restrictions to, and to develop and create, new investment opportunities for the full utilization of the human resources in the unit.

Which Theories Do Managers Actually Hold?

While surveys of managerial attitudes and opinions have been increasing in number and scope since World War II, it has been in only the last decade or so that managers' theories, as such, have been the target of systematic research.

The first major studies of managers' theories, including their assumptions about people and their views toward management policies and their effects, were begun at about the same time at Stanford University, under the direction of Dale Yoder, and at the University of California, Berkeley, under the direction of Mason Haire, Edwin Ghiselli, and Lyman Porter. Having had a part in the Stanford studies and having followed the Berkeley studies closely, I subsequently began a series of studies designed to clarify points which they had raised and to probe more deeply into certain findings. My own studies have now involved over 1,000 subjects, including managers from public and private organizations, labor union leaders, medical administrators, and executives from a variety of other types of organizations. Taken together, these three researches have covered several thousand managers, and a brief examination of the general pattern of findings is in order.

Not too surprisingly, one of the more clear-cut findings is that managers appear to hold not one but two theories of management—one theory concerning how they should behave with and manage those below them and a second theory concerning how they themselves should be managed by their own superiors. Moreover, these two theories appear closely related to two of the models described here.

A Theory for Subordinates   When we look at managers' views of how their subordinates should be managed, two points seem clear. (1) Managers generally accept and endorse the use of participative concepts. (2) However, they frequently doubt their subordinates' capacity for self-direction and self-control and their ability to contribute creatively to departmental decision making.

In the Stanford studies, an overwhelming majority of managers indicated agreement with statements emphasizing the desirability of subordinate participation in decision making. In the Berkeley studies, a majority of the managers in each of eleven countries, including the United States, indicated agreement with such concepts as sharing information with subordinates and increasing subordinate influence and self-control. Similarly, in my recent studies, managers overwhelmingly endorsed participative policies.

On the other hand, while managers appear to have great faith in participative policies, they do not indicate such strong belief in their subordinates' capabilities. For example, the Berkeley group, in their international study, found that managers tended to have a "basic lack of confidence in others" and typically did not believe that capacity for leadership and initiative was widely distributed among subordinates. In my own studies, managers in every group have rated their subordinates and rank-and-file employees well below themselves, particularly on such presumably important managerial traits as *responsibility, judgment,* and *initiative.*

But if managers do not expect creative, meaningful contributions from their subordinates, why do they advocate participative management? A reasonable answer seems to be that they advocate it as a means of improving morale and satisfaction. This interpretation gains support from my own studies. In them, managers were asked to indicate their agreement or disagreement with statements predicting improved morale and satisfaction, and statements predicting improved performance, as the result of following various participative management policies. In connection with each of these policies, managers indicated consistently greater agreement with the predictions of improved morale than with the predictions of improved performance.

The fact that managers appear to have serious doubts about the capabilities of those reporting to them seems to rule out their acceptance of the human resources model for use with their subordinates. On the other hand, the fact that they do endorse participation and seem quite certain about its positive impact on morale suggests a close relationship between their views and those expressed in the human relations model. Moreover, the types of participative policies which managers most strongly advocate seem to support this interpretation.

In my research, managers indicate strongest agreement with policies that advocate sharing information and discussing objectives with subordinates. However, they tend to be somewhat less enamored with policies which suggest increasing subordinate self-direction and self-control. This pattern of participation seems much closer to that of the human relations approach than to that of the human resources model.

A Theory for Themselves When we examine managers' views toward their relationships with their own superiors, a much different pattern of responses becomes evident. (1) Managers in my studies tended to see little, if any, difference between their capabilities and those of their superiors. In fact, they tended to rate themselves equal to, if not higher than, their superiors on such traits as *creativity, ingenuity, flexibility,* and *willingness to change.* (2) When asked to indicate at which levels in the organization they feel each of the participative policies would be most appropriate, managers invariably felt most strongly that the full range of participative policies should be used by their own superiors. More important, they also tended to be most certain that these participative policies would result in improved organizational performance *at their own level.*

Thus, when managers discuss the type of practices their superiors should follow with managers at their own level, they appear to espouse the human resources model. They see themselves as reservoirs of creative resources. Furthermore, the fact that they frequently see themselves as more flexible and willing to change than their superiors suggests that they feel their resources are frequently wasted. Correspondingly, they expect improvement in organizational performance to result from greater freedom for self-direction and self-control on their part.

Which Theory Should Managers Hold?

It is appropriate, as suggested at the beginning of this chapter, that we should close this brief discussion by at least raising the question of which theory managers *ought* to hold. Having raised it, we are obliged to provide at least the beginnings of an answer, which we will do with what will appear to be typical professorial evasiveness. Managers *ought* to hold that theory which most accurately describes the real world.

Let us be more precise. If the assumptions underlying the traditional model are more accurate than those of the human relations and human resources models in their description of the actual needs and capabilities of most people, then a manager's theory of management ought to be built upon these assumptions. If they are not, if, say, the human relations assumptions more accurately describe the way most people really are, then they should be the foundation for a manager's theory of management.

If we can agree with this not terribly profound observation—that the theories managers hold ought to be built upon the most accurate set of assumptions possible—we can then attempt to deal with two questions which have probably already formed in the reader's mind. The first question might be framed as follows: "So what if the manager's assumptions are accurate? Isn't it true that, given his particular organizational environment, he may not find it possible or profitable to behave in line with them or to carry out the policies that logically follow from them?" The answer, of course, is yes. The manager may be right and his world wrong, but if so, his charge is clear—he must try to restructure his environment so that he can behave in the best long-run interest of the organization. Moreover, while engaged in this continuing, long-term process, he can make a variety of small adjustments which together may bend the constraints within which he operates toward a better alignment with his personal theory of management. There is obviously much more to be said with regard to this question and its corollaries, and we will deal with these in detail in later sections.

The second question which is very likely in the reader's mind at this point may be posed in these terms: "Agreed, the manager should hold those assumptions about people which are most accurate and should build his theory of management in accordance with them, but doesn't this force him to behave ineffectively with some people—to miss the mark with those for whom his assumptions are not most accurate?" The answer is, again, yes. No single set of assumptions about people will encompass the full range of individual differences in the areas of needs or abilities. It is probably equally true, however, that within broad limits managers do not and cannot take this acknowledged continuum of human capabilities and desires into account. Managers, for example, establish control systems which apply to large numbers, or groups, of individuals without attempting to determine their appropriateness for every individual affected. Similarly, theories of management influence the way in which department and task assignments are structured and which may encompass any number of individuals with unique characteristics on one dimension or another. Our argument, then, is simply that managers should obviously try to adjust their behavior to fit the needs and capabilities of individuals and groups to a much greater extent than is typically done today. At the same time, we hold that the manager will, and must, choose a basic posture, a general approach to management, which will be reflected in many of the broad policies he sets and follows with regard to the full set of integrative mechanisms discussed earlier. Within these broad boundaries, there is much room for adjustment to individual needs and abilities, but the main thrust of his behavior will reflect his basic theory of management. Again, the chapters that follow will enlarge on this argument, but it is perhaps well to establish this premise now.

In framing beginning answers to these two questions, we have purposely avoided the broader, overriding issue—which set of assumptions is most accurate? If the evidence were clear-cut and easily mustered, we would address this question straightforwardly. But in fact, as is true with most important issues in the real world, the available evidence is rather messy, fragmented, and more than a little complex in its interpretation. Therefore, we choose a less direct approach. In the chapters which follow, we will focus separately on the integrative mechanisms which form the substance of the manager's role, examining for each the prescriptions implied by each of the three management theories, tracing out their logical implications, and broadly examining the evidence which is available. In every instance, we will discuss the impacts of both organizational and human variables and explore the range of alternatives which may be open to managers to accommodate these two sets of variables in a coherent and consistent theory of management. Hopefully, this process will help the reader to formulate his own answer to the question of which set of assumptions is most accurate, or at least to develop his own theory of management with its own set of assumptions uniquely applicable to his particular organizational setting.

BIBLIOGRAPHY

Bendix, Reinhard, *Work and Authority in Industry*, 2d ed. (Berkeley: University of California Press, 1974), see particularly chap. 5 and Introduction.

Gerth, H. H. and C. Wright Mills, *From Max Weber* (New York: Oxford Press, 1958), chap. 8.

Haire, Mason, Edwin Ghiselli, and Lyman Porter, "Cultural Patterns in the Role of the Manager," *Industrial Relations*, vol. 2, pp. 95–118 (February 1963).

Homans, George, *The Human Group* (New York: Harcourt, Brace and World, 1950), chap. 3.

McGregor, Douglas, *The Human Side of Enterprise* (New York: McGraw-Hill, 1960), chaps. 1–4.

Miles, Raymond E., "Conflicting Elements in Managerial Ideologies," *Industrial Relations*, vol. 4, pp. 77–91 (October 1964).

Pugh, D. S. (ed.), *Organization Theory* (Baltimore: Penguin Books, 1971).

Taylor, Frederick, *The Principles of Scientific Management* (New York: Norton, 1967).

Yoder, Dale et al., "Managers' Theories of Management," *Journal of the Academy of Management*, vol. 6, pp. 204–211 (September 1963).

Chapter 4

Job Design

Following the precedent begun in Chapter 3, we should invest a few lines in clarifying where we have been and where we are going. We have constructed a general conceptual framework describing some of the more important determinants of management's role and behavior and ultimately of organizational performance, a framework which for analytical purposes treats organizational variables and human variables as separate factors. In addition, we have examined at even greater length a third factor, managers' own theories of management, which we argued has a substantial impact on the way in which organization members are directed, controlled, rewarded, etc.

Our task here and in Chapter 5 is to illustrate and analyze how these variables may interact to determine managerial behavior in one specific area—the way in which managers design individual jobs and the manner in which these jobs are combined into units, departments, and organizations. It should be made clear that a complete explanation of the complex interrelationships among these variables is not only beyond the scope of these chapters, but quite likely beyond the limits of current knowledge. We will, therefore, declare our task complete following exploration of some of the more important patterns of interaction and impact.

JOB DESIGN UNDER THE THREE MANAGERIAL MODELS

We can begin our analysis of job design and organization structure by moving back over familiar ground, tracing out in more detail the prescriptions for job and organization design which are stated and implied in our three alternative theories of management. Also, recall that the assumptions underlying these theories focus almost exclusively on human variables, and thus their directives would seem to be primarily aimed at adjusting the structure to fit the needs and abilities of its members.

A closer examination reveals, however, that for each set of explicit assumptions about people, there is an implicit, related set concerning the nature of the world in which people exist—the environment in which the organization functions, the impact of that environment on the goals and objectives of organizations, and the technological systems and procedures most appropriate for achieving those ends. We will focus first on the prescriptions for job and organization design that are derived directly from the models' stated sets of assumptions about human attitudes and capabilities and then develop the related sets of implied assumptions about organizational variables.

The prescriptions for job design stated or implied by our three theories of management can be illustrated as shown in Figures 4-1, 4-2, and 4-3. You may wish to examine and compare these diagrams before proceeding with the text.

Job Design under the Traditional Model

Based on its assumptions about the attitudes and abilities of the typical organization member, the traditional model, as illustrated in Figure 4-1, prescribes a complete separation of thinking and doing. The manager or his staff assistants are responsible for determining not only the precise duties for each job but also for establishing standard procedures and methods for carrying them out. Moreover, the manager is expected to specify the flow and pace of work moving through the job—to determine which steps should be taken in what order and to establish time and quality standards appropriate to each step.

A basic principle of job design under this model holds that jobs should contain a limited number of related tasks, each requiring similar skills and roughly comparable learning periods. The job holder is thus

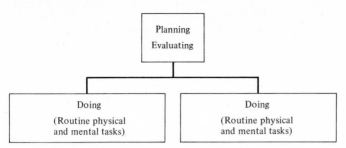

Figure 4-1 Job design under the traditional model of management

expected to be able to learn quickly and to follow precisely the methods prescribed. Included in these methods are detailed decision rules to be applied to the routinized alternatives with which he may be faced. He is expected to turn to his superior for direction in case of any unspecified occurrence. In fact, the primary work relationship of each organization member is designed to be dyadic—one to one with his superior. Work-related contacts with peers are formalized and controlled—the scheduling and pacing of sequential work flow are the responsibility of the superior.

If the typical organization member is, as the assumptions of this model suggest, neither particularly interested in nor capable of exercising self-direction and self-control, he should perform best under conditions in which he is told precisely what to do and how to do it. Moreover, as he is assumed to be more interested in what he earns than in what he does, he should be pleased to be relieved of all possible responsibility—providing, of course, that he is paid well, in accordance with his output, and treated with basic fairness.

Job Design under the Human Relations Model

The prescriptions for job design stated or implied in the human relations model are essentially unchanged from those of the traditional model. Given its assumptions about human needs, the human relations model tends to focus more on the context of the job, the conditions under which the work is performed, than with the actual content or makeup of the job itself. Thus, as shown in Figure 4-2, job design under this model still calls for the basic separation of thinking and doing—the manager is still responsible for most if not all work-related planning, scheduling, and control activities, and the employee is responsible only for carrying out his directives. The manager's task is *broadened*, however, to include concern for the human needs of his department members. He is expected to respond, wherever possible, to each individual's desires to feel important

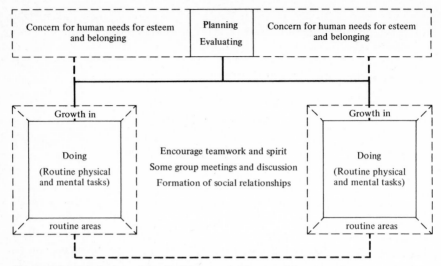

Figure 4-2 Job design under the human relations model

and to receive recognition as a person rather than being simply another part in the organizational "machine."

In Figure 4-2, the manager's human relations responsibilities are shown by the dotted-line squares. These squares are not drawn with solid lines because, although these responsibilities are considered important, they are still considered secondary to the manager's prime task of structuring and directing the work itself. Similarly, the interaction between department members and their superiors is shown with dotted lines to indicate that their participation in the affairs of their units, although seen as an important means of satisfying their needs and improving morale, is not seen as central to the actual accomplishment of their jobs or of departmental objectives. Participation and consultation *must not interfere with task accomplishment or affect the flow and pacing of work.*

Finally, Figure 4-2 illustrates two more aspects of the human relations view of job design—the development of relationships among peers and the provision of some opportunity for growth (both again designated by dotted lines). The superior is urged to work toward the development of a cohesive, supportive work group so as to minimize personality frictions which might impede departmental performance. His efforts to promote a friendly and cooperative atmosphere are not intended, however, to be carried to the point of allowing department members to coordinate their own activities or determine the nature of joint efforts or the linking of sequential work activities. Similarly, the superior is encouraged to allow for some on-the-job growth activities, including, for example, rotation of members among similar positions and work stations, and occasional opportunities to interact with other units or departments. Such activities are viewed as a means of reducing boredom and enhancing feelings of importance and may, of course, make it easier to reschedule work during vacation periods, illnesses, other temporary absences, and so on.

If organization members fit the assumptions of the human relations model—that is, if, even though they are limited in capacity for self-direction and self-control, they still seek to satisfy their needs for belonging and importance on the job—they should respond positively and cooperatively to work environments similar to that portrayed in Figure 4-2. The manager's efforts to make his department a warm and friendly place in which to work, and his efforts to consult members whenever possible concerning working conditions and minor aspects of the work process, should result in a loyal work force which tries to carry out its assignments as directed.

Job Design under the Human Resources Model

Job design under this model is, as illustrated, more complex than it is with either the traditional or human relations approaches. This is because the manager is expected to achieve high levels of performance by using his department members' creative talents and their capabilities for self-direction and self-control, while at the same time providing opportunities for them to satisfy their individual needs. In fact, this model assumes that it is *through* the utilization of their abilities in self-directed and self-controlled activities toward jointly planned objectives that members obtain satisfaction. Thus, the manager is not urged to seek out opportunities for consulting his subordinates so that their needs for belonging and importance may be satisfied. Rather, he is urged to create mechanisms by which their contributions will directly improve departmental performance. Satisfaction, if it occurs as expected, is therefore a desirable *by-product* but not the direct target of managerial activities.

As shown in Figure 4-3, joint planning of work objectives and schedules is considered a crucial part of the manager's job under the human resources model. He is expected, from the day a new member enters his department, to work with that member to broaden the area over which he can exercise self-direction and self-control. That is, the new member may initially need substantial guidance and assistance, but the manager's task is to move him as quickly as possible to the point where he is able to structure and control many of his own activities, determining his

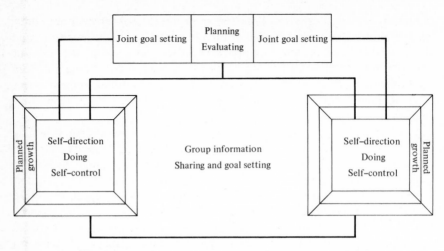

Figure 4-3   Job design under the human resources model

own work pace and scheduling in line with general objectives set jointly with his superior.

Further, he will be expected to move rapidly to the point where he can contribute effectively to joint planning with his peers and with his manager in setting priorities and in scheduling and coordinating the flow of work within the department as a whole. Throughout his tenure in the department, each member is expected to be the recipient of a substantial investment of time in training, covering a wide range of tasks and activities, from his peers as well as from his superior, an investment again intended to have a joint payoff (i.e., to the member and to the department).

It should be noted that, under the human resources model, the manager is not asked or allowed to share his responsibility for or to minimize his contributions to the planning, scheduling, and controlling of department activities. Rather, he is asked to upgrade and expand his concern in these areas. If department members are able, as expected, to plan and coordinate most of their own activities, the manager is freed to work with individual members and with the group as a whole in seeking methods of improving overall performance. Thus, if this model's assumptions concerning people's untapped resources are accurate, the manager and his unit should be able to pursue a course of continued growth, development, and improvement up to limits set by the broader organization structure and technology. These limits are not explicitly developed in the human resources model or in either of its two counterparts and, therefore, are not illustrated in Figure 4-3. Nevertheless, job design must take into account organizational as well as human variables, and it is to these that we now turn our attention.

THE IMPACT OF TECHNOLOGY AND THE ENVIRONMENT

The traditional, human relations, and human resources models build their prescriptions for job design not only on their explicit assumptions about people's attitudes and abilities but also on a set of implicit assumptions concerning the environment in which these jobs exist. The traditional and human relations models tend to share a common view of the organization's environment and its goals and technology, a view which is substantially different from that of the human resources model.

Assumptions of Stability

Under the traditional and human relations models, jobs are designed to fit into a stable and predictable environment. The development of standard tools, methods, and procedures is predicated on the assumption that the core technology of the unit, and presumably of the organization, will remain constant long enough for the investment in analytical time and energy to be repaid. Similarly, under these models, on- and off-the-job training is restricted to specific skills and knowledge needed to operate a narrow segment of the current technology, and thus these types of training both limit the flexibility of the system and are forfeited if change occurs.

The assumption that technology will remain reasonably constant dictates the corollary assumptions that the organization's environment and basic objectives will also remain stable—that is, the needs and behaviors of the groups with which the organization interacts will remain relatively fixed. In other words, if the needs and demands of the organization's customers or clients tend to remain, or can be forced to remain, relatively constant, the design of the organization's product or service can be fixed. And, if the core product, or service, remains stable, the organization's technology can be designed and refined to achieve machinelike articulation.

The emphasis here on *stability* of environmental factors and organizational goals and technology, rather than on their degree of complexity or sophistication, is intentional. Within broad limits, it is the stability of product and process rather than the complexity which serves to constrain job design under these models. Even the most sophisticated products can be produced by minimally or at least narrowly trained personnel if a sufficient investment is made in special-purpose equipment and assembly processes. Stability, of course, need not be present across the entire system. If departments or units can be shielded from external turbulence or goal instability, they may continue to produce parts, components, or lines of products with relatively stable technological processes.

Stability in the organization's (or unit's) environment, goals, and technology might, therefore, be considered a necessary but not sufficient condition for efficient job design under the traditional and human relations models. A stable technology is essential for routinization of physical and mental activities, for thinking to be separated from doing, and for members to be trained to perform repetitive, narrowly defined collections of tasks. Whether people *will* perform most effectively and efficiently under these conditions depends on the extent to which the assumptions of these models are accurate.

Recognition of Variability

Under the human resources model, on the other hand, the prescriptions for job design are not based on the assumption of stability in organizational goals or processes. The reverse is true—job design is explicitly dynamic. The continued upgrading and broadening of members' skills is a basic responsibility placed on the manager and his unit. This growth is viewed as a capital investment leading to improved performance and flexibility. Thus, change is not only presumed but is in fact demanded if the full benefits of this investment are to be realized.

Similarly, under this model the emphasis on self-direction and self-control also reflects the acceptance and encouragement of change. The skills acquired in planning and controlling the bulk of one's own activities in one situation are at least partially transferable to new circumstances, and the confidence gained through successful self-direction is a prerequisite to the acceptance of new challenges.

Finally, the human resources model calls for joint planning of departmental objectives, schedules, and procedures. For this to be successful, members must be well informed not only about what is expected or is happening but also about why and how their unit's activities fit into the broader organizational process. Understanding *why* as well as *how* things operate not only promotes adaptability to externally generated change but is likely to stimulate internal pressure for change and improvement.

In sum, job design under the human resources model anticipates change and reaps its full benefits under circumstances which demand flexibility and creative adaptation to new problems and objectives. Where the environment is turbulent and changes in goals and technology are frequent, this approach to job design appears to be more appropriate than that of the traditional and human relations models, *whether or not its assumptions about people's attitudes and abilities are entirely accurate.* Where conditions are stable, the choice of this approach over its counterparts depends on the accuracy of its assumptions. If people do have untapped capabilities, ignoring these even where it is technologically feasible to do so would appear to represent a hidden cost akin to that of maintaining excess funds in unproductive reserve accounts. But we will have more to say on the economics of job design in a moment. We must first attempt to put the comments made thus far in perspective by looking at some examples of the way in which jobs are designed and by examining the characteristics of both the organizational and human variables present in each instance.

SOME EXAMPLES OF JOB DESIGN

Our first two examples are of jobs designed in the traditional model. In both examples, environmental and organizational conditions appear to be reasonably well in line with the assumptions of this model—basic objectives, including product design, have remained relatively constant, and it has been possible to hold core technology essentially stable. Following this, we present two additional examples. In each of these two examples, the organizational environment is relatively stable, but jobs have been designed using the assumptions of the human relations and human resources models. (These and subsequent examples are based on actual cases, modified to provide anonymity. Modifications include shifts from one organizational site, location, or industry to another.)

> ORGANIZATION A—(Stable Environment, Traditional Job Design) The main plant of organization A is devoted to assembling a fairly small piece of mechanical equipment. The product moves down a conveyor belt in the middle of a series of long workbenches. Workers pull parts from bins beneath their bench and perform their fractional part of the assembly process, fitting in screws or nuts and bolts, soldering, or using a fast-drying-cement and clamp procedure.
>
> Engineering studies have determined the speed at which the line can move, and the number of operations performed at each position is in turn determined to fit the speed with which the product must move past that station. The product is produced in several sizes and styles, but all basic assembly operations are essentially the same. The style and location of parts bins, the tools used in assembly, etc., have also all been determined by engineering studies. When products flow off the end of the line, they are

transported directly to a separate quality control group which inspects for defects and moves the products on to the packing section.

Product design and thus the basic technology have remained reasonably constant for the past two or three years. The organization is beginning to be concerned about competition from a foreign manufacturer and is considering moving to a cheaper style of product made entirely of plastic. This would eliminate many of the current assembly operations and would hopefully reduce the present level of defects—a source of constant friction between quality control and the line department.

Most of the line employees in the assembly plant are women and are presently nonunion. Quality control personnel and all supervisors are men. Turnover and absenteeism among the assembly crew present troublesome though not severe problems, but the rates in both instances have increased in the last year. A union which represents the warehouse personnel in this organization claims to have signed up over half the men working in the quality control group (four of seven) and nearly 30 percent of the assemblers.

The organization is worried about the threat of unionization and concerned over pay rates, which, although fair for the area, are a problem in the face of cheaper, foreign-made competitive products. There has been considerable discussion among top management concerning the possibility of moving the plant to another area where the likelihood of unionization might well be lower and where employees might be more satisfied with the present level of wages. As one of the plant managers remarked, "It used to be that women, particularly those from minority groups, were delighted to get the chance to work in a plant like this, where wages are reasonably good and working conditions are much better than average. We still have a pretty good group, but we now have far fewer applicants and many of those you just wouldn't want to hire."

ORGANIZATION B—(Stable Environment, Traditional Job Design) Organization B is a public utility. It has a sizable engineering department, including a large group whose responsibility includes designing and preparing drawings and specifications for power generation and transmission facilities. Design, in this instance, actually refers to the making of simple modifications in accordance with standardized decision rules—the basic design of major components is handled either by the equipment manufacturer or by a senior staff of engineers. Further, work assignments for this group are handled in such a way that each member is expected to specialize in one small segment of the generation-transmission system. As the basic technology has remained relatively constant for the past several years, many members have become so experienced that they can practically turn out drawings and write specifications from memory.

A substantial number of the engineers in this group are products of European universities who have been attracted to this country by high salaries. The flow from abroad has slowed a bit in the past two or three years, and there is some concern in organization B over recent difficulties in recruiting engineers from United States institutions.

At least two points should be emphasized concerning the above examples. First, both the production plant in organization A and the engineering group in organization B are performing effectively. Although management in each instance would presumably welcome improved levels of output, reductions in costs, or increased profitability, it is not at present dissatisfied and is faced with no compelling reason for modifying the current approach to job design. Second, besides having environmental and technological conditions which make it possible to achieve high levels of job specialization and routinization, it would seem that these two organizations have employees whose behavior for the most part has not been out of line with the assumptions of the traditional model; they have appeared to be satisfied with their pay and working conditions and have made few overt demands for increased responsibility or autonomy.

Of course, it is possible that these organizations have tended to select their employees from somewhat special populations. The women on the assembly line in organization A may view their jobs as temporary or else simply as a source of secondary income for their families, and, therefore, these jobs may well meet their aspirations. Further, it may be that many of the engineers in organization B have been molded by their cultures to expect, and perhaps prefer, relatively high levels of centralization of authority and responsibility.

In both instances, however, management's concern about the future is worth noting. While they do not have reason to expect dramatic changes in organization goals or technology, they do appear concerned about maintaining a flow of people whose characteristics fit their current approach to job design.

ORGANIZATION C—(Stable Environment, Human Relations Job Design) Organization C is an assembly plant located in a suburb of a medium-sized Eastern city. Its main task is putting together a small and relatively simple piece of electronics equipment from parts manufactured in other plants of the same firm and by outside suppliers. Here again, many of the operations—particularly those involving wiring and soldering connections—are handled by women. Parts move through several assembly areas on overhead conveyors and are removed, then replaced following work at each station. As in organization A, inspection is handled by a special test group which is responsible to a manager outside the production-line organization. Each assembler performs a narrow range of operations according to product style and specifications. Production engineering has designed a unique system of color coding which allows the assemblers to make connections or link parts after briefly glancing at an instruction card attached to the part.

The current production system was installed in 1969. During the next two years the plant manager became concerned about the "growing evidence of poor morale" in the main assembly room. Turnover and absenteeism increased during late 1969 and again in 1970. The percentage of defective assemblies increased only slightly but had been expected to *decrease* following the installation of the new production system and the color-coded instruction sheets. Moreover, work-floor supervisors reported numerous complaints that, whereas the assembly instructions were clear, the sequencing of steps on the cards was difficult or even impossible to follow. As one supervisor put it, "My girls think the engineers don't know one end of the product from another."

After discussing the situation with his personnel manager, the plant manager decided that the key problem was one of boredom, coupled with an unnecessarily rigid position on the part of the methods engineers concerning assembly steps at the individual work stations. At a meeting with his floor supervisors, they hit on two ideas. The first involved a system of rotation in which the assemblers would be scheduled to work in different but related work stations each day. (Following the suggestion of one supervisor, it was agreed that if two women were especially good friends they should be allowed to rotate to adjacent positions wherever possible.) The second suggestion involved the formation of a "methods" committee which would be charged with collecting suggestions for changes in the assembly steps at various work stations and sending these along to engineering. Presumably, engineering would agree to follow any suggestions which did not appear to violate good design principles.

The rotation system took some time to implement, but, as each station's operations could be learned quickly, it presented no problems. Assemblers have seemed generally appreciative of management's efforts to make their work more interesting and supervisors have reported a general reduction in the level of complaints. Turnover did not increase in 1971 but did again slightly in 1972 (the last year for which figures are available), a factor which the personnel manager attributed to the opening up of new jobs in the community.

The "methods" committee is still operating but in the view of the plant manager has "not worked out exactly as was hoped." Some modifications in methods were made following the first few weeks of activity by the committee, but fewer and fewer have been made since that time, even though the rate of suggestions continued to increase for several months. In fact, the plant manager has had a number of difficult moments pacifying the engineering group, particularly when one strongly supported suggestion questioned the whole conveyor layout. All suggestions are now routed through the plant manager's office, and he is toying with the idea of trying to shift the committee's concern away from methods as such and into the general area of working conditions (such as heating, lighting, etc.). At one point he planned to abolish the committee entirely but was cautioned against that move by his personnel manager.

In this organization, product design and basic technology have, as indicated, remained basically stable for the past several years, and management has never questioned the basic efficiency of its approach to job design.

Overall performance is satisfactory, although it never quite reaches the goals set for the new system, and no complaints have been received from higher management. The plant manager and his assistants are generally proud of their efforts to "satisfy human needs as well as the needs of output efficiency" and regularly point out that their plant is one of the few in the area which has never had a serious threat of unionization.

ORGANIZATION D—(Stable Environment, Human Resources Job Design) Organization D is the main manufacturing and assembly plant of a medium-sized firm in a Midwestern city. A number of related products in varying sizes and styles are produced to stock in this organization. Its products are sold to a nationwide market and have an outstanding reputation for quality at a competitive price. Although the demand fluctuates from year to year, it can be forecast with reasonable efficiency, and thus output levels can be stabilized. Similarly, because organization D keeps closely abreast (and usually ahead) of its competitors in product design, year-to-year changes can be programmed without major difficulty, so that the basic manufacturing and assembly technology can be held reasonably constant.

Despite the fact that conditions are such that jobs could be designed to maximize routinization and specialization, organization D has held to the basic concept that employees can and should be made responsible for their own quantity and quality of output. Implementing this philosophy, the organization has attempted to retain work assignments that allow individual or small-group accountability. Individual work stations are designed to accommodate in-process stocks of parts and products, and workers are expected to maintain their own inventory of supplies and materials. In most instances, individual workers or small teams of two to four employees can determine the pace with which they will draw items out of in-process storage, complete their stage of the process, and move these ahead to the storage area at the next work station. Moreover, the work at each station is designed to allow completion of some operationally meaningful stage of the manufacturing-assembly process so that usually, when the work is completed, the product can be tested and certified as to proper functioning. The individual worker or small team does the testing and places its certification mark on the product before moving it ahead to the next storage station.

Organization D claims to have an output-per-worker ratio significantly higher than its leading competitors and, as pointed out above, enjoys an unchallenged reputation in terms of product quality. It is, for the moment at least, apparently willing to forego the possible advantages of further mechanization and routinization in the belief that its present system is more efficient overall.

Our remaining examples describe job designs in turbulent environments—where for some reason environmental conditions demand fairly rapid adjustments in the form of changes in the nature and design of products and services. In the first instance, the organization has attempted, with predictable results, to maintain a traditional approach to job design.

ORGANIZATION E—(Turbulent Environment, Traditional Job Design) Organization E is the order-processing section of the marketing department of a firm which manufactures a line of testing devices used by many small manufacturers and repair shops. The ten-man sales force covers fourteen states and is trained both to sell the equipment and to make minor repairs in it, or at least to diagnose the nature or source of malfunctions so that new parts or components can be ordered. They consider themselves "field engineers" and not salesmen and have strongly resisted efforts to get them to follow standard order-taking procedures. They tend to write up orders by part name without attaching the part number and seldom bother to verify prices. The organization attempts to carry a full line of replacement parts for all models sold during the last seven years.

The order-processing section employs twelve full-time clerks, eight of whom are women. In addition to processing orders from the field sales force, they also write up orders which are phoned or mailed in directly by customers. All phone orders are transferred to one of three senior clerks. Similarly, all phone correspondence with field salesmen is handled by either the division manager or one of the three senior clerks.

When an order is received or has been transferred to the multiple-copy standard order form, it is placed in the in-basket of the appropriate clerk. If the order is for a standard model in current production, it is processed by one of three "standard" clerks (usually those newest on the job). If it is for replacement parts it goes to one of the six "parts" clerks. If the order contains both current product and parts requests, it goes first to the "standard" clerk and then to the "parts" clerk. If it is a complex request, it will most likely be handled by one of the three senior clerks (all men). Orders are apportioned to "standard" and "parts" clerks by the division manager, or by the senior clerks, in such a manner that the numbers of orders in the in-basket piles are as nearly equal as possible at all times. Once received, orders are typed, prices verified, availability checked against stock records, and entries made to update stock records.

The multiple copies of the order form are sent to warehouse-shipping, billing, and, in the case of orders for currently produced devices, to the production scheduling department. In addition, copies are filed in the processing section under the customer's name and in the file of the salesman who took the order. Finally, the processing clerk keeps a desk copy of the order which is held in a current file until notice of shipping has been received. Notices of delays in shipping or of parts out of stock are sent to the processing section, and the division chief or one of the senior clerks is then responsible for sending an appropriate form to the field salesmen or, in the case of direct orders, to the customer.

The system used in the order-processing section has been in effect for just over four years. It was instituted at the same time that the clerical force in the section was doubled (from six to twelve) in response to a rapid increase in sales associated in part with the acquisition of a smaller firm making a related line of test devices. Before the current system, each clerk handled orders from one or two salesmen, processing both new-model and parts orders.

According to its severest critics, the field salesmen, the new system "has just never worked out." They claim that delivery promises are seldom met and that parts orders are often delayed for weeks—delays which are considered intolerable by customers who depend on the test devices. Moreover, they complain, even simple orders are regularly "screwed up," with the wrong part arriving even after the delay.

The division head is also upset because he "can't get all the bugs out of the system" but lays much of the blame on the "warehouse crew" (which he claims "sits on orders for days without processing them or letting us know that something is wrong") and the "kind of clerks you get nowadays—by the time you get one that knows a standard valve from a gauge dial, she gets married, pregnant, or just leaves." The division chief, who is only a few years from retirement, notes that he and his senior clerks "try to be as nice as possible to the new girls—help them learn the system and the stock and try to get them to be more concerned with correcting their mistakes 'before they happen.'" Nevertheless, he feels that he is caught between the mistakes and lack of commitment of his staff and the warehouse-shipping force and the increasing demands for rapid service from the field sales force. He has been meeting with the marketing manager and a representative of a local data processing firm to explore the possibilities of buying new equipment to handle part of the order-processing work load. The marketing manager simply feels "something has to be done—we are losing, or coming close to losing, important business and have already lost one or two good salesmen we shouldn't have lost."

Clearly a substantial portion of the "turbulence" experienced by the order-processing section in organization E comes from inside rather than outside the organization. The sales force could greatly aid the processing section's quest for order and efficiency by being more precise in the handling of orders and by cutting back on promises of delivery and services to customers. They see this, however, as a direct violation of their proper role—they feel they work for their customers as much as for their firm, and they point out that it is their personalized, specialized service which has kept them ahead of their competitors.

Similarly, the warehouse-shipping crew could improve its performance. The men claim, however, that they are doing their best. They point out that most of the delay has occurred before they get the forms and that when they do have questions or problems it takes "all day to get through to anyone who knows what the hell is going on up there."

ORGANIZATION F—(Turbulent Environment, Human Resources Job Design)   Organization F is the process-engineering department of a manufacturer of complex electronic equipment. The firm manufactures a number of items to stock, but items are regularly combined or modified to special order in small lots. In addition, advances in the field are extremely rapid and product design changes are constantly being made in order to incorporate the latest innovations. This is considered a matter of necessity, not of choice, as many small competitors are constantly seeking to syphon off sales on the basis of "improved design."

It is the task of the process-engineering group to build prototype models of new products and to devise efficient methods for manufacturing these in sizable quantities. In addition, the group is responsible for preparing manufacturing orders for special-product requests which require only minor modifications or a combination of existing designs.

Until three years ago, all drawings and orders were prepared by graduate engineers. A group of thirty technicians then built the prototype equipment and prepared special tools, jigs, and fixtures required in the manufacturing process. The technicians were nearly all former members of various line departments who had shown unusual skills and who in most cases had some college or technical school training. Most of these technicians were in their late twenties or thirties, although a few were older employees who had some training as machinists or toolmakers (none were journeymen in these trades). In addition, the technicians often completely handled single-item special orders.

As the press of product innovation increased, along with the inflow of special orders, the technicians were frequently held up by delays in the preparation of drawings. Sometimes, without formal approval, the engineer working on a special order would sketch out the requirements and discuss them with a team of technicians, and they would then proceed to complete the product without further instructions. Success with these efforts led some engineers to use the more experienced technicians in completing drawings and manufacturing orders for some of the less-complex standard items. When this was done, the technicians would then follow up their work in the line departments, working out bugs in the manufacturing process.

The manager of the process-engineering department was well aware of these deviations from procedures but adopted a wait-and-see posture. As he became more and more impressed with the skills and capacity for growth shown by many of the technicians, he proposed consideration of a formal redesign of procedures in the department. In open discussion with his engineering staff, he found general agreement that much greater use could be made of the technician group. The engineers quickly identified five or six technicians who could, they felt, handle "damn near any project on their own." They also felt that many of the remaining technicians could be quickly trained to carry out much broader assignments.

Discussing the issue with those technicians considered most qualified, the department manager began to draw out ideas for broadening their roles. The technicians felt that often they were better able to carry out liaison with the line departments than were the engineers—they knew many of the men by name, and, since they had actually built models themselves, they knew firsthand some of the more difficult problems involved in putting the final products together. Moreover, they had ideas for simplifying some of the detail work on drawings and manufacturing orders: "The guys in the shop don't need all that extra crap—they just laugh about it anyway."

Using these and other suggestions, the technicians' jobs have been reformulated. For the most part, they now work in teams headed by an engineer. The most experienced technicians do much of the write-ups of manufacturing orders, but only after they have worked through one model with the line department assigned to build it. The less experienced technicians work along with the more competent and remain with the line department for a few days as each new start-up is carried out. According to the department manager, it is becoming increasingly difficult to call any but the newest technicians inexperienced, they are all developing skills so rapidly. Special-order products are now being handled almost exclusively by technicians. They turn to the engineer only when highly specialized help is needed. In fact, as the market for special products is increasing, the firm is drawing more men off the line to work with the technicians, and it is expected that a whole new department may emerge.

In organization F the rapid changes in product design and the increase in special orders appeared almost to force changes in job design in the process-engineering department. Recently, the department manager remarked that he did not feel they could have met the requirements of their current level of business if they had continued to operate as they once had. He is impressed enough with the success of this venture so that he is arguing that most of the line departments could benefit from major job redesign. "Given the direction business is taking," he argues, "we ought to be raising at least half of the line operatives up to the level of competence of the technicians, and I don't see any reason why we can't."

CONCLUDING REMARKS

We have, up to this point, described alternative approaches to job design flowing from our three theories of management and examined their operation under varying environmental conditions. It is appropriate now to attempt to draw some conclusions concerning the present and future state of job design. (As we do so, the reader may note a shift in emphasis from description to prescription—from an analysis of what *is* to the passing of judgments concerning what *might be*. The shift is intentional.)

Our discussion of alternative approaches to job design implies that management has the option of choosing among these alternatives, an implication reinforced by those examples which illustrated movement from one approach to another. This implication is regularly challenged. It is argued by some—expanding on our earlier point that form follows function—that the task to be done dictates the technology to be used and that this in turn constrains or fixes the nature of job design. This argument is usually bolstered by pointing to situations, such as automotive assembly lines, where enormous investments have been made in special-purpose machines and materials-handling equipment and where many jobs are apparently inextricably intertwined with the form and pace of the total process. Such conditions obviously do exist, and the manager faced with them does in fact find most of his alternatives eliminated or severely constrained.

Nevertheless, two points should be made in response to this challenge. First, job design decisions are made in these circumstances—before and during the time at which the overall technology is being constructed. At any given point management may appropriately refuse responsibility for problems which may result from inherited technologies. Managers may not, however, ignore the role they play in the continuing set of decisions to renew, refurbish, and expand such processes. Second, and more important in the long run, the number of jobs which may be judged to be more or less fixed by the surrounding technology is a small and probably shrinking proportion of the total job population in our economy. By generous estimation, some 5 million workers may operate in or about heavily mechanized assembly-line processes, less than 10 percent of our total work force. Moreover, as we move along the line toward what some have called a "postindustrial economy," we may expect a relative if not absolute decline in the semiskilled, blue-collar work force associated with mass production industries. Jobs in the future may still be designed according to principles of specialization and routinization, in the office as well as the plant, but they will be so designed by intent and not by default—the "absolute" constraints of mass production technologies on job design can be expected to decline.

In addition to the just-defended implication that management has options, whether or not exercised, in the area of job design, we have suggested through discussion and example that each of these options may be effective if the assumptions underlying it are met. The traditional approach appeared to be working successfully in our first two examples, under stable environmental conditions, although there was some evidence of a declining supply of employees whose attitudes and career expectations fit the nature of their jobs. In the third example, again under stable conditions, the organization had adjusted to employee discontent by moving with apparent success from a traditional to a human relations approach to job design. Finally, in our next to last example, the traditional approach appeared to be creating problems, but this was understandable given the turbulent conditions in the department's environment. Conversely, the movement of the organization in our final example from a traditional to a human resources approach appeared to be dictated, in part at least, by necessity—increased demands for flexibility in product design and manufacture.

This suggestion that conditions vary and that the assumptions underlying each model may be more or less well met from one situation to another is also regularly challenged. Advocates of the human relations approach tend to hold that all employees want and expect to develop warm personal attachments to their peers and superiors. Further, some advocates of the human resources approach argue that *all* organization members are actively seeking opportunities for self-fulfillment, growth, and autonomy in their work environments and that the environmental conditions appropriate for the traditional approach no longer exist. Both these challenges deserve rejection simply on the basis of their inclusiveness. One need not search far for organization members, including many in the growing ranks of professionals and scientifically trained personnel, who neither expect nor want complete fulfillment of their social needs on the job. Similarly, organization members who work well under conditions in which they are told precisely what and how much to do, and who seek to satisfy their growth and fulfillment needs off the job, can be readily found. Finally, many organizations (or at least many organization units) continue to enjoy stable environmental conditions with no immediate threats to this stability on the horizon.

Nevertheless, these challenges, particularly the challenge of the human resources advocates, deserve attention. There is evidence that the pool of people who may be anxious, or at least willing, to accept narrow, routinized positions is declining. Over half of the current high school students in most states will attend college, and this proportion is expected to continue or increase. Minority group members and women are demanding that equal opportunity become a reality rather than a slogan—a demand that frequently can be translated to mean opportunity to move beyond low-level routinized positions.

Obviously, not all workers are, or are likely to be, equally interested in, or responsive to, efforts to enlarge the scope and challenge of their jobs. Some researchers claim, for example, that "alienated" workers, primarily those from urban settings with large ghettos or depressed areas, respond much less positively to increased job responsibilities than do their "nonalienated" counterparts from suburban or rural areas. Others argue that future generations may reject career aspirations and treat jobs as merely instruments through which they can achieve a minimal complement of necessities, leaving them free both physically and psychologically to pursue their broader interests.

On balance, however, the evidence seems to suggest that many, if not most, organization members will respond positively to meaningful job enlargement along the lines suggested by the human resources approach. Further, projecting the trends indicated above (always a risky business) suggests that the proportion of members presently satisfied with or suited for heavily routinized positions is declining, although not perhaps uniformly across the population. The precise percentages of members who might fall into varying categories of readiness for, or responsiveness to, job redesign is, of course, unknown.

Once again the manager is faced with the task of evaluating and acting on his own assumptions about people. If his assumptions match those of the traditional model, he will tend to play it safe with current repetitive and routinized designs, running the risk of some degree of dissatisfaction from the more capable of his subordinates and ignoring the hidden losses incurred from failing to use their capabilities. If his assumptions parallel those of the human relations model, he will attempt some measure of job redesign, stopping short of meaningful increases in the actual level of self-direction and self-control. This tactic runs a lower risk of damaging the existing system and may minimize some symptoms of dissatisfaction. It does not, however, face up to the larger issue of possible waste of human resources. Finally, if his assumptions are close to those of the human resources model, he will attempt to design and redesign jobs so as to maximize his subordinates' opportunities to use their capacities for self-direction and self-control, providing for expansion of job responsibility in line with increasing capacity. In so doing he will spend additional time and energy in development activities, investments which will probably not be repaid fully by every member of his unit. He will run this risk, however, in the belief that the total amount of resources tapped—the energy and commitment released by this process —will be jointly beneficial to the organization and to the typical member.

The manager's freedom to design jobs is obviously constrained to some extent by the environment in which his unit operates—the broader organization structure in which it is embedded. Again, rather obviously, the degree of constraint he feels will depend on the amount of congruence which exists between his concepts and policies of job design and those underlying the general form which his organization structure takes. These types or general forms of structure reflect, as do the types of job design, both environmental and technological variables, and real and/or perceived human attributes. This parallelism will be demonstrated in the following pages as we address the topic of organization design.

BIBLIOGRAPHY

Davis, Louis E. and J. Taylor (eds.), *Design of Jobs* (Baltimore: Penguin Books, 1972).

Dowling, W., "Job Redesign on the Assembly Line: Farewell to Blue-Collar Blues?" *Organizational Dynamics*, vol. 2, pp. 51–67 (Autumn 1973).

Ford, Robert N., *Motivation Through the Work Itself* (New York: American Management Association, 1969).

Hackman, J. R. and E. E. Lawler, III, "Employee Reactions to Job Characteristics," *Journal of Applied Psychology*, vol. 55, pp. 259–285 (June 1971).

Hulin, Charles L. and Milton R. Blood, "Job Enlargement, Individual Differences, and Worker Responses," *Psychological Bulletin*, vol. 69, pp. 41–55 (January 1968).

Chapter 5

Organization Design

In this chapter we move from an analysis of the ways in which jobs are designed to an examination of the ways in which positions, units, and departments are structured to form organizations. As we do so, our task becomes more complex. Most organizations contain many jobs and designing them is more complex than simply designing jobs by accumulation. The problem of relationships between any given set of positions within an organization is likely to be compounded by the broader set of relationships between each of those positions and numerous other positions, units, departments, etc.

Given this complexity, we will regularly be forced to retreat into more abstraction in our descriptions of organization structures and the processes by which they are created and modified. This statement is not a veiled request for indulgence but rather a means of serving notice to the reader that some hard work may be required to relate our discussion to the real world organizations with which he is familiar. A comment or two may clarify this notice.

Organizations are often described as "collections of people grouped together in pursuit of a common goal." They are much more than this, however. They are also complex collections of at least momentarily fixed and more or less well-understood roles, relationships, and responsibilities. Organizations are designed and redesigned not only by arranging and rearranging people but also by establishing and modifying the larger structures within which people carry out their duties. Managers expect to specify some sizable portion of the behavior of organization members simply by placing them in specific positions within the structure—positions which define who their boss is supposed to be, who their subordinates are presumed to be, and the nature of their work-related contacts with their immediate peers and, laterally, across to other units and departments.

The modifying terms "supposed" and "presumed" are used purposely here to underscore the obvious. People, even at low levels in organizations, do not behave precisely as defined by their positions. To some degree they shape and modify their own roles; they create, ignore, and alter relationships between their own and others' positions; and they accept, decline, expand, and otherwise adjust the responsibilities placed on them by their positions.

All this is more than just a lengthy way of saying that organizations do not actually work exactly as they are or were designed to—which is, of course, a well-documented fact. It is also an introduction to a less-obvious notion. People violate their positional constraints for many reasons. They do so because of their own needs and desires—for security from threat and pressure, to develop or modify social ties, to satisfy needs for recognition and esteem, and so forth. They also do so simply because their positions appear unclear or unworkable—poorly described or defined and, from their point of view, dysfunctional for unit or departmental objectives. Thus, organizations not only may work less well than they were designed to work because of the interaction of people and their positions, but they may also work much better than they have the right to perform, given their prescribed structure, and precisely because people do not accept their roles, relationships, and responsibilities as immutable.

These partially obvious insights should be held at the ready as we examine the assumptions about human attitudes and abilities which appear to underlie various types of organization structures and as we analyze the ways in which technological and environmental variables may constrain or otherwise affect these structural forms. They should remind the reader that our generalizations mask much of the detailed dynamics of real organizations. As stated, a structural form which appears appropriate to a given set of conditions may be made less effective by members who try to bend relationships to suit their own needs or views. On the other hand, structures which are in fact unsuited to their technological and environmental conditions may survive on paper, if not in practice, simply because people create their own workable order within the inappropriate design. Obviously, the manager's goal should be to create a structure which both meets the demands of its environment and makes greatest use of its members' capabilities, a task which should become clearer as we examine some of the alternative forms available.

THE PROCESS OF ORGANIZATION DESIGN

In theory, organization design can proceed from the top down or from the bottom up. In the top-down procedure, broad organizational goals would be translated into specific objectives—means of achieving the desired end. These objectives might become the focal point around which a series of departments could be organized. Positions within such departments would then be established to serve as the means of attaining the objectives. Further, many of the tasks assigned to each position might require considerable time and might, therefore, necessitate the development of additional positions or even units or departments. Through this deductive process of establishing ends and the means to them, a full-blown organization structure could be developed.

In the bottom-up approach, the basic process(es) of the organization would be established, defining simultaneously the core technology to be used. As positions were formulated to operate the process, the requirements of a superstructure would begin to emerge. Lower-level managerial positions are needed to coordinate activities, and these in turn require coordination by higher levels if the process is at all complex. Similarly, expert help would be required at various points, thus dictating the development of specialized technical groups with their own coordinating superstructures.

Even as described in theoretical terms, these two procedures are not, in fact, independent of each other. Broad goals must be established even before the basic process is determined, and the core technology chosen clearly becomes a means to the overall organizational ends. In practice, as suggested in Chapter 2, the two procedures are merged beyond separate identification. Even where new organizations or segments of organizations are being designed, key processes either already exist or are considered almost coincidentally with ultimate objectives. Most often, the manager is faced with situations in which all or some aspects of the structure are already established and thus the term organization "re-design" is more appropriate than organization design.

Moreover, because the manager is usually faced with some sort of existing structure, most redesign efforts are carried out in a fragmented fashion. Adjustments which are made tend to affect only portions of the structure—a department is shifted from here to there, groups are re-aligned, reporting procedures are modified, and so on, but only in rare instances is a redesign effort aimed at totally revamping an existing structure. Given this fragmented approach, managers—even those at the top—seldom have the opportunity to step back and examine the form which their organization has assumed, the total pattern of relationships which has resulted from their design efforts. Our discussion here is aimed at providing (perhaps "demanding" is a better word) such an opportunity.

TRADITIONAL ORGANIZATION STRUCTURE

Logically enough, the traditional organization structure illustrated in Figure 5-1 appears to be little more than a hierarchical combination of modules based on concepts of traditional job design. That is, if we pulled out any given segment of the structure (a unit, department, division, etc.) and examined it closely, the jobs and basic superior-subordinate relationships would resemble those described in our earlier section on traditional job design. These modules are linked together by solid lines indicating reporting (communications and control) responsibility.

The general shape of the traditional structure, although influenced by the specific technology of a given organization, is essentially pyramidical. In labor-intensive traditional structures (say a post office or assembly line), the pyramidical shape, with its broad base of low-level operative positions, would be clearly visible. On the other hand, also shown in Figure 5-1, a capital-intensive traditional structure (such as a chemical plant, oil refinery, or automated production facility) might contain few low-level positions, and one might visualize the structure as more diamond shaped than pyramidical. The overall form is still pyramidical, however, as Figure 5-1 illustrates; low-level operatives have simply been supplanted by machines or automated equipment while the shape of the superstructure remains essentially intact. (Some have suggested that the advent of the computer will greatly modify the shape of the middle and upper levels of traditional structures, a point to which we will return shortly.)

Relationship to Traditional Theory

A structure of this general form flows naturally from the assumptions of the traditional model. It allows maximum specialization and routinization

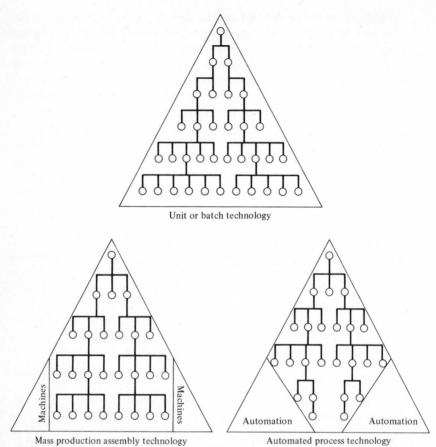

Unit or batch technology

Mass production assembly technology

Automated process technology

Figure 5-1 Organization design under the traditional model [Suggested in part by data from Joan Woodward, *Management and Technology* (London: HMSO, 1958)]

of decisions and activities, even within the managerial portions of the hierarchy. Coordination and planning (thinking activities) are forced upward by the shape and structure of the organization—problems involving two or more low-level units may, in line with the structure, find their logical formal point of resolution only at or very near the top of the pyramid. Further, in line with the assumption that most people are least capable in the area of exercising responsible self-direction and self-control, this type of structure facilitates the establishment of formal review procedures and requirements for obtaining higher-level approval before taking action.

The pyramidical shape and the rigid linkages binding the pieces of the structure are both essential to the key characteristic of the traditional structure—accountability. The holder of any given position in the hierarchy is presumed to be accountable, in theory and in fact, for the actions of all of those below him in the hierarchy and whose positions are directly linked to his. This accountability is assumed to be a necessary precondition to control and thus, in turn, to stability and predictability within the structure. Emphasis on accountability tends to pull the locus of decision making toward the top of the pyramid. That is, if the manager is held responsible for the actions of his subordinates, he may institute or maintain procedures to force them to obtain his approval before taking "important" actions, even if he tends to feel they are reasonably capable. Similarly, rigid lines of responsibility are not only essential to accountability but are reinforced and maintained by it. It is reasonable for people in such structures to wish to know precisely the limits of their accountability, as designated by lines of reporting responsibility, and "stray" positions and units must be rounded up and "branded" so that they will belong somewhere in the system. Further, the pyramidical form of the traditional structure is both a cause and an effect of accountability. The pinnacle positions provide a point of ultimate arbitration of decisions and disputes ("the buck stops here") and a point of central initiation of new directives and objectives for which they and those below them will be held accountable.

A final and partially redundant comment on the relationship between accountability and structural form and shape may be helpful. Note that positions at the same level within a given unit or department in the traditional structure (see Figure 5-1) are not linked together directly. They are joined only by their common attachment to their superior's position. This formal arrangement (whether or not observed) is essential to the concept of accountability. If persons at the same level are allowed to coordinate their own activities and to plan jointly, it then becomes difficult to assign responsibility for possible mistakes or shortcomings. Further, their common superior will not have the built-in opportunity to review actions and decisions for which he too will be held accountable. The traditional structure provides no direct linkages across departments or between positions at the same level. Thus, as indicated earlier, even though such positions may have contact in the course of carrying out assignments, the first formal point of linkage between them may exist two or more levels up the hierarchy. While such an arrangement can and does cause delays in resolving problems, it is held essential to the preservation of accountability.

Delegation and Decentralization   We have suggested at several points that the traditional structure tends to promote centralization of decision making. In fact, however, neither traditional management thinking nor the traditional structure necessarily precludes delegation or decentralization—the formal acknowledgment of the right of a subordinate to carry out actions under his own direction or the formal assignment of the right of the head of a unit or department to make certain types of decisions as the need arises. Rather, despite the assumption of the traditional model concerning the lack of subordinate capability in terms of judgment and long-range perspective, and despite the fact that the traditional structure is designed to both push and pull decisions upward, delegation and decentralization are accepted as appropriate *under certain circumstances*. For example, where units are separated geographically from the "home office" some degree of local autonomy is seemingly dictated by the constraints of time and space. Similarly, where a subordinate is dispatched to perform an assignment out of sight and contact with his superior, it is acknowledged that he must be granted a certain degree of freedom to adjust on his own to the demands of the situations he may face. In fact, if the limits of autonomy are prescribed in advance and enforced by the establishment of regulations, decision rules, and budgetary constraints, neither limited decentralization nor delegation violates the basic concept of accountability.

Nevertheless, although decentralization and delegation are viewed as acceptable under the traditional approach, they are never viewed as ideal. The manager *must* delegate. He cannot be everywhere at once—but the theory holds that it would be best if he could. Circumstances *demand* that some decisions be made at outlying points. It would be too slow and cumbersome to collect the information centrally, though better decisions might well be made if it were possible to do so. The manager is also forced to grant the professional or the technically trained employee a measure of autonomy in those areas where he himself does not have the knowledge to evaluate alternative courses of action, but he must at least exercise budgetary control so that things do not get out of hand.

During the 1940s and 1950s, when many organizations embarked on programs of diversification in both location and line of products and services, some decentralization appeared to be forced upon them. However, many traditionally oriented managers have viewed the advent of the computer era and the possibility of rapid electronic data processing as the means of bringing to a close the period of forced decentralization. It is now possible, they note, to recentralize many functions which had been forced downward or outward. Centralized computers can be programmed to schedule day-to-day activities at remote locations, and the expenditure of money and material at many points can be closely tracked.

Impact of the Computer   As noted earlier, some have argued that the computer will tend to take over many of the duties currently performed by middle-level managers and staff personnel. If this should occur, the pyramidical shape of the traditional structure would be greatly altered (on paper at least, although one could argue that the basic form would still be intact—the functions of middle management would still be performed). It seems likely, however, that the urge to recentralize may offset these tendencies. Middle management can now maintain personal control over many activities previously delegated or decentralized, control which mechanically can be exercised by the computer but which, if accountability is to be preserved, requires a manned review point. The evidence to date concerning the actual impact of computers on middle management is fragmented and difficult to interpret. It is impossible to determine whether the management functions are being electronically usurped more rapidly than new ones are being added, or vice versa. There is at least no indication that middle-management ranks are being depleted, and thus the report of their demise, like the report of Mark Twain's death, appears exaggerated.

Departmentalization by Function   We have said virtually nothing so far concerning one of the most frequently mentioned topics under the general heading of organization design—the structure and interaction of line and staff departments. We have avoided this topic because we feel the terms line and staff and the concepts built around them are no longer particularly useful. In the modern, merger-oriented business firm and in the complex public or private service organization, the bases for designation of all but a few departments by these terms are at best complicated and unclear, and at worst nonsensical. The issue of line and staff appears much better handled under the broader concepts of *functional specialization* and *lateral relationships*. Moreover, when the traditional structure is examined through the lens of these two concepts, one of its more interesting paradoxes becomes apparent.

Departmentalization by function is the logical goal of specialization in traditional design. The accumulation of similarly trained persons carrying out related—if not identical—duties in a single department not only increases opportunities for standardizing and routinizing their activities but also (in theory at least) enhances accountability. Thus, for example, in a manufacturing firm, engineering, production, quality control, and purchasing are most often maintained as separate departments, even though each initiates activities for the others. Similarly, in a welfare office, both the probation department and the aid-to-dependent-children unit are likely to have a separate chain of reporting responsibility, even though each may frequently be servicing all or some portion of the same household. Designers of traditional organizations are of course aware that such functionally organized departments tend to come into contact with each other at various levels within the structure. The difficulty, however, is that if they are to carry functional specialization to its logical limits, formal linkages between such departments, i.e., points of resolution of conflict, are raised upward toward the top of the pyramid. Thus, as suggested earlier, a point of contention between departments near the bottom of the structure may have to be carried through several levels of the hierarchy before it is resolved.

The Traditional Organization and Its Environment

From our discussion to this point, one can draw an analogy between the traditional organization structure and a playground jungle gym with a shortage of low-level lateral braces. The structure is rigid, and one can reach any given point from any other point but only by climbing to the top, across, and down again. The structure can be shifted or turned but only if the force is applied carefully at the apex—at the top center. Force applied at any other point may well wrench or tear the structure.

This analogy is intended to illustrate the fact that traditional structures, as designed, are primarily suited to stable, predictable environments. In the business firm, if consumer demands can be accurately anticipated (or regulated), the marketing department can send its forecasts upward for dissemination to engineering, production, and other departments which can then use the provided lead time to schedule their activities with high-level coordination. On the other hand, if the firm's environment is unstable, if demand for goods or supplies of materials, for example, cannot be forecast nor controlled, severe strains can be placed on the structure. In a public service organization, if client needs can be defined (manipulated or regulated) to fit neatly into the categories of specialized services which are offered, and if the total demand for services can be forecast, a traditional structure can be effectively maintained. However, if client needs are complex, users may become disgruntled or antagonistic toward fragmented, uncoordinated services.

As was noted in Chapter 2, all organizations try to reduce their dependence on the environment. Where possible they try to regulate the demands placed on them or, barring this, at least to influence them.

Where such efforts are impossible, the organization seeks to forecast environmental forces and thus provide some lead time or slack between actions in the environment and reactions in the organization. No structural form could withstand the stress of a completely unregulated environment, and a good portion of every organization's activities is aimed at stabilizing these organization-environment linkages. It should be obvious that the traditional structure is not only extremely vulnerable to such forces but that it must, therefore, spend considerable resources and energies to protect itself from their dysfunctional consequences. It is possible, although difficult, to estimate the amount of an organization's resources devoted to the creation of slack between it and its environment (for example, ordinarily unused production capacity, inventories of materials and finished goods, and so on). Similarly, it is theoretically possible, although perhaps even more difficult, to measure the amount of energy spent in a traditional organization to maintain its structure in the face of internal stresses and strains: an approximation can be achieved by enumerating the number of individuals, groups, and departments whose duties are defined, in part at least, as "coordination," "facilitation," "liaison," and so on.

In sum, traditionally structured organizations tend to operate with apparent effectiveness when their environments are reasonably stable or can be accommodated through the creation of organizational slack. Whether such organizations are efficient depends on at least two factors: (1) the total amount of organizational energy required to maintain the structure in the face of external and internal stresses, and (2) the degree to which the structure uses the full range of capabilities of its resources, including the abilities of all its members. Traditional structures are likely to be inefficient in highly turbulent environments, both in terms of the quality of their response to the demands of their environments and in terms of the energies which they must spend in maintaining themselves. Whether they are efficient under stable environmental conditions depends, in the main, on the extent to which the assumptions about member attitudes and abilities which underlie their structural form are accurate.

HUMAN RELATIONS ORGANIZATION STRUCTURE

In describing the human relations organization structure we draw attention again to Figure 5-1, because the human relations model advocates no major changes in the formal structure of the traditional model. Its assumptions about human capabilities are, as we have said, not substantially different from those of the traditional model, and it therefore accepts specialization, routinization, and the separation of planning from doing as essential characteristics of the effective organization.

The human relations model does, however, explicitly acknowledge that people do not behave precisely in line with their formally structured positions and relationships. It calls management's attention to the existence of the "informal structure" (to which we alluded earlier) that exists within and across the organization's various elements. It points out that members ascribe status, form contracts and relationships, and even control one another's behavior in ways quite apart from those prescribed in their formal position descriptions. Further, it cautions management that, although it can fit physical contributions together rather neatly within the system, it cannot so regulate the emotions of its members— their human, social needs obtrude constantly upon the system.

Nevertheless, while the human relations model acknowledges these imperfections, it does not suggest that the formal structure be modified to accommodate them. Instead, it advocates a variety of "off line," nonstructural adjustments, techniques, and behaviors. A few of these will illustrate the main thrust of the human relations view of organization structure.

First, and most important, the human relations model calls upon the manager to use his leadership ability to help reduce the friction between people and their positions and to build cooperative relationships among the organization members who report to him. He is urged to be warm and supportive, to listen to complaints, and to attempt to resolve or remove the sources of conflicts, where this can be done without damage to the overall system. He is urged to have frequent contacts with his subordinates, to get to know them as individuals so that he can, where possible, make minor adjustments in routines, regulations, or assignments to fit their particular needs and desires. Further, he is urged to meet with his subordinates as a group, on occasion, to allow them to raise questions, discuss problems, and generally "blow off steam."

Second, the human relations approach suggests that the manager, where possible, make use of the informal organization within his department—that he respond to it cooperatively rather than combatively. He is told to seek out and to gain the confidence of informal leaders, to recognize and make use of informal channels of communication, to generally maintain the cohesive personal attachments which may be formed among his subordinates. Working through informal leaders can enhance their prestige and make them feel important and, hopefully, at the same time make them and their followers more cooperative. Maintaining a happy, cohesive work force will presumably reduce complaints and make members somewhat more tolerant of pressures and demands within the system.

Third, the human relations approach is identified with a number of techniques, or programs, usually under the jurisdiction of the personnel department, which are designed to serve the needs of all organization members. For example, suggestion systems are frequently advocated as a means of providing members with a chance to feel they are participating in running the organization. Positive suggestions may be recognized in the organization newsletter, perhaps along with a small cash bonus, thus not only boosting the morale of the contributing employee but encouraging his friends as well. Employee credit unions are recognized as a low-cost means of maintaining loyalty and positive feelings toward the organization, along with off-the-job activities such as company athletic teams, picnics, and parties. Sometimes the organization may use member committees to advise it on such matters as the operation of cafeteria and concession facilities, the coordination of car pools, vacation tours, etc.

More directly, the personnel department may include a professional counseling service. The only visible change at the Western Electric plant following the famous Hawthorne experiments was the implementation of a counseling service where employees could take their job and personal problems for discussion and assistance. These counselors were, of course, outside the formal "line" organization and could take no direct action on work-related issues.

In sum, the core concepts of human relations did not deal directly with organization structure. Rather, structure was taken as a given—the environment within which interpersonal attitudes and behaviors were displayed. Human relations theories, in the main, attempted to provide the manager with techniques and mechanisms which would help him and his subordinates adjust to structural constraints, rather than to provide principles to guide the design of structure itself.

The Human Relations Organization and Its Environment

The human relations theorists accepted, either without question or as a matter of necessity, the essentially machinelike form of the traditional structure. Their prescriptions were aimed primarily at providing means of lubricating the machine, oiling away the frictions between persons and groups. Thus, structures built on human relations concepts may be expected to react to their environments in much the same manner as those based on traditional theory. Reporting relationships are still rigidly defined, and issues must still be pushed upward in the hierarchy to find a common point of resolution. The jungle gym analogy used earlier is still appropriate, although we may imagine the cold steel to be warmed by some degree of friendliness and concern. Informal lower-level linkages may be accepted and even encouraged, but these are not viewed as appropriate coordinating mechanisms for anything other than routine matters. Participative mechanisms, which might be viewed as bridging devices, or at least as adding flexibility to unit and departmental linkages, are designed to reduce conflict and ease tensions but not to alter work flow and processes in any way. In fact, in times of crisis, managers operating under the human relations model tend to feel that they should strip the structure back to its bare bureaucratic bones—trim away the participative fat and return the structure to its fighting form.

If, as our analysis suggests, human relations organizations tend to forfeit much of their emphasis on involvement in periods of crisis and to emphasize the more rigid, formal sets of relationships, they may be as unsuited as their traditional counterparts to turbulent environmental conditions. Flexibility and adaptation, if they occur, depend on interpersonal skill rather than on planned structural mechanisms.

Under reasonably stable conditions, the combination of "off line" participative mechanisms and concern for human feelings associated with the human relations theory may aid an organization in performing effectively. However, as these mechanisms are aimed at preventing and/or resolving conflict within the structure rather than at utilizing the full range of capabilities of members, inefficiency will exist to the degree that these capabilities are undervalued by management's assumptions. Moreover, if the participative devices divert work-relevant energy and capability rather than use them, a double cost is incurred.

HUMAN RESOURCES ORGANIZATION STRUCTURE

The implications for organization structure contained in the human resources model, although abstract, are nevertheless clear. The model argues that, in the main, people are capable of exercising more creative self-direction and self-control than their present jobs allow and that the manager's task is that of creating an environment in which they can contribute up to their capacities. Thus, the prime implication is that management must design a structure which, in contrast to the traditional hierarchy, is aimed more at facilitating positive contributions than at controlling deviant performance.

In line with these broad concepts, a human resources design would try to maximize flexibility both within and between interacting positions. Constructive flexibility requires that organization members have (1) an operational level of goal consensus, (2) access to relevant vertical and horizontal information sources, and (3) the ability to respond to this information with efficient goal-directed decisions and behavior. The third requirement, the ability to respond efficiently, is dealt with in the model's assumptions, so that our attention is directed at means of achieving goal consensus and access to information. These two conditions are clearly not independent and, therefore, mechanisms designed to affect one will in most cases affect the other. Some of these mechanisms have already been discussed, both in previous sections here and in other sources.

In our earlier discussion of job design, we noted that the human resources model prescribed joint goal setting between the manager and his subordinates. Following this prescription, it is part of the manager's regular task to discuss with each of his subordinates the key objectives they feel should guide their decisions and behavior. In this process, both the superior and the subordinate have an obligation to verify the alignment between individual objectives and unit or departmental objectives and priorities. This obligation is discharged primarily through the sharing of relevant information and attitudes. An agreement between the superior and the subordinate that sound objectives and priorities have been set provides the charter for creative self-direction and self-control. It should be noted that "agreement" does not necessarily imply perfect alignment of views and values. It is sufficient that each understand the other's constraints and reservations and the reasons for them. Part of the "obligation" discussed here is that of making these reservations and constraints clear and discussing the ways in which they may impede performance. We will have more to say on this issue in Chapter 6.

Joint goal setting obviously transforms the boss-subordinate relationship prescribed by the traditional and human relations model, allowing the subordinate to respond flexibly to the demands of his job rather than merely carrying out directives. The rigid, order-giving–reporting relationship is largely removed and is replaced by a commonly shared vision of what must be accomplished.

Nevertheless, the transformation of the individual superior-subordinate relationship is only one aspect of the broader modification demanded by this model. Not only must the superior-subordinate roles be restructured, but the relationships between positions at the same level must also be transformed. Much of the behavior of any organization member depends at least as much on the decisions and actions of those adjacent to him as it does on those above and below him. He must coalign his activities with his peers, particularly those in his own unit, but also with those in other departments who initiate or control inputs into his unit or receive its output. The traditional structure precludes, on paper at least, self-directed efforts at lateral coordination. The diadic, one-to-one relationships demand that coalignment be achieved only by working upward through the superior.

Again, joint goal setting is prescribed in the human resources model as the means of achieving lateral alignment and flexibility. Here, however, the goal-setting–information-sharing relationship is not between individual boss-subordinate pairs but between the superior and his group of subordinates. In regularly scheduled meetings and at other points dictated by the inherent characteristics of project, process, or environmental demands, group goals, priorities, and problems are reviewed and worked through. Again, the aim is to create a level of agreement that will facilitate self-directed coordination of activities. An operational level of agreement requires neither perfect consensus nor loss of individual identity. It does require that areas of necessary interaction be recognized and understood and the foundations for a reasonable working relationship established.

The superior-subordinate(s) role relationships described here have been presented in diagrammatic form by Likert. As shown in Figure 5-2, Likert pictures an effective organization as one made up of a set of interlocking groups, with the interlocking achieved through various "link-pin" positions. Figure 5-2a illustrates the basic transformation from dyadic one-to-one linkages between superiors and each of their subordinates to a group relationship in which the superior plays the linking role between his group and that above it. Having been a part of a joint goal-setting procedure with his superior, and having been a fully functioning member of his superior's group, the manager has the information and understanding to aid *his* subordinates in setting individual and group objectives. The agreements he achieves with his superior reflect his own thinking and that of his subordinates and thus establish the framework within which his group can exercise discretion.

Further, as Figure 5-2b illustrates, the link-pin role need not always be performed by the group superior. Where units regularly interact, one or more members of each unit may become, in effect, fully functioning members of both units, participating in group goal setting and problem-solving sessions in both settings. Such lateral link-pin roles, as Likert notes, are not compatible with traditional organization principles or practices. They can flourish only in an environment in which control systems, appraisal procedures, reward policies, etc., are all in alignment with the human resources approach. More will be said on this point later.

Finally, as illustrated in Figure 5-2c, the link-pinning process may cut widely across functional and departmental lines. To bring expertise to bear on given projects or problems (on both a one-shot or sustained basis) and to effect coordination in implementation, a manager in one unit may serve as the leader of a group whose members are not tied to him in

(a) Vertical linkages

(b) Horizontal linkages

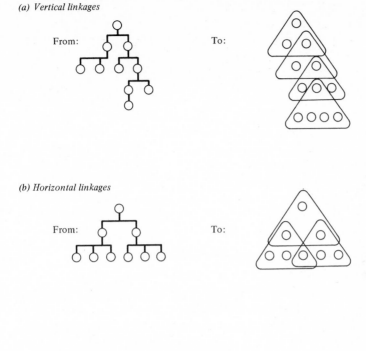

(c) Cross-departmental linkages

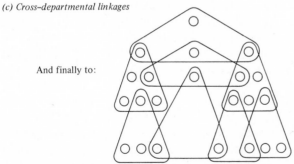

Figure 5-2 Likert's linking-pin structure [Adapted from Rensis Likert, *The Human Organization* (New York: McGraw-Hill, 1967), figures 4-2 and 10-2*a* and *b*)]

any traditional superior-subordinate relationship, but who are in fact members of departments in other areas of the organization. These linkages are established with full knowledge of all units concerned and further increase flexibility and responsiveness.

Figure 5-2*c*, while exotic in appearance, is in fact descriptive of real practices even in traditionally structured departments. Committees which

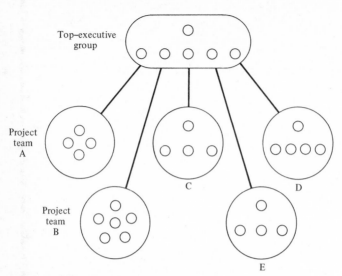

Top–executive group

Project team A

C

D

Project team B

E

Figure 5-3   The "project team" organization structure

cut across departmental lines are not infrequently formed and special "task force" arrangements are not at all unknown. However, within traditional structures, such cross-functional groupings are not only usually temporary but are seldom vested with anything other than advisory powers. In contrast, the cross-functional linkages envisioned by Likert are designed to actually solve problems and facilitate effective interaction.

Another organizational arrangement which is both in line with human resources implications and in many respects similar to Likert's cross-functional linkages is the project team. In this arrangement, most common in high-technology organizations, members of a number of specialties may be pulled together to work‚on a particular project or problem. For example, a design engineer might be placed with a physicist, a methods specialist, and an experienced production supervisor, and this newly formed team (under the direction of, say, a higher-level member of the engineering group) might then be charged with the task of developing a major product modification and carrying it through to production. In many small organizations in electronics, aerospace, and related industries, it is not uncommon to find structural arrangements similar to that illustrated in Figure 5-3, where most personnel are members of a project team. This arrangement provides each team member with a clear-cut objective and the opportunity to use his full range of capabilities—

including those outside his functional specialty—in the accomplishment of the team goal.

Finally, in its most highly developed form, the human resources structure would allow every member increased freedom to guide and direct his own activities, responsible only to the broad set of goals which he has helped establish. In such a structure, every member would be directly linked to every other member and would thus be equally responsible for sharing information and coordinating activities. Structures such as these are only approximated in reality and then usually only in extremely small organizations or in subunits of larger structures. The most common example of this form is that of the university department where a collection of colleagues may share a common though loosely defined set of objectives and enjoy roughly equal status. Or a group of doctors or lawyers in joint practice may develop an arrangement similar to that described here.

Note that in each of the above instances, specific sets of credentials are required for entry, credentials that are assumed to attest to the capability for self-directed, self-controlled behavior. Further, in the broadest sense, goal consensus is based on professional ethics and values, presumably acquired along with the credentials essential to entry. Finally, appropriate collegial behavior, including information sharing and cooperation, is expected as part of the professional norm. However, although it is most closely associated with professional groupings, the collegial form of structure, illustrated in Figure 5-4, is also found in other settings. For example, a squadron of pilots, or an infantry team, may well adopt such a structure and maintain it through lengthy periods of real or presumed danger. Status differences are minimized and each member is expected to bend his full resources to the achievement of group goals. Similarly, within business organizations or public agencies, some units may have arrangements approximating the collegial form. However, such arrange-

Manager or professional   A

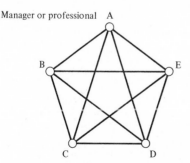

Figure 5-4 A collegial form of organization structure

ments in nonprofessional settings are usually not supported by the norms of the overall structure and are usually temporary.

The Human Resources Organization and Its Environment

The human resources model, with its emphasis on developing and utilizing the full range of capabilities of organization members, is ideally suited to situations that demand flexible, responsive behavior. For example, the collegial structure is predicated in part on the assumption that the problems which its members face do not appear in standard sizes and shapes adaptable to preset solutions. Each member is expected to correctly diagnose the situation and to process through his full range of knowledge and skills to provide the most appropriate response. Similarly, the project-team structure is designed to handle unique or special classes of problems, usually under a specific set of time demands dictated by the environment. Finally, the group link-pin arrangements described by Likert are aimed at providing mechanisms for intra- and interdepartmental problem solving and coordination.

However, although each of the forms associated with the human resources model is aimed at promoting flexibility, some appear more organic and adaptive than others. Maximum self-direction in response to the situation at hand might be expected to occur in the collegial form, with project team and link-pin arrangements following in that order. Thus, if the organization is trying to operate in an extremely complex and unstructured environment with only general and abstract goals to guide its behavior, something approaching the collegial form of structure might be most appropriate. Or, if the environment is relatively stable, so that reasonably clear-cut goals and objectives may be set and many elements of the technology fixed to respond to a standard set of demands, something akin to the basic link-pin arrangement may be suitable.

These relationships between structural form on the one hand and environmental conditions, goals, and technology on the other are diagrammed in Figure 5-5. In this schema, environmental conditions are allowed to range from more stable, on the left, to more turbulent, on the right. And following our discussion here and in Chapter 1, which illustrate their likely linkages to environmental conditions and to one another, organizational goals and technology are also characterized from fixed and standardized on the left to more ambiguous and unprogrammed on the right. The organizational forms which might be associated with points along these continua are ranged, as suggested above, from the basic link-pin structure on the left to the collegial form on the right.

Note, however, that a fourth form has been added. The mixed, or

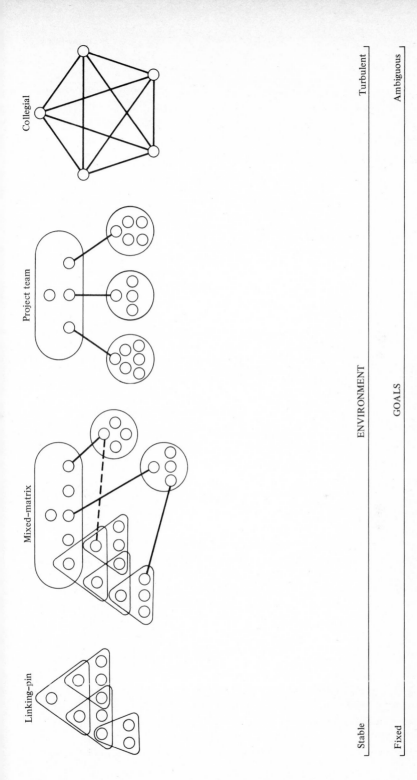

Linking–pin   Mixed–matrix   Project team   Collegial

Stable   ENVIRONMENT   Turbulent

Fixed   GOALS   Ambiguous

Standardized   TECHNOLOGY   Unprogrammed

Figure 5-5 Human resources structures and environmental conditions. (This figure is based on a diagram developed by Robert Biller, though my explanation and use of it here differ in many ways from Biller's interpretation.)

matrix, model (second in Figure 5-5) combines portions of the basic link-pin structure and the project-team arrangement. This form might be (and is in fact) found in some, generally sizable, organizations with a wide range of products, clients, or environments. For that portion of its environment that can be stabilized, or that set of products and/or clients with predictable specifications or requirements, a basic link-pin arrangement may be suitable, whereas for the more turbulent, unprogrammable demands, something like the project-team arrangement may be required. Within an organization of this sort, individuals may move out of assignments in functional departments, into project-team assignments, and back again as the task of the project team is completed.

The fourth form added in Figure 5-5 is important in its own right, but its addition is also significant as an indication that any number of possible structures can be imagined that meet demands of various sets of conditions associated with environment, goals, and technology. Thus, the continuum of forms suggested in Figure 5-5 might well be expanded to include additional mixed models—for example, one can easily imagine (and find examples of) structures combining the project-team arrangement with an executive group at the top, structured in something close to the collegial form. However, if such forms are to remain in line with the prescriptions of the human resources model, it should be clear from our discussion to this point that the following set of core conditions must be met:

1 Individual tasks and unit tasks will be structured in a manner so that they not only allow but also encourage self-direction and self-control.

2 The prerequisites for the exercise of self-direction and self-control will be met. That is, members will participate in setting their own goals and objectives and those of their unit and will have access to the information essential to guiding their efforts to achieve these goals and objectives.

3 Members within each unit will be expected to coordinate their activities in line with unit goals—to work out the mechanisms for such cooperation, including procedures for sharing work loads and utilizing special expertise.

4 The structure will take into account the pattern of interaction between units and will have designed-in lateral-linking mechanisms. These mechanisms may include link-pin individuals who are members of adjacent departments, or perhaps the cross-functional arrangement suggested by Likert. At any rate, lateral-linking mechanisms will be developed at the actual points of interaction and not forced upward to the top of the organization.

CONCLUDING REMARKS

Every organization structure effects some balance between stability and creativity, both of which are essential to effective and efficient performance. Tasks are grouped into positions and these in turn are linked together into groups, units, or departments to provide stability, or, more accurately, predictability, which is crucial to rational behavior such as planning, scheduling, etc. Every organization member gains some assurance from the fact that, at least on a temporary basis, he knows what he is working on, with whom, and where. Without such predictability, in large organizations anyway, each day would provide a new adventure in search and discovery. On the other hand, in striving for stability, the organization runs the risk of unduly restricting responsiveness and initiative.

The traditional structure sought to maximize predictability, taking the view that responsiveness and creativity could be exercised sufficiently by those at or near the top. The human relationists recognized that this approach produced dysfunctions but defined these primarily in terms of unfulfilled human needs for belonging and recognition. Human resources theorists have challenged the basic balance sought in the traditional structure and have argued that high levels of responsiveness and initiative can and should be developed at all points in the structure, not just at the top. They argue that traditional structures waste basic human capacity for self-direction and self-control and thus accrue huge (usually hidden) losses. They further argue that operational levels of stability and predictability can be achieved in more flexible structures, structures which, because they emphasize creativity and adaptiveness, actually result in improved performance.

Under stable conditions, the choice between traditional and human resources structures rests primarily on management's assessment of the accuracy of their assumptions. If management doubts the existence of widespread capacity for self-direction and self-control, it will opt for a balance weighted heavily on the side of stability. Moreover, because costs of underuse or misuse are generally hidden, they are not likely to arise in such a form as to disprove the accuracy of management's choice. Similarly, doubts about the capability of members to exercise judgment and initiative may be confirmed as "poorly informed," and perhaps poorly motivated members do make a predictable quota of errors. Finally, any possible gains from the human resources structure under stable conditions depend, obviously, on the accuracy of its assumptions and on management's willingness and skill in following its prescriptions.

On the other hand, under more turbulent, less-predictable environmental conditions, where goals are under regular reassessment and technology cannot be heavily routinized, the correctness of management's choice between traditional and human resources structures may be more easily evaluated. As suggested earlier in our jungle gym analogy, a rigidly joined structure with few low-level braces cannot be easily tipped, turned, or rotated. The only alternative is to fix it firmly in place and hope that environmental forces can be constrained or controlled. However, building on this analogy, each human resources structure has some degree of built-in flexibility. Imagine, for example, that the link-pin positions in Likert's model represent pivotable joints rather than rigid connections. Now, unexpected pressure on a given unit does not rock the entire structure but can, within limits, be absorbed by the unit itself. Or imagine that the connecting lines in the project-team structure are cables attached at each end by snap-on swivel joints, thus greatly increasing the ability of the organization to adjust to environmental demands. Finally, the collegial structure, with its complete network of internal bracing, can be imagined as completely rotatable. Any point (any member) can be turned to meet a particular environmental demand, or a number of demands from various directions can be dealt with simultaneously. Thus, if, as many theorists predict, the environments of many organizations are becoming or are likely to become increasingly complex and turbulent, efforts to retain traditional structures may prove costly, and managers may be forced toward human resources structures whether or not they accept their basic assumptions.

We have not dealt specifically in this section with two issues which are usually covered in discussions of organization design. The first of these, the issue of whether units should be structured around functional specialties or around definable products or problems, was dealt with in part in our discussion of traditional theory but was not raised again here, and thus a brief comment is in order. There is no fixed answer to this issue. Grouping positions or units by functional specialties may tend to increase predictability and perhaps efficiency within such units. On the other hand, grouping various skills around a product, service, or problem may increase coordination and adaptability. However, these gains or losses must be evaluated on the basis of the situation at hand and a broad prescription based on this issue alone is probably unwarranted. It is suitable, however, to challenge the traditional model's basic reliance on functional specialization, as we did earlier, and to suggest that the issue be regularly weighed on scales calibrated for each new set of conditions.

The second issue we have failed to deal with explicitly is that of centralization versus decentralization. This issue will be raised directly in Chapter 6 where we examine communications and control systems.

However, it has been covered here implicitly and a few lines may illustrate how. When the economist examines this issue he does so on the basis of costs and benefits. However, he may also expect that more efficient decisions could be made at a central source, primarily because of the opportunity to accumulate information and utilize the most capable decision makers. Thus, the variables he considers—responsiveness, predictability, capability, etc.—and his expectations concerning them are precisely those we have been discussing. If the economist discovers that low-cost mechanisms exist for providing decentralized units with the information necessary to make good decisions, and that decision-making talent capable of processing this information is generally available, his cost-benefit analysis would clearly fall on the side of increasing responsiveness.

We have dealt with the issues of job and organization design at some length because, in our view, they establish the framework in which management and member behavior occurs and are greatly influenced by managers' theories of management. Many of the concepts expounded here will appear in slightly different form in later chapters, in line with our stated purpose of tying together in a systematic way managers' theories and the mechanisms through which they are applied.

BIBLIOGRAPHY

Avots, Ivars, "Why Does Project Management Fail?" *California Management Review*, vol. 12, pp. 77–82 (Fall 1969).

Kover, A. J., "Reorganizing an Advertising Agency: A Case Study of a Decrease in Integration," *Human Organization*, vol. 22, pp. 252–299 (Winter 1964).

Likert, Rensis, *Human Organization* (New York: McGraw-Hill, 1967), chap. 10.

Lorsch, Jay W. and Paul R. Lawrence, "Organizing for Product Innovation," *Harvard Business Review*, vol. 43, pp. 109–122 (January-February 1965).

Thompson, James D., *Organizations in Action* (New York: McGraw-Hill, 1967), chaps. 4–6.

Walker, A. H. and J. W. Lorsch, "Organizational Choice: Product vs. Function," *Harvard Business Review*, vol. 46, pp. 129–138 (November-December 1968).

(Also see references related to Goals, Technology, and Structure listed at the end of Chapter 1.)

Chapter 6

Communications
and Control Systems

The transition from a discussion of job and organization design to one of communications and control systems is not very difficult. The key variable differentiating one approach to job design from another is the amount of self-control built into the position. Similarly, types of organization structure are defined primarily in terms of the way in which positions and departments are linked together, and the linking mechanisms, whatever their shape, are essentially nothing more than recognized and established lines of communication over which pass control information—orders, progress reports, instructions for corrective action, and so on.

Thus the material in this chapter on communications and control systems will build directly on the previous chapter's analysis of job and organization design. Hopefully, by taking a separate and detailed look at these topics, we will both develop some useful new concepts and add substance to our earlier discussion.

ONE VIEW OF COMMUNICATIONS AND CONTROL SYSTEMS

As our comments have already suggested, we are treating communications and control systems as if they were identical, or, if not identical, at least inseparably intertwined. The aim of any control system is to maintain behavior in line with preset objectives, and the mechanism by which this is accomplished is communication. Or turned around, the purpose of most communications in formal organizations is the exercise of control. Our view of these systems and how they are related can be illustrated with a pair of brief examples.

EXAMPLE 1—(The Line Supervisor) John Roberts is in charge of a subassembly department in a large manufacturing plant. His group prepares special components for a number of other departments. We meet him first on Monday morning as he discusses with his six leadmen the weekly schedule which has been sent down by the production control department for his group. A question arises concerning an apparent shift in priorities from the previous week's schedule and a phone call to production control verifies that the shift was intentional and was caused by a reshuffling of final-assembly schedules.

John and his group are visibly upset by these changes, which they feel will force them to shut down and restart operations several times more than their previous schedule would but without producing any significant changes in actual completion times. They agree, however, that, based on past experience, trying to get the priorities changed is difficult and time consuming.

Later the same morning we see John meeting with three other department supervisors and their joint superior, the general production superintendent. They are discussing the weekly report on defective assemblies, which is prepared by the quality control department. The data indicate a slight increase in defective subassemblies produced by John's department. John points out that he predicted earlier that this would happen when his request for a new in-process testing device was turned down during preparation of the current year's budget. His boss agrees that they will have to reopen this issue and seek permission to replace the old equipment even if it means going over budget. He is not, however, optimistic, as John can see from his expression. What John cannot see is the memo in his boss's top drawer which indicates that not only will no capital expenditure items be considered during the remaining quarter of the fiscal year but that the maintenance budget for the coming months is likely to be cut by one-fourth.

Near midafternoon that same Monday, we find John in conversation with Pete Ramsey, the assistant director of training in the personnel department. The two men are attempting to work out a schedule which will allow three of John's leadmen to attend a supervisory training program during the following week. He is reminding John that the director of manufacturing has ordered that all leadmen attend these sessions during the year and points out that the three in John's department are among the few remaining who have not attended.

Finally, at the very end of the day we see John performing a final bit of communication. He is filling out a required form for the payroll department to explain the reasons for unscheduled overtime work during the weekend performed by two members of his department.

In each of the situations in our example, John is communicating—upward, downward, and laterally—along established reporting and information channels. In each instance he is giving or passing along orders, providing or being provided with data relevant to previous instructions, or using information to take corrective action toward established objectives or to make plans to adapt to new requirements. His role in these episodes has been in large measure predetermined by his place in the overall structure and, more specifically, by the system of controls his organization has established and the procedures they have designed to make it operate.

The system within which John operates has developed over a period of time in response to organizational needs, interpreted through management's framework of concepts and theories. The process by which a control system can be established and procedures set is suggested in part by our second example.

EXAMPLE 2—(The New Cost-Control Unit) Jamison Enterprises is a rapidly growing organization which can best be described as a miniconglomerate. It began around the manufacture of a line of plastic novelty products which were sold to many firms to be used as sales-promotion items. Because of rapid fluctuations in this market, the organization quickly sought a more stable source of income. About four years ago they bought out a small but stable building-maintenance operation which had a number of firm, long-term contractual arrangements. In the last two years they have acquired a rug-and-drapery-cleaning firm and have set up a small plant in which they are using their basic technology in plastics to manufacture components for firms in the electronics industry.

As these new operations have been acquired or begun, the practice has been to operate them as if they were independent businesses, each proposing and receiving approval for its own general capital and operations budget, and each providing quarterly reports to corporate headquarters. This practice has been followed as much by necessity as by design. The accounting-controller staff at corporate headquarters was not large initially, and the acquisitions and expansions have occurred so rapidly that little could be done except to extend whatever control procedures were in operation.

At corporate headquarters there is growing concern that one or more of the operating organizations may inadvertently jeopardize the entire structure by overextending its budget. These concerns have been heightened by the fact that the most recent venture in plastic component subcontracting drew heavily on reserve funds during its start-up period, thus reducing liquidity in a period of tight money and general easing of demand. Because of these concerns, corporate staff members have been exploring several possible control systems. All have agreed that the corporate controller's operation must be enlarged and the analysis has focused on the relationship between this unit and the management of the operating organizations. One of the alternate proposals would establish, at corporate level, a general cost-control unit. This unit would receive and summarize weekly reports of expenditures at each operating unit and would alert management to any dangerous trends. A second proposal would go further than this. It would call for centralizing all accounting and would demand that all expenditures for other than budgeted payroll and supplies be cleared with corporate officials. A third proposal, running counter to the first two, suggests that each new division be given the resources to develop more effective internal information systems and that these groups in turn work with the central staff to develop an overall system which will be responsive to the particular needs of the operating units while still providing more frequent and accurate data to corporate head-quarters.

It should be noted that managerial decisions and behavior here are occurring in response to a variety of environmental and technological developments. Some members of the corporate staff feel that the combination of increased operating complexity and demand uncertainty is pushing them toward a much more centralized control system. Others, however, apparently feel that the situation demands a system which provides both flexibility at the operating level and increased flows of aggregate data upward. In each instance, managers are processing and evaluating information from their internal and external environment within the framework of their own concepts and philosophies of management.

Obviously, the decisions which result from the present studies at Jamison, whatever their final form may be, will have far-reaching effects on the roles and behaviors of organization members throughout the organization. These decisions will establish the basic structure of control for the entire system and will dictate, in large part, the nature of communications channels and reporting relationships.

Against the backdrop of these two examples, one illustrating the behavior of a manager within a fully developed communications and control system and another suggesting the pattern of forces which may help shape the development of such a system, we should now bring back to center stage our three theories of management so that we may analyze some of their implications in the area of communications and control.

COMMUNICATIONS AND CONTROL UNDER THE TRADITIONAL MODEL

The reader will recall that the assumptions of the traditional theory hold that most organization members lack both the capacity to exercise reasonable discretion concerning organizational objectives and the motivation to pursue these objectives unless they are threatened or enticed to do so. At least four key implications for the design of communications and control systems can be derived from these assumptions.

First, the assumptions imply that members require specific objectives to guide their behavior and specific standards against which their performance can be measured and to which they can be held accountable. These objectives and standards, logically, must be set for each organization member (and for each organization unit) by some superordinate person or group. That is, if members are allowed to influence the objectives toward which they work, the expectation would be that they would seek objectives which would enhance their own well-being rather than that of the organization and standards which would require minimal outputs of energy and attention.

Second, the assumptions imply that once objectives and standards are set for members and their units, the evaluation of performance against them must be made by someone external to the actual operating unit. If not, if units are allowed to take their own measurements, there will be no assurance that the standards will be imposed rigorously and objectively or that corrective action will be diligently pursued.

Third, and corrollary to these first two implications, the assumptions imply secrecy. That is, if we assume that members may try to manipulate or subvert objectives and measurements, it follows that all planning and control information should be carefully guarded. Therefore, members should have access only to that information required for their immediate duties and should receive feedback on performance only as is necessary for corrective action.

Fourth, the assumptions force us to focus specifically on the issue of capacity. If, as the traditional model states, the capability of most members to effectively exercise discretion is limited, then it follows that the points at which objectives are set and corrective action initiated should be located as near the top of the organizational hierarchy as is feasible.

Turning back to our initial example, the communications and control system within which supervisor John Roberts operates appears in part at least to have been designed in line with these implications. Note first that the schedule under which his group operates has been established by someone outside the unit (in this instance by the production scheduling group) and that John's unit has little choice but to accept it as given.

Second, we see that John's group does not receive information concerning the proportion of defects produced in that group until long after they have occurred. Inspection data from his unit have been collected by inspectors from the quality control department, aggregated by specialists in the quality control unit, and fed back through the director of manufacturing, two levels above John. This control linkage, though long and complex, is considered necessary to preserve both the integrity of the evaluation process and the chain of command in the production area. To John and his group, the system is simply cumbersome—so cumbersome in fact that he and his leadmen keep their own separate charts on quality (with the illicit aid of inspectors in his area) and frequently take corrective action as needed on the basis of these figures rather than waiting for response from the formal system.

Third, we see that John and his group are not privy to information held by their superior or by the several control groups who initiate action for them. The communications system is not designed to provide John and his group with the information which would be necessary for them to efficiently plan or schedule production, maintenance, or even the manning requirements of the unit. This arrangement is, of course, not illogical, given that John's role and that of his unit is viewed essentially as one of implementation—planning has been explicitly withdrawn or designed out of his operation and assigned to special functional planning groups.

Finally, we see an element of anomaly in the scene played by John and Pete Ramsey, the representative of the personnel department's training group. John is being asked to respond to decisions made several levels above him with regard to training needs among leadmen, but Ramsey is apparently attempting to be as accommodating as possible to avoid forcing on John a training schedule which will be disruptive. This posture, however, is the personal strategy of Ramsey and does not reflect either normal practices with personnel or a special policy. In fact, John has in the past frequently been handed a completed training schedule (with starting dates close at hand) which he has neither seen before nor been consulted about.

Somewhat similarly, in the Jamison Company example, we see the basic planning for a communications and control system with a staff group at headquarters, with little or no consultation with the heads of the operating units. Moreover, most of the alternatives being given close attention appear to be aimed at moving the exercise of measurement and discretion up from the operating units to headquarters staff. If one of these alternatives is implemented, the resulting system may well have many of the characteristics of that under which John and his group now operate.

In sum, the communications and control system in John's organization, and that which seems likely to emerge at Jamison, appear to reflect the assumptions of the traditional model and to flow logically from its prescriptions. Across such systems, therefore, we might expect to find most if not all of the following characteristics:

1   Standards and quotas will tend to be set unilaterally for individuals and groups and stated in absolute terms. Thus, communications flowing downward will be made up primarily of orders, directives, and instructions. Upward flows will be made up primarily of progress reports, explanations, and requests for special treatment.

2   Many of the communications will be written, with special forms dictating the nature of the data transmitted and specifying routing and priorities. (Putting things in writing helps to assure accountability.)

3   Feedback loops will tend to be long and complex—that is, in many instances data reported from operating units will flow first to special functional groups whose task it is to aggregate them, compare them to preset objectives, and then route the comparisons up to some official for review and corrective action. Feedback to operating units will ordinarily occur at established intervals (e.g., weekly, monthly, quarterly, etc.).

4   Direct lateral communications between operating units will not be provided for in the formal system—instead, information will be routed up from each unit to central control points, and then selected information and directives will be routed down to the operating units.

5   When information or action is required at a pace or in a form not provided for in the formal system, special liaison roles will be established. In time, these may grow into formal positions and even into formal departments.

COMMUNICATIONS AND CONTROL UNDER THE HUMAN RELATIONS MODEL

As repeatedly noted, the assumptions underlying the human relations theory do not challenge those of the traditional theory with regard to the distribution of capacity for self-direction and self-control. The superior's role as planner and evaluator and the subordinate's role as doer are accepted as given and presumably justified. Nevertheless, the human relations theory recognizes that the interaction of these roles may produce dysfunctional consequences, particularly when the superior carries out his role in an impersonal and autocratic fashion so that basic human needs for belonging, support, and recognition are unfulfilled, and member efforts to satisfy these needs outside the formal system may impede performance and goal accomplishment.

Given these assumptions, the implications for communications and control systems contained in the human relations theory have to do more with the implementation and operation of these systems than with their design. For example, managers operating under the human relations model might be expected to stress that standards and quotas ought not to be set unilaterally; they should be "sold." The manager should meet with his subordinates and attempt to explain these requirements and to develop enthusiasm for them. Similarly, human relations prescriptions would not modify the superior's prerogative to initiate corrective action, but they would suggest that he go about it in a diplomatic fashion, praising good points as well as indicating areas of needed improvement.

However, while most of the implications for communications and control flowing from the human relations model concern implementation, a number of mechanisms widely employed have their origins in this theory. A brief comment on three of these will illustrate their nature, that of those related to them, and their linkage to the model, thus setting the stage for a concluding generalization.

Suggestion Systems In addition to the formal channels of work-related communications, many organizations have suggestion and complaint programs. Organization members are provided with ways (e.g., the familiar slotted box on the corridor wall) whereby they can easily route ideas, questions, or concerns to some central group. (Provisions are usually made to guarantee the anonymity of members using the system, if they so wish.) In more sophisticated versions of this mechanism, members may be encouraged to make suggestions to improve work methods and may also receive bonuses or other forms of recognition if their ideas are deemed meritorious and practical. Similarly, a number of organizations have one or more special positions or units charged with supplying answers to members' questions and/or attempting to obtain redress for legitimate complaints. One organization, for example, runs an "action line" column in its weekly newsletter in which answers are given to selected questions and follow-up action on specific complaints is described.

Newsletters and Magazines Related to our last comment, we should note that many if not most medium-size and large organizations publish regular issues of an in-house newsletter or magazine. Two or three features are common across such media. First, positive developments within the organization are prominently featured (e.g., new products, new facilities, etc.). Second, personal accomplishments of organization members and their families are noted (e.g., receipt of a thirty-year service pin, the birth of triplets, the decoration of son for valor in military service, etc.). Finally, the "house organ" is often used to provide background information and justification for changes in specific policies and methods.

Special Committees A large number of organizations have established committees made up of members from across their several units or departments and charged with a variety of tasks and duties related to member needs and activities, particularly in the areas of health and safety. In this area it is not too unusual for these committees to receive and make recommendations on member suggestions concerning safety and health hazards. More commonly, however, committee members serve primarily as communications links between professional health and safety units and their own work groups and departments.

Each mechanism described here tries to broaden and humanize the downward flow of communications, while providing at least a minimal amount of responsiveness to member needs for individual recognition. Nevertheless, these mechanisms and their variations are all *outside the formal communications and control system*. They are not a part of, nor are they expected to interfere with, day-to-day operations. Management, for the most part, chooses the information which is channeled down through these devices and can respond selectively to upward flows. While member participation is encouraged in most of these mechanisms, participation carries no responsibility, or at least no direct authority to exercise discretion.

Finally, an analogy may be useful in describing how these mechanisms tend to operate and how they link to theory. If the main communications and control system is viewed as a complex set of electrical circuits, the wiring diagram would show these human relations mechanisms as disconnected from the main flow of current. They can be tied in when needed to absorb excess energy in the system or to supplement flows to areas with excess demand. Member energy poured into the suggestion circuit, for example, can be allowed to simply cycle there, channeled off from the main system until it dissipates. Or, when resistance appears at some point in the main circuit, say to a particular policy or directive, the secondary circuits provided by certain of these mechanisms can be used to partially bypass the source of resistance, providing additional flows and thus perhaps taking part of the load off that line. (As noted earlier, the counselors at Hawthorne provided just such secondary circuits.)

COMMUNICATIONS AND CONTROL UNDER THE HUMAN RESOURCES MODEL

The human resources model assumes the existence of untapped member capabilities for the exercise of responsible self-direction and self-control. Its implications for the design of communications and control systems flow directly from these assumptions and are, logically enough, aimed at tapping these resources.

Specifically, as we noted in the preceding chapter, the existence of member capability is not enough to assure the successful exercise of discretion; there must also exist goal consensus and access to performance information. That is, if members are to creatively direct and control their own behavior, they must fully understand what it is they are working toward and why, and they must have a central position in the flow of data relating their behavior to these goals and standards.

Recognizing these requirements, a communications and control system designed in accordance with the human resources model would be expected to have most of the following characteristics:

1 There would be full disclosure of information. All information related to the setting of any goal or standard would be available to members working toward these objectives.

2 Although performance goals and standards set under this approach may be stated in precise or absolute terms, explicit recognition would be given to expected variation around these figures. Normal patterns of variation (e.g., week-to-week, seasonal, etc.) would be noted, along with discussion of possible contingencies.

3 Standards would ordinarily be set through joint planning between superiors and subordinates. In addition, goals or objectives affecting more than one member or unit would usually be set after consultation between members of units and their joint superior.

4 There would be short feedback loops. Performance information collected in a unit or department would ordinarily be fed back directly to that group so that corrective action could be taken immediately and directly by unit or departmental members.

5 Substantial freedom to exercise discretion would be allowed lower-level positions with regard to decisions affecting the operation of their units.

Human Resources Concepts Applied—Management by Objectives

The above-listed characteristics take on operational meaning in organizations which make successful efforts to "manage by objectives." The concept of management by objectives was given form and substance by Peter Drucker in the mid-1950s and supported with eloquent examples and discussion by Douglas McGregor a few years later. The concept has a wide array of supporters and critics today and has been implemented in a growing number of organizations with varying degrees of success.

The principal component of management by objectives is joint planning between superiors and subordinates. In planning sessions, the superior shares with the subordinate his own values, priorities, and goals for the unit, along with all the current information he has regarding the present and future operation of the organization, or at least that portion of it which provides the environment of his unit. Similarly, the subordinate shares his views about his job or unit—his own information needs, resource requirements, individual aspirations, etc. (This process of information sharing may well extend over several meetings, particularly in those instances where such sharing has not occurred in the past or where the relationship is undergoing or has undergone some strain.)

Following this initial phase, the subordinate is asked to look closely at his own job or unit and to develop for it both a long-run plan and a set of specific short-run objectives. The plan and objectives will then be discussed with his superior and will likely go through one or more revisions. In these sessions, both the superior and subordinate will focus on how accomplishment of objectives may be measured and on what schedule measurement will occur. The act of specifying criteria sharpens objectives and brings to light contingencies which may not have been considered, along with the need for additional information. When agreement is reached on the subordinate's plan, it becomes his guide for action over the specified period. He may return to the superior with questions or to discuss unforeseen developments, but in the main he will be expected to exercise discretion within the framework of the plan, measuring his progress against the agreed-upon criteria.

Joint planning of the sort described here is not easily done. It requires substantial time and energy and an orientation toward planning as well as a set of planning skills which, surprisingly, many managers do not have. Superiors may find it difficult at first to fully share the information they possess, and subordinates may find it hard to believe that they can help set a course of action to guide their own behavior. More pointedly, both superiors and subordinates may find it difficult to shift away from thinking about global—but unmeasurable—goals such as "doing a better job," and toward clear-cut objectives and criteria for their measurement, such as a "10 percent reduction in turnover to be achieved through a program of job enrichment."

Because this approach is demanding, it is seldom achieved in practice. Instead, something which might be called a "human relations" approach to management by objectives develops. Such efforts are typically supported primarily by members of the personnel or training department and are viewed as essentially a means of building morale or improving superior-subordinate relationships. With this orientation no real joint planning occurs, subordinate objectives are put forth in general terms and approved without analysis, and are then used by neither the superior nor the subordinate as real guides for behavior.

The communications and control characteristics embodied in the "human resources" approach to management by objectives may be seen in operation in a group setting, as well as in the relationship between a single superior-subordinate dyad, in the following examples which are based loosely on actual organizational practices. (As before, names are fictitious and organizations are on occasion shifted from one industry to another.)

EXAMPLE 3—(Jordon Press)   Jordon Press handles complex special-order printing assignments, using a number of large, expensive, multicolor presses. The work force is organized into press teams with certain teams responsible for a single mammoth press and others responsible for operating two or more slightly smaller units. Once each week (usually on Thursday afternoons) the press team leaders meet with members of the production planning group to review progress on current orders and to plan and approve future schedules. No estimates of time for any given order are fixed (and thus no final prices established) until the press team leader has judged them to be reasonable. If he is in doubt concerning any estimate, he will call in one or more members of the team and clear the figures with them. At this meeting, priorities of each order are discussed and a tentative schedule agreed to. Following this meeting, each team leader returns to his group and discusses the schedule. It is not certified as final nor are delivery dates guaranteed until the team agrees that the assigned times and priorities are workable. Once the schedule is accepted, meeting the delivery date with a product of approved quality is the team's responsibility up to the point of delivery to the shipping group. Teams for the most part are responsible for ongoing maintenance of their own equipment and are expected to notify appropriate groups if unforeseen contingencies develop.

EXAMPLE 4—(Lectocom)   The heads of the five operating divisions of Lectocom meet regularly once each quarter at corporate headquarters. Before the meeting, each division head has reviewed with his own staff the division's progress toward agreed-upon objectives and has explored with them developments which may affect the coming quarter's operations. A brief summary of these discussions has been sent ahead to corporate staff members and to the other division heads. At the two-day meeting, the division heads are briefed on market trends and on product-development activities in the central R & D group. (Conversely, division heads report on product and process innovations which may have application in the other units.)

As two of the divisions supply components to the other three, major scheduling problems and priorities are worked out on the spot. Similarly, needs for major expenditures are discussed against the most recent information concerning the corporation's financial position. When competing needs exist, the allocation problem is also resolved by the full group. The division managers return to their units with an updated plan of action and an updated picture of the way in which the plan for each unit fits into the broader framework of corporate needs and activities.

For two further examples of communications and control systems flowing out of the human resources model, we can return to our earlier discussion in Chapter 5 of project-team and matrix organization structures. In each of these structures, organization members with various skills are grouped together around specific projects and problems and are expected to use discretion in completing or solving them in accordance with a general set of criteria and within a broad set of constraints. In the pure project-team structure, usually associated with smaller organizations, team leaders discuss the team's assignment with top staff members. Ideally, they leave with an understanding of the requirements which need to be met and the budget constraints under which they are to operate. Within this framework, the team is, in effect, on its own, and it is expected that, in the main, contacts between it and top staff will be initiated by the team. In the more complex matrix structure, specific projects are again the focal point of the control system. Typically, a project is funded and then those in charge in effect "purchase" the manpower they will need from the more stable, functionally organized segments of the organization. If the adage "control goes where the money is" is accurate, then project leaders should be able to operate with maximum discretion and flexibility under this system.

BUDGETING UNDER THE THREE MANAGERIAL MODELS

As implied in the discussion and examples above, much of the communications and control activity in any organization revolves around the budget. If we examine a few of the many methods by which budgets are established in organizations, we can see elements of our three models at work.

The Competitive Approach One common budgeting procedure is to ask all operating units to submit their projections for the coming period's operating expenses and capital expenditures to a central budgeting group. This group reviews the full range of requests and then returns a fixed dollar schedule to each unit. As the central group is usually well removed from the actual arena of operation of most units, it cannot judge requests precisely on their merit but must operate primarily by comparing projected figures with past expenditures. In periods of rising costs the central group will attempt to hold the line as nearly as possible and in harder times may attempt to reduce budget items by some percentage across all units. Recognizing this behavior pattern, operating units are tempted to "pad" their requests to provide for contingencies and to build a larger base for subsequent periods. If the "padding" is allowed to stand, operating units then take great care to spend the allocated funds somehow, as unspent funds are a certain target for reduction. Conversely, central budgeting groups, anticipating padding, frequently adopt the position that any request can safely be reduced by some amount. Again, alert to this response, operating units may raise the amounts by which they pad requests, etc.

The Hard-Line–Soft-Practice Approach A second common approach finds the central budgeting group adhering to a firm line in the initial allocation of funds. Through this procedure, certain "reserves" are established, and it is made known that well-argued requests will be met during the period of the budget. Under this procedure, groups which complain loudly (or through favored channels) may find funds available to pacify their demands. Similarly, cooperative groups can be rewarded with special allocations and dissidents can be righteously denied. In time, however, this approach tends to honor more and more special requests in order to maintain harmony, so that operating groups tend to anticipate and count on a certain percentage of "slack" in the established budget.

The Multiple-Level–Contingency Approach A less-frequently employed approach asks each operating unit to prepare its budget with upper and lower limits indicated for each major category, rather than absolute figures. The forecast is then presented in a budget meeting with the unit's superior. Factors which could push expenditures toward the upper or lower limits are discussed, and contingencies not described in the budget are considered. Having convinced himself of the accuracy of these figures, the superior aggregates the budget for his larger group and then carries this forward to the next level for approval. The success of this approach depends primarily on the extent to which contingencies are recognized and discussed in advance and to which expenditures falling at the lower limits are the subject of recognition rather than retribution— that is, to the extent that unusual success in one period does not become the basis for restricting allocations in the next.

Rather clearly, the traditional model is influencing budgeting practices in the competitive approach. Final decisions are made autocratically and within a framework of suspicion concerning the motives of unit managers. Some combination of the traditional and human relations model appears to be influencing budgeting behavior in our second example, the hard-line–soft-practice approach. Those in charge of budgeting do not allow meaningful participation in setting the initial dollar limits, perhaps indicating their doubts concerning the capabilities and motivation of most operating managers. Nevertheless, they recognize that some will openly rebel against such strictures and must be appeased if the system is to operate with reasonable harmony. Examining these two approaches, one could argue that the budgeting process serves to promote the very behaviors it seeks to control. That is, such a process appears to reward those units which are most creatively and/or aggressively self-serving, and it appears to invite subterfuge and to discourage efforts to produce honest, least-cost estimates.

The multiple-level–contingency approach reflects, at least in part, the influence of the human resources model. It views budgeting as a logical extension of the joint planning process and emphasizes the explicit recognition of both normal variations in department needs and the possibility of unusual variability which is not precisely predictable. Under this approach, members of a unit can set high standards for themselves with the recognition that they have "the freedom to fail"—gaining recognition in advance that a variety of factors essentially outside their control may influence their performance.

CAPITAL EXPENDITURES AND THE CRISIS SYNDROME

The current trend toward acquisition and merger suggests that the control relationships between corporate headquarters and division management are an increasingly important subject for analysis. A few lines on this issue are thus in order, particularly as they point up a key dimension of managerial behavior related to our models.

It is not uncommon for an independent organization to be acquired by another organization and set up as an operating division of the larger unit. When this occurs, the previously independent unit may be allowed to operate for a time pretty much as it has in the past. (See our earlier Jamison Enterprises example.) This frequently happens because the larger unit has no choice. It desires to maintain operating continuity within its newly acquired division—continuity which would be threatened by major changes rapidly implemented. Thus, the corporate group may simply allow the division to extend its pattern of operating expenditures into subsequent periods. One area for corporate control is available, however, almost from the beginning—that of capital expenditures (investment in buildings, machinery, equipment, etc.), with life spans extending considerably beyond current operating periods. Division managers are not likely to view control in this area as inappropriate. In fact, they recognize along with the corporate staff that major investments must be carefully analyzed, and that even if they were operating completely on their own they would be required to demonstrate to stockholders or loaning institutions that a given expenditure was essential and profitable.

Where conflict occurs—and it frequently does—is over the definition of what must be classified as "capital" expenditures and what size the expenditure must be before it requires corporate clearance. The division manager obviously wants the "requires approval" dollar limit set as high as possible to allow him maximum freedom to meet the needs of his unit. Corporate executives, however, may want this requirement set very low so that they can maintain close control over division developments and prevent possible aggregate overcommitment.

Observing practices in this area, it is not uncommon to find a cyclical pattern emerging. Division managers may initially be given a rather sizable amount of discretion—that is, they will be allowed to make capital expenditures and commitments up to some large dollar amount without corporate approval. Then, if times are good and the divisions are profitable and growing, the amounts may even be extended upward, either explicitly or else implicitly by simply approving rapidly—and almost automatically—requests that run above the established figure. This pattern may be reversed, however, by either of two events, or a combination of both. First, one of the division managers may make a poor decision, committing the corporation to a losing venture. Or, second, a general drop in demand may reduce the corporation's reserves to the point where top officials become concerned. When poor decisions occur or demand slackens, the reaction is frequently severe. The "without approval" capital expenditure or commitment figure is sharply reduced or even removed completely. In either instance, the policy is usually uniform across all divisions and the managers of those divisions which have been and are likely to continue to be highly successful are subject to the same restrictions as those who have erred or whose units will be hit hardest by the reduced level of demand.

The more creative division managers frequently adopt innovative behaviors to evade what they may feel are unreasonable constraints. For example, as operating and maintenance expenditures fall outside these limits, managers may, on finding that they cannot purchase a new machine, simply purchase enough "replacement" components to build the needed equipment. Similarly, a warehouse extension may appear on the books as "repairs." To counteract this tendency, corporate headquarters may accompany their new regulations with the assignment of a new controller at the division level, reporting jointly to the division manager and to the corporate controller group.

Again, in time the cycle may shift upward again. As economic conditions improve and as the memory of some past overcommitment fades, managers at the division level may once again be given a higher dollar limit under which to operate. This process may occur, as suggested, either explicitly or, more commonly, implicitly through corporate leniency in approving requests.

Two things are worth noting regarding such fluctuations in the degree of discretion allowed at the division level. First, the shift toward tighter figures is ordinarily much more abrupt than is the shift toward greater freedom. Quick action in the face of real danger is of course reasonable, in fact mandatory—survival is the prime requisite for any organization. The willingness to move equally rapidly to restore discretion and responsiveness may be just as desirable, however. Second, and perhaps more important, the imposition of substantial restrictions as the result of a single mistake may be quite dysfunctional. When this occurs, the organization loses much of its responsiveness and division growth may be seriously retarded. Moreover, such behavior may "teach" division managers to avoid risk rather than to maximize division performance.

CONCLUDING REMARKS

The preceding comments lead us to a pair of concluding observations. First, both traditional and human relations communications and control systems tend to be aimed more at preventing deviations from established practices rather than at promoting creative responsiveness. That is, they focus, much more than does the human resources system, on the *methods* by which things are done. The human resources communications and control system tends to focus on *goals*, or *objectives*—the ends which the organization is seeking—and to leave the choice of means, as far as possible, to the individual or unit charged with the task. This is highlighted in the philosophy of management by objectives and in the budgeting examples described earlier. Second, by focusing on and responding primarily to negative stimuli, traditional and human relations control mechanisms generate a substantial amount of subterfuge—they tend to guarantee that upward flowing communication will, wherever possible, minimize shortcomings. Lower-level personnel will try to tell those above them what they want to hear—that things are going smoothly, that all is well—until problems can no longer be hidden. Thus these approaches tend not to be oriented to problem solving but to problem hiding or avoidance. The human resources approach makes it clear that some mistakes are a normal outgrowth of high-level performance. The emphasis on goal accomplishment through creative response at the unit or individual level, anticipating problems where possible but dealing with them openly when they occur, can place a positive cast on the entire communications and control system. As we noted in Chapter 3, the fact that control is exercised at lower levels does not mean that any less control is exercised at upper levels. Instead, it may mean that the total amount of control over and concern for organizational performance is substantially increased.

BIBLIOGRAPHY

Allen, Stephen, III, "Corporate-Divisional Relationships in Highly Diversified Firms," in Jay W. Lorsch and Paul R. Lawrence (eds.), *Studies in Organization Design* (Homewood, Ill.: Irwin, 1970), pp. 16–35.

Argyris, Chris (abridged from *The Impact of Budgets on People*, prepared for the Financial Research Foundation), "Selections from the Impact of Budgets on People," in Joseph A. Litterer (ed.), *Organizations: Structure and Behavior* (New York: Wiley, 1969), pp. 282–295.

Drucker, Peter, *The Practice of Management* (New York: Harper & Brothers, 1954), chap. 11.

Granick, David, *The Red Executive* (Garden City, N.Y.: Doubleday, 1960).

Likert, Rensis, *The Human Organization* (New York: McGraw-Hill, 1967), chaps. 8 and 9.

McGregor, Douglas, *The Human Side of Enterprise* (New York: McGraw-Hill, 1960), chap. 5.

Miles, Raymond E. and Roger C. Vergin, "Behavioral Properties of Variance Controls," *California Management Review*, vol. 8, pp. 57–65 (Spring 1966).

Tannenbaum, Arnold, "Control in Organizations: Individual Adjustment and Organizational Performance," *Administrative Science Quarterly*, vol. 7, pp. 236–257 (September 1962).

Thompson, James, *Organizations in Action* (New York: McGraw-Hill, 1967), chaps. 7 and 10.

Chapter 7

Leadership Styles and Subordinate Responses*

To many people, management and leadership are synonymous. We have argued, particularly in Chapters 1 and 2, that such is not the case. Our contention has been that managers' theories of management are reflected in the way in which they design jobs, structure units, put together communications and control systems, set up appraisal and development efforts, establish and operate reward mechanisms, etc. Our main point has been that these systems and mechanisms are all part of an overall approach, or model of management, within which direct, face-to-face relationships with subordinates are only one aspect.

Thus, we have sought to de-emphasize leadership as it is usually conceived and to indicate that designing a job or establishing a control

*Much of this chapter is drawn from or based on an article, "Participative Management: Quantity vs. Quality," authored by Professor J. B. Ritchie of Brigham Young University and myself, and which appeared in the *California Management Review*, Summer 1971. I appreciate the *Review's* permission to use the material here. I also appreciate Professor Ritchie's willingness to allow me to blend his ideas with mine in this manner.

system is as much an act of leadership as consulting with a subordinate (or not consulting with him) on a matter of departmental business. We have taken this position because we believe that variables other than interpersonal behavior have too frequently been left out of discussions of leadership style. However, in adopting this stance, we may well have swung the pendulum hard to the opposite side, implying that the way the manager interacts with his subordinates is unimportant. If we have done this, the present chapter should serve to erase that implication. For what we hope to show here, by discussion and by examination of research data, is that subordinates' attitudes toward their superior are indeed affected by the manner in which he interacts with them—specifically by the extent to which he consults them regarding departmental issues and by his attitudes concerning this consultation process.

As we noted in Chapter 3, research indicates that most managers today pay at least lip service to the concept of participative management. That is, most would agree that some amount of consultation with subordinates is probably useful. Nevertheless, even though it is widely accepted, managers' responses indicate that a heavy pall of confusion hangs over the whole concept of participation.

We feel that a prime source of the confusion surrounding the concept concerns its *purpose*. Our research suggests that most managers tend to hold at least two "theories" of participation. One of these, which we labeled the human relations concept, viewed participation primarily as a means of obtaining cooperation—a technique which the manager could use to improve morale and reduce subordinate resistance to policies and decisions. The second, which we labeled the human resources approach, recognized the untapped potential of most organization members and advocated participation as a means of achieving direct improvements in individual and therefore organizational performance. Perhaps predictably, managers regarded the human relations model as appropriate for their subordinates although they preferred the human resources model for themselves.

Our recent research draws attention to a closely related and probably equally important source of confusion involving the *process* of participation. Our earlier descriptions of the *purpose* of participation under the human relations and human resources models implied that it is not only the *degree* that is important but also the *nature* of the superior-subordinate interaction. Upon reflection, the notion that both the quality and quantity of participation must be considered seems obvious. Surprisingly, however, the quality variable has been infrequently specified in management theory and even more rarely researched.

The lack of specific focus in theory or research on the quality aspect of the process has led, in our view, to the promulgation of a simple quantity theory of participation, a concept which, whether intended or not, appears to lump all participative acts together in a common category, which is therefore open to much justified criticism. Clearly, a theory which implies only that some participation is better than none, and that more is better than a little, ignores individual and situational differences. It is just such a simplified view that allows its more vitriolic critics to draw caricatures extending the participative process to include a chairman of the board consulting with a janitor concerning issues of capital budgeting—the sort of criticism which brings humor to journal pages but contributes little to our understanding of this managerial mechanism.

Recognizing these key sources of confusion, our current studies have been aimed at increasing our understanding of the process of participation under the human relations and human resources models. Specifically, we have attempted, within a large sample of management teams, to identify and measure (1) the amount of superior-subordinate interaction, and (2) a dimension of the quality of this interaction—the superior's confidence in his subordinate's capabilities. In our theoretical framework both the quantity and quality of participation are important determinants of subordinate satisfaction and performance. For these analyses, we have focused on the impact of these variables, both separately and jointly, on the subordinate's satisfaction with his immediate superior. We believe our findings clarify the role that quality plays and add substance to the human relations–human resources differentiation.

In the following sections we will explore further the concepts of quantity and quality of participation, integrate these into existing theories of participative management, and examine the implications of our research for these theories and for management practice.

THE QUALITY ASPECT OF PARTICIPATIVE MANAGEMENT

A simple, and we believe familiar, example should assist us in firmly integrating the quantity-quality variables into the major theories of participative management and perhaps demonstrate, in part at least, why we are concerned with this dimension. Most of us have had the following experience:

> We receive an invitation to attend an important meeting. (We know it is important because it is carefully specified as such in the telephone call.) A crucial policy decision is to be made and our views and those of our colleagues are, according to the invitation, vital to the decision. Having done our homework, we arrive at the meeting and begin serious and perhaps even

heated discussion. Before too long, however, a light begins to dawn and illuminated in that dawning light is the fact that the crucial decision we had been called together to decide . . .

The typical organization member completes the final sentence in our example with a cynical, knowing smile: ". . . had already been made." It is helpful, however, to push aside the well-remembered frustration of such situations and examine the logic of the executive who called the meeting and the nature of the participative process flowing from his logic.

We can easily imagine—perhaps because we have frequently used the same logic—the executive in our example saying to himself, "I've got this matter pretty well firmed, but it may require a bit of selling. I'd better call in the troops and at least let them express their views." He may even be willing to allow some minor revisions in the policy in order to overcome resistance and generate among his subordinates a feeling of being part of the decision.

Managers' Attitudes and the Purposes of Participation

Clearly defined in our example is the tight bond between the purpose of participation and the quality of involvement which ensues. And underlying the purpose is the executive's set of assumptions about people— particularly his attitudes concerning the capabilities of his subordinates.

Three theoretical frameworks describe this linkage between the manager's basic attitudes toward people and the amount and kind of consultation that he is likely to use with his subordinates. (Two of these were discussed in another context in Chapters 2 and 3 but deserve amplification here.) It is worth a few lines to compare these theoretical systems and to apply them to our example. Listed chronologically, these frameworks are (1) the theory X–theory Y dichotomy described by the late Douglas McGregor, (2) the system I, II, III, and IV continuum defined by Rensis Likert, and (3) our own traditional, human relations, human resources classification.

McGregor's theory X, Likert's system I, and our traditional model describe autocratic leadership behavior coupled with tight, unilateral control, and obviously little or no subordinate participation in the decision process. Theory X and the traditional model explicitly delineate the superior's assumptions that most people, including his subordinates, are basically indolent, self-centered, gullible, and resistant to change and thus have little to contribute to his decision making. Focusing more on descriptive characteristics and less on an explicit set of assumptions, Likert's system I manager is pictured only as having no confidence or trust in his subordinates.

At the other extreme, theory Y, system IV, and the human resources model define a style of behavior which deeply involves subordinates in the decision process and emphasizes high levels of self-direction and self-control. Again, both theory Y and the human resources model make the logic underlying such behavior explicit—that most organization members are capable of contributing more than demanded by their present jobs and thus represent untapped potential for the organization, potential which the capable manager develops and invests in improved performance. A system IV superior is described simply as one having complete confidence and trust in subordinates in all matters.

In between these extremes fall Likert's systems II and III and our human relations model. Systems II and III describe increasing amounts of subordinate participation as their superior's attitudes toward them move from "condescending" to "substantial, but not complete" confidence and trust. Our human relations model views the superior as recognizing his subordinates' desire for involvement but doubting their ability to make meaningful contributions.

Comparing these frameworks to our example, it is clear that the executive calling the above-mentioned meeting was not operating at the theory X, system I, traditional end of the participative continuum. Had he followed the assumptions of these models he would simply have announced his decision and, if a meeting were called, used it openly to explain his views. Similarly, it seems doubtful that our executive was following the theory Y, system IV, or human resources models. Had he been, he would have called the meeting in the belief that his subordinates might well have important contributions to make and that their participation would possibly result in the construction of a better overall policy. He would have had confidence in their ability and willingness to generate and examine alternatives and take action in the best interest of the organization.

Instead, the meeting in our example, as well as many from our own experience, seems to be defined almost to the letter by our human relations logic and the behavior described in Likert's systems II and III. The casual observer, and perhaps even the more naïve participant, unaware of the motives of the executive calling the meeting, might observe a high level of involvement during the session—participation in both quantity and quality. Most of the participants, however, would be much less charitable, particularly about the meaningfulness of the exercise. They would sense, even though the guidance was subtle, that at least the depth of their participation was carefully controlled if not the entire strategy of the meeting itself.

SUBORDINATE SATISFACTION UNDER THE THREE MODELS

Having described various degrees of quantity and quality of participation flowing from alternative theories of management, and having attempted to link to a common experience through our meeting example, it is not difficult to conjecture about the relationships between these variables and subordinate satisfaction. We would expect subordinate satisfaction to move up and down with both the quantity and the quality of participation, and there is already some evidence (with regard to amount of participation, at least) that it does. Thus, we would expect, particularly within the managerial hierarchy, that satisfaction would be lowest when both quantity and quality of participation were lowest, i.e., as the traditional model is approached, and highest when both quantity and quality are high—when participation moves toward the type described in the human resources model.

Predicting satisfaction under the human relations model is less easy. If the superior's behavior is blatantly manipulative, perhaps close to that in our example, one might expect satisfaction to be quite low, even though the amount of participation was high. On the other hand, if the superior's logic were less obvious, even to himself, we might expect his subordinates to be somewhat pleased to be involved, even if their involvement was frequently peripheral.

While we cannot precisely test the impact of these models on subordinate satisfaction, our recent research does provide some evidence with regard to these conjectures, and we will therefore briefly describe the method of our investigation and look at some of our findings.

Research Approach

The findings reported here were drawn from a broader research project conducted among superior-subordinate management teams from five levels in six geographically separate operating divisions of a West Coast firm.

From extensive questionnaire responses, we were able to develop measures of the three variables important to these analyses: (1) quantity of participation, (2) quality of participation, and (3) satisfaction with immediate superiors. Our measure of quantity was drawn from managers' responses to questions concerning how frequently they felt they were consulted by their superior on a number of typical department issues and decisions. This information allowed us to classify managers as high or low (compared to other managers at the same level) in terms of the amount of participation they felt they were allowed. For our measure of quality, we turned to the responses given by each manager's superior. The superior's attitudes toward his subordinates—his evaluation of their capabilities with regard to such factors as judgment, creativity, responsibility, long-range perspective, etc.—were analyzed and categorized as high or low compared to those of other managers at the same level. Finally, our satisfaction measure was taken from a question on which managers indicated, on a scale from very satisfied to very dissatisfied, their reactions to their own immediate superiors.

Findings

The first thing apparent in our findings, as shown in each of the figures discussed below, is that virtually all the subjects in our study appear reasonably well satisfied with their immediate superiors. This is not surprising, particularly since all subjects, both superiors and subordinates, are in managerial positions. Compared to members lower in the hierarchy, managers generally respond positively on job satisfaction scales. Moreover, the organization in which our research was conducted is reputed to be forward looking and well managed. In a similar vein, and supporting the organization's reputation, most participants reported generally high levels of consultation, and superior's scores on confidence in their subordinates were typically higher than the average scores in our broader research.

Nevertheless, differences do exist which, given the restricted range

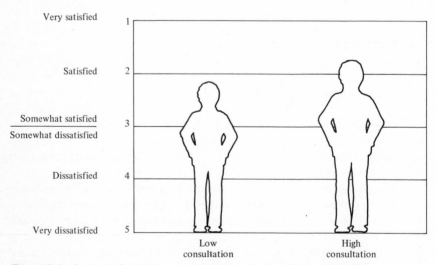

Figure 7-1 Amount of superior consultation and subordinate satisfaction

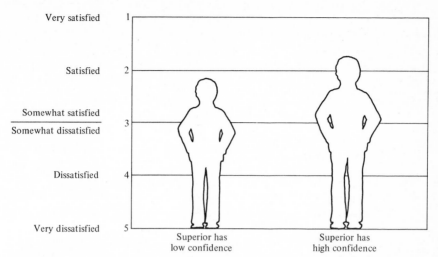

Figure 7-2 Superior's confidence in subordinates and subordinates' satisfaction

of scores, are in most instances highly significant in statistical terms. Moreover, they demonstrate that both the quantity and the quality of participation are related to managers' feelings of satisfaction with their immediate superiors.

As shown in Figure 7-1, the quantity of participation achieved is apparently related to managers' feelings of satisfaction with their superiors. Managers classified as low in terms of the extent to which they are consulted by their superiors are significantly less satisfied than those classified as high. The average score for the low consultation group falls between the satisfied and the so-so (somewhat satisfied–somewhat dissatisfied) categories. For the high consultation group, the score falls between the satisfied and the highly satisfied.

A slightly stronger pattern of results is apparent when managers are regrouped in terms of the amount of confidence their superiors have in them (Figure 7-2). Managers whose superiors have relatively high trust and confidence scores are significantly more satisfied than are their colleagues whose superiors have relatively lower scores on this dimension.

Finally, our results take on their most interesting form when managers are cross-classified on both the quantity and quality dimensions. As shown in Figure 7-3, the progression in satisfaction is consistent with our theoretical formulation. Especially obvious is the comparison between managers classified as low both in amount of consultation received and in the extent to which their superior has confidence in them and managers

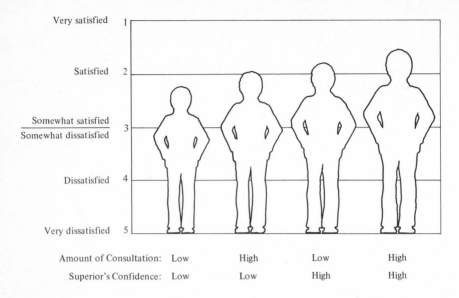

Very satisfied 1

Satisfied 2

Somewhat satisfied
Somewhat dissatisfied 3

Dissatisfied 4

Very dissatisfied 5

Amount of Consultation: Low   High   Low   High

Superior's Confidence: Low   Low   High   High

Figure 7-3 Effects of amount of consultation and superior's confidence in subordinates on subordinate satisfaction

who are rated high on both these variables. Interestingly enough, and relevant to our later discussion, managers whose superiors have high confidence in them but who are low in amount of participation appear slightly more satisfied than their counterparts who are high in amount of participation but whose superiors have less confidence in their subordinates.

Linking Findings to Theory

The bulk of our findings, particularly as illustrated in Figure 7-3, appear to support our conjectures. Managers who place the least value in their subordinates' capabilities and who least often seek their contributions on departmental issues have the least-satisfied subordinates. Although it would probably be incorrect to place the traditional (theory X, system I) label on any of the managers in our sample, those who lean closest to these views do so with predictable results in terms of subordinate satisfaction.

Similarly, managers who are high in their respect for their subordinates' capabilities and who consult them regularly on departmental issues also achieve the expected results. Again, although precise labeling is probably inappropriate, managers whose attitudes and behavior are closest to the human resources (theory Y, system IV) model do in fact have the most satisfied subordinates.

Further, those managers who consult their subordinates frequently but who have little confidence in their ability to make decisions, and who thus fall nearest to our human relations model, have subordinates who are more satisfied than those under managers who lean toward the traditional model but are significantly less satisfied than those under human resources managers.

Although the majority of our findings support the major formulations of participative management theory, they also suggest the need for elaboration and clarification. This need is brought to attention by the total pattern of our findings and particularly by the results for one of our categories of managers—those high in superiors' confidence but relatively low in participation. If you recall, although the differences were not large, this group had the second highest average satisfaction score in our sample—the score falling between that of the human relations group (high participation, low superior confidence) and the human resources group (high on both). Moreover, for the two groups characterized by high participation, there is substantially higher satisfaction for those whose superior expresses his confidence in his subordinates. Clearly, any theory which focused on the amount of participation would not predict these results. Rather, for these managers at least, the quality of their relationship with their superiors as indicated by their superiors' attitudes of trust and confidence in them appears to modify the effects of the amount of participation.

Implications for Theory

Although the quality dimension of the theory of participative management has not been fully developed, its outlines are suggested in our own human resources model and in McGregor's theoretical framework. McGregor stressed heavily the importance of managers' basic attitudes and assumptions about their subordinates. Expanding on this point in his more recent writing, he suggested that a manager's assumptions about his subordinates' traits and abilities do not bind him to a single course of action. Rather, he argued that, taking circumstances into account, a range of behaviors is appropriate under theory Y assumptions—i.e., a manager with high trust and confidence in his subordinates could and should take into account a number of situational and personality factors in deciding, among other things, when and how to consult with them. Extending this reasoning, one can even imagine a theory Y or human resources manager actually consulting with his subordinates less often than some of his colleagues. Nevertheless, the nature and quality of participation employed by such a manager, when it occurs, would presumably be deeper and more meaningful, which would be reflected in high levels of subordinate satisfaction and—hopefully—performance.

This view of the superior-subordinate interaction process, emphasizing as it does the quality of the interaction rather than only the amount, can be used to provide an answer to three of the more pervasive criticisms of participative management. These criticisms, each of which is probably most accurately aimed at the simple quantity theory, focus on the inappropriateness of extensive consultation when the superior is constrained by time, technology, and temperament (his own or that of his subordinates). Let us discuss these criticisms further.

The Time Constraint   "In a crisis, you simply do not have time to run around consulting people." This familiar explication is difficult to debate and in fact would receive no challenge from a sophisticated theory of participation. In a real "burning building" crisis, consultation is inappropriate and unnecessary. A crisis of this nature is recognized as such by any well-informed subordinate and his self-controlled cooperation is most likely willingly supplied. The behavior of both superior and subordinate in such a situation is guided by the situation and each may freely turn to the other, or to any available source of expertise, for help in solving the problem at hand.

Many crises, however, do not fit the "burning building" category and in fact may be much more real to one individual or to one level of management than to those below them. Our experience and some very tentative research findings suggest that managers may not be nearly so bound by their constraints as they frequently claim, or at least if they are constrained, these limits are either known in advance or are open to modification if circumstances demand. In many instances it appears that managers employ the "time won't permit" argument primarily to justify autocratic and risk-free behavior—if he succeeds the credit is his; if he fails, he can defend his actions by pointing out that he had no time to explore alternatives.

Such self-defined, or at least self-sustaining, crises are, it seems to us, most frequently used by the manager with a human relations concept of participation—one who views participation primarily as a means of obtaining subordinate cooperation and who focuses mainly on the amount of formal involvement required. The crisis itself can be employed in place of participation as the lever to obtain cooperation, and there is clearly no time for the sort of routine, frequently peripheral consultation in which he most often indulges.

On the other hand, the manager with high trust and confidence in his subordinates' capabilities, the human resources manager, is less likely to use time constraints as a managerial tactic. In real crises, he moves as rapidly as the situation demands. He is, however, more likely, because of his normal practices of sharing information with his subordinates, to have a group which is prepared to join him in a rapid review of alternatives. He is unconcerned with involvement for the sake of involvement, and his consultation activities are penetrating and to the point. His subordinates share his trust and feel free to challenge his views, just as he feels free to openly question their advice and suggestions.

The Technology Barrier   "Look, I've got fifteen subordinates scattered all over the building. What do you expect me to do—shut down the plant and call a meeting every time something happens?" This argument is obviously closely linked to the time-constraint argument—technology is a major factor in determining the flow and timing of decisions. Similarly, it too flows from a human relations–quantity-oriented view of participation.

Of course a good manager does not regularly "stop the presses" and call a conference. He has confidence in his subordinates' abilities to handle problems as they appear and to call him in when the problem demands his attention. This confidence is, however, reinforced by joint planning, both one to one and across his group of subordinates, before the operation gets under way. Having agreed in advance on objectives, schedules, priorities, and procedures, involvement on a day-to-day basis may be minimal. The manager in this instance does not seek participation to obtain cooperation with his views. The regularly scheduled work planning and review sessions are viewed as important by both parties because they result in well-considered solutions to real problems.

The Temperament Barrier   "I'm simply not the sort who can run around to his subordinates asking them how things are going. It's just not my style." The manager who made this statement (a participant in one of our earlier studies) did so somewhat apologetically. In fact, there was little for him to be apologetic about. He had a high-performing group of subordinates in whom he placed great trust and confidence, and who were in turn highly satisfied with him. Further, while he did not seek their views on a variety of routine departmental matters, and his subordinates did not drop into his office to chat, he freely shared all departmental information with them and, on a regular basis, worked with his subordinates in coordinating departmental plans and schedules. In addition, he practiced a somewhat formal but effective form of management by objectives with each of his subordinates.

This manager and, unfortunately, many of the more outspoken critics of participative management, tend to feel that consultation must be carried out in a gregarious, back-slapping manner. Quite the contrary— joint planning is a decision-making technique and not a personality attribute. Extreme shyness or reserve may be an inhibiting factor, but it is not a complete barrier. Trust and confidence in subordinates can be demonstrated at least as effectively by actions as by words.

Similarly, as suggested earlier, the manager who holds a human resources view of participation acknowledges personality and capability differences among his subordinates. He feels a responsibility to the organization as well as to his subordinates to assist *each* to continuously develop his potential. He recognizes that individuals move toward the free interchange of ideas, suggestions, and criticisms at different paces. However, by demonstrating his own confidence in his subordinates' capabilities, he tends to encourage more rapid growth than other managers.

CONCLUDING REMARKS

Our continuing research on the purpose and process of participative management has, in our view, contributed additional support for the human resources concept of participation. It has emphasized that when the impact on subordinates is considered, the superior's attitudes toward the traits and abilities of his subordinates is at least as important as the amount of consultation in which he engages.

This not-so-startling finding allows expansions and interpretations of modern theories of participation to counter criticisms which may be properly leveled at a simple quantity theory. However, while our findings have obvious implications for both management theory and behavior, they too are open to possible misinterpretation. One can—and some surely will—read into our findings that subordinate consultation may be neglected—that all that matters is that the superior respect his subordinates.

Our findings do not support such a view, and, in fact, it has been tried and regularly found wanting. Such a philosophy is embodied in the frequently heard statement, "All you need to do to be a good manager is to hire a good subordinate and turn him loose to do the job as he sees fit." Such a philosophy, in our view, abdicates the superior's responsibility to guide, develop, and support his subordinates. The most satisfied managers in our sample were those who received high levels of consultation from superiors who valued their capabilities. We feel that effective participation involves neither the "selling" of the superior's ideas nor the blanket approval of all subordinate suggestions. Rather, it is most clearly embodied in the notion of joint planning where the skills of both parties are used to their fullest.

While our findings emphasize the importance of feelings of trust and confidence in subordinates, they do not indicate their source. It is possible of course that those superiors in our sample who reported the highest levels of trust and confidence in their subordinates did so because their subordinates were of higher caliber than those of their colleagues. However, this seems to us a bit unlikely. Rather, within our large sample of managers, several indicators suggested that the capabilities of managers were roughly evenly distributed across levels and divisions within the organization.

Another possible reason for differences in superior attitudes on this dimension is that they are caused by interaction with subordinates in the first place, rather than being a determinate of the nature of this interaction. That is, the manager who attempts consultation which is highly successful increases his confidence in his subordinates and thus develops broader involvement. This explanation seems to us to be a highly plausible one which has implications for management development. In fact, there is growing evidence that managers who experiment with participative techniques over lengthy periods of time do develop both a commitment to such practices and additional trust in their subordinates.

BIBLIOGRAPHY

Bowers, D. G. and Stanley E. Seashore, "Predicting Organizational Effectiveness with a Four-Factor Theory of Leadership," *Administrative Science Quarterly*, vol. 11, pp. 238–263 (September 1966).

Fiedler, Fred E., "Engineer the Job to Fit the Manager," *Harvard Business Review*, vol. 43, pp. 115–122 (September-October 1965).

Heller, Frank A., "Leadership, Decision Making and Contingency Theory," *Industrial Relations*, vol. 12, pp. 183–199 (May 1973).

McGregor, Douglas, *The Professional Manager* (New York: McGraw-Hill, 1969).

Miles, Raymond E. and J. B. Ritchie, "An Analysis of Quantity and Quality of the Participative Decision Making Process," *Personnel Psychology*, vol. 23, pp. 347–359 (Autumn 1970).

Roberts, Karlene, Raymond E. Miles, and L. Vaughn Blankenship, "Organizational Leadership, Satisfaction, and Productivity: A Comparative Analysis," *The Academy of Management Journal*, vol. 11, pp. 401–414 (December 1968).

Strauss, George, "Human Relations—1968 Style," *Industrial Relations*, vol. 7, pp. 262–276 (May 1968).

Vroom, Victor and Philip Yetton, *Leadership and Decision Making* (Pittsburgh: University of Pittsburgh Press, 1973), chaps. 5 and 6.

Reward Systems

We have examined a number of important factors influencing the role and behavior of managers and other members of work organizations—the way in which their jobs are designed and linked to other positions, the manner in which performance information is routed and appraised, the degree of trust and confidence existing between superiors and their subordinates, etc. We have referred to these factors—job and organization design, control systems, leadership—as integrative mechanisms, i.e., processes aimed at structuring and drawing together human capability and focusing it on organizational objectives. We have noted the logical linkages among these integrative mechanisms, pointing out that what is attempted with one will surely affect what is feasible with another. Similarly, we have called attention to the fact that choices among alternative designs of these integrative mechanisms are influenced by the nature of the organization's environment, the capabilities and attitudes of its members, and the basic assumptions of its managers concerning how people behave and how they should be managed. We have done this so far without direct attention to the topic of motivation. Thus, we have yet to address what is frequently considered the most important integrative mechanism of all, the organization's reward system.

We have deferred attention to the topic of rewards to this point for two reasons. First, discussion and analysis of reward systems require some examination of theories of motivation, theories which we believe are more easily understood and take on additional meaning within the broader conceptual framework we have been attempting to develop. Second, and more important, our earlier discussions of job design, control systems, and leadership provide a foundation on which we can build some of the more abstract pieces of motivation theory.

Most of us are smugly secure in our understanding of organizational reward systems and how they operate. I suggest that this confidence is, on the surface at least, rather surprising because the hard evidence in this area is both meager and fragmented. On the other hand, it is frequently true that we are most certain about those subjects where the least is known—e.g., the existence of God and His relationship to man, or whether Babe Ruth could have hit as many home runs against modern pitching. This perhaps unwarranted confidence frequently leads managers to build and maintain reward systems without ever attempting to measure their efficacy—genuinely close analysis is discouraged and experimentation is considered an unnecessary or perhaps even threatening venture, something most likely to result only in creating unrest.

REWARD SYSTEMS—A BROAD CONCEPTUALIZATION

As employed here, the term "reward system" includes the total package of benefits which the organization makes available to its members and the mechanisms and procedures by which these benefits are distributed. Wages, salaries, pensions, vacations, promotions to higher office (and to higher salary and benefits) are clearly included. But so are such rewards as assurance of job security, lateral transfers to more challenging positions or to positions leading to additional growth and development, and various forms of recognition for outstanding service. Finally, included in this package of benefits is the structure of tasks and processes—to the extent that the organization can and does add, delete, or adjust features of the work itself to enhance its intrinsic attractiveness.

Not only is this broad array of factors, of which a full listing was not attempted, included in the concept of a reward system, but so is the means by which these are allocated. That is, the reward system not only includes promotions and merit wage increases but also the basis on which these are granted and the perceptions of members at all levels concerning the process.

REWARD SYSTEMS IN OPERATION

Some brief examples will help illustrate our concept of a reward system and provide the foundation on which we can construct an analytical framework for viewing motivation and rewards.

> EXAMPLE 1—(Jo Ann Myers) Jo Ann Myers works for an insurance company in a large office which processes customer claims. She has been employed for ten months, and as summer is approaching she is planning ahead for her vacation. The company's vacation policy is spelled out in her employee handbook. She knows that having worked for the company for over eight months but fewer than eighteen qualifies her for one week's paid vacation. According to the policy, by next summer she will be eligible for two weeks' vacation, and after five years she will receive three weeks off. She also is aware, from the policy statement, that senior employees get first choice at vacation dates. Jo Ann's excitement over her coming vacation is blunted a bit by the fact that her scheduled dates do not correspond perfectly with those of the two girls with whom she rooms and with whom she was planning a trip. She is considering the possibility of simply calling in sick for the three days before her vacation starts so that she can leave with her friends but wonders whether she dare approach Mrs. Besselink, her supervisor, with a request for special scheduling. She knows that special scheduling is permitted if it is recommended by the supervisor and approved by the personnel department, but she also knows that Mrs. Besselink has the reputation of being generous to her favorites but snippy with those she doesn't care for or who "ask for too much too soon." Jo Ann at this point simply doesn't know for sure how Mrs. Besselink feels about her, although she believes that her work has been as good as, if not better than, those whom Mrs. Besselink appears to favor.

In this example, the nature of the reward which the member is expecting to receive in return for almost a year of service is clear, as is the basic mechanism by which the reward (a week's vacation) is determined and allocated. A portion of the reward system in this instance, however, remains ambiguous. Mrs. Besselink's standards of performance are not spelled out in the handbook, nor are her personal attitudes toward Jo Ann.

In our second example, the rewards being sought and the basis on which they are provided are even more complex and ambiguous.

> EXAMPLE 2—(Charlie Hutton) Charlie Hutton is thinking about leaving the office a couple of hours early this afternoon. It's been a rather dull day.

He spent the morning with two of his subordinates wrapping up details on his department's portion of a major project and has in the last hour or so cleaned up the accumulated correspondence and routine reports on his desk.

While the day has seemed dull to Charlie, a thirty-two-year-old executive in a large manufacturing organization, it has in fact been a momentous one in his career. For while Charlie was cleaning up project details and correspondence, his personnel file was the subject of careful consideration in a meeting on the fourteenth floor of the "headquarters" building across the street.

Charlie and a group of his peers, all of whom are considered "top executive caliber," have been undergoing evaluation by a team of upper-level executives—an evaluation which can result in promotion, lateral transfer, being held for another year of seasoning, etc. In Charlie's case, the executive team has been quite impressed with his record of performance over the past eighteen months—particularly the way in which he stepped in to get a lagging maintenance project back on schedule. Interestingly, Charlie's immediate superior (who is not a member of the executive team reviewing the records of Charlie and the others), while writing glowing memos concerning Charlie's problem-solving ability and drive, noted that a certain amount of hard feeling had resulted among the older production and engineering personnel because of his handling of the maintenance project. Nevertheless, the executive team felt that this was a small price to pay for completing the work on time and, as one of them noted, "It's probably a good thing to put a tiger like Charlie on their tail now and then."

Following their review, the executive team reached the decision that Charlie was precisely the man to push into the number two spot in a recently acquired manufacturing plant—one that supplies crucial parts for the main plant and in which many of the previous management personnel had been retained. The recently acquired plant had always been a dependable supplier, "but with a guy like Charlie in there pushing, we should have no worries about them keeping up." The move for Charlie is a definite promotion, with a substantial increase in salary. The plant is located over 300 miles from the headquarters plant where Charlie now works, but moving expenses for him and his family will be paid.

"Give Charlie a couple of years out there and then we can move him back in here to take Luther Tolan's place [Luther Tolan is head of plantwide planning and is scheduled for early retirement a year from May, a decision also made by the executive team]."

While Charlie has been unaware of the proceedings at the meeting determining his immediate future, if not the course of his entire career, he has been expecting to be reviewed. And while he has anticipated a positive outcome, he has been a bit concerned about his relationship with his immediate superior. Charlie felt that he and his boss had never quite communicated on the handling of the maintenance project, but it was his guess that his boss (who is also nearing retirement) wouldn't have the final say anyway. Moreover, Charlie has had a feeling that the headquarters team would want to move someone from the main plant into the recently acquired plant and has wondered if he might be considered. The opportunity to "build a record" looks good there, but he is rather certain his wife will not be excited about such a move. Thus, rather obviously, the exact value of this reward, the criteria used to determine it, and the mechanism by which these criteria have been applied are neither simple nor explicit.

In our third example the reward system is well understood by those involved in it, but their understanding of the system and the effects it has on them are not precisely those which the designers of the system had in mind.

EXAMPLE 3—(Centerville Community Hospital) All nonsupervisory, nonmedical personnel in the Centerville Community Hospital are covered by a merit pay plan which calls for an annual review of their performance by both their department head and his immediate superior. Based on these reviews, an employee's work can be classified as outstanding, satisfactory, or acceptable. The system, begun three years ago, was intended to allow departments to reward outstanding performance with pay increases above those given for normal attention to duties and to provide minimal increases for work judged to be merely or, perhaps, barely adequate. Thus, presumably, those employees performing at high levels would be pleased with their exceptional rewards and those performing at lower levels would be encouraged to give additional effort to their jobs so that they might qualify for a larger raise next time.

In fact, the reward system does not appear to be achieving its anticipated goals. Department heads discovered an initially unwritten but now explicitly coded rule that no more than 20 percent of the employees in any unit may be classified as outstanding in any given year. Moreover, they have learned that if any employee in their unit is to receive an increase above the average figure budgeted for all employees, some other employee in their unit must receive a proportionately lower amount. In the first two years of operation of the plan, department heads and their superiors filed numerous complaints with the central salary committee, arguing that the 20 percent restriction and "equalization" formula were undermining the plan. They argued that in some units there might well be numerous employees performing at an outstanding level and few if any performing below quite acceptable levels. The central salary committee countered by pointing out that they had to budget a fixed percentage amount for all employees and that if one department received more than this percentage (averaged across all members of the department), then other departments would surely complain. The salary committee did agree to allow some "outstanding" awards to be made without proportional reductions in other employees' increases if unusual justification could be provided.

To meet these constraints, department heads and their superiors have regularly prepared elaborate cases for their most deserving employees, hesitating (particularly during periods of considerable inflation) to give any employee less than the "average" percentage increase. The salary committee, in turn, has tended to deny all but a few of these requests, apparently building up a set of criteria of its own by which to discount some outstanding designations and accept others.

Some sample statements from members at various levels indicate how the plan is presently perceived to be working:

From department head A: "I worked for three full days documenting an 'outstanding' claim for a young man in my department, a guy who has worked through his lunch hours and come in early when he saw the need, who has taken a course in office management and contributed numerous ideas on improved planning and scheduling. I turned it in, confident that it could not be denied—so confident that I was not even worried that the young man knew he was being recommended (he had to know because I had to get information from him about the course he took). What happened? You guessed it—denied, with a note that next year he would receive prime consideration. Well, there won't be a next year. He's leaving at the end of the summer."

From an "outstanding" award recipient: "Of course it was nice to receive the merit award, but it's really not a big deal. I got a little over a 7 percent increase while most people got 4 to 5 percent. I suppose I came out a little ahead of prices, but not much. What you wonder is, if your work is all that good, how come it's not worth more?"

From an "average" award recipient: "My boss explained that he could not put me up for an outstanding award this year even though he felt I deserved it because two other girls were already on the 'deserving' list ahead of me. I don't really mind. The amount of money isn't worth crying over anyway, but it does gripe you a bit to think you have been doing well and no one can do anything about it."

And, finally, from a resigning member of the central salary committee: "Look, the damn system is perfectly designed to make everyone unhappy. The department heads hate to go to all the trouble demanded and then not have it pay off. They hate to listen to the complaints of their subordinates, many of which they know are justified. The people who do get the outstanding awards don't consider them to be very awe inspiring, and those who don't get them but feel they should have are madder than hell. I'm recommending we drop the whole thing."

While some of the features of the reward systems in the three cases described here are obvious, as are their behavioral consequences, a more complete understanding can be achieved with the guidance of a theoretical framework linking concepts of motivation to types of organizational rewards.

A Need-Path-Goal Model

A model of purposive behavior in organizations can be built around three basic variables: (1) a need felt by the organization member, (2) a goal or reward which can satisfy that felt need, and (3) a path—a perceived route—to the goal (receipt of the reward).

Such a model, illustrated in its simplest form in Figure 8-1, might help describe the behavior of a probationary employee who feels very insecure (who "needs" security) and who believes that by volunteering for extra assignments (a path or route) he will be retained at the end of the probationary period and thus achieve permanent employee status (his goal or reward). Or, conversely, the model might help us characterize the behavior of a fifty-five-year-old middle manager who has little formal education (feels insecure) and is a bit unsettled by the bright young men being hired in adjacent positions. He may feel that if he runs his department quietly without taking any risks (a path or route), he can hold onto his position until retirement (his goal or reward).

Logically, managers may be expected to establish an array of rewards which organization members will find attractive and to specify for each reward a method of attainment which will prove beneficial to the organization. Such an ideal arrangement does not always occur, however, for a number of reasons. First, the rewards the organization decides to offer may not be a good match for its members' needs. Second, the paths which the organization specifies for the attainment of certain rewards

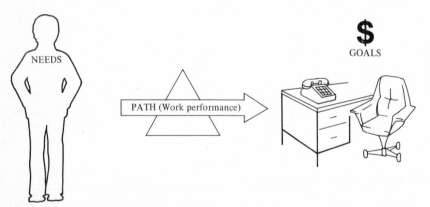

Figure 8-1 A need-path-goal concept of motivation

may be unclear or may not be viewed as acceptable by its members. Third, members may not, for one reason or another, believe that rewards are actually distributed on the basis that management claims—that is, they may perceive that other paths, perhaps paths which are ultimately dysfunctional to the organization, are the actual routes to achievement of rewards. Fourth, rewards may not be clearly visible to all members, performance expectations may not be clearly specified, etc.

This simple model can be expanded and diagrammed so that the relationships among variables can be examined and the viability of certain reward-system features analyzed. To expand this model, we need to define an array of organizational rewards and to link to them some generally accepted paths. Further, we need to specify some list of human needs which might be satisfied by the rewards in our array.

Developing a list of rewards is not difficult. The actual nature of rewards offered from one organization to another varies, but they can be easily classified into some representative package. Similarly, paths to these rewards, while not always well marked or certain, are generally specified in at least broad terms by most managements.

Specifying a list of human needs, however, is not so easily accomplished. People's needs are not spelled out for us but must be inferred from their behavior. It is not clear whether there may be a few or many needs, whether they are innate or learned, or whether and how they might vary with time. To expand and diagram our simple need-path-goal model of motivation and rewards, we will use one conceptualization of the nature and structure of human needs, the hierarchical classification of the late psychologist, Abraham Maslow. We will use Maslow's hierarchy of needs because it is widely known (and thus will probably be recognized by many of the readers of this book) and because it is highly relevant for the sort of explanation we are attempting here. We are not using it because it is a proven theory—in fact, recent studies have not lent precise support to the concept. Neither, however, has anyone else provided a more plausible explanation of human needs, and Maslow's formulation does exhibit a certain amount of face validity. We will briefly review Maslow's hierarchy before building it into our model.

The Maslow Need Hierarchy

Maslow defined five classes of human needs: (1) physiological needs—the basic requirements for survival, such as food, clothing, shelter; (2) safety needs—the requirements for some level of security, freedom from threat, etc.; (3) social needs—the requirements to feel wanted, loved, cared for, to belong; (4) esteem needs—the requirements for a sense of personal worth and identity, for status, for personal recognition, etc.; and (5) self-actualization—the requirement for self-fulfillment, to become what one is capable of becoming. Maslow indicated that these needs could be thought of as existing in a hierarchy of prepotency. That is, he felt that the basic needs (e.g., the physiological needs) would require some degree of satisfaction before some higher level of need (e.g., esteem) would become fully active. Or, stated differently, people would tend to be relatively unaware of needs near the top of the hierarchy until the more basic needs had been reasonably well cared for. In addition, Maslow felt that once a particular need was satisfied, it no longer motivated behavior.

On the surface, Maslow's conceptualization is broad enough and logical enough to be widely persuasive. For example, this scheme can be easily linked to generalizations about human development—much of an infant's life is focused on needs for food, shelter, and security; much of an adolescent's concern focuses on the need for acceptance and belonging; young adulthood is frequently associated with efforts to find one's place or to make one's mark in the world; and many people reach a point where ambitious strivings are put aside and efforts are made to "do what I really always wanted to do." Similarly, the shipwreck survivor washed ashore on a deserted island might be expected to worry about food and shelter before companionship and to be little concerned initially about self-actualization. Finally, the truly destitute are regularly forced to sacrifice social acceptance and esteem in the quest for survival.

Of course, exceptions to this model can be quickly pointed out. The artist may forego food to buy paint, and the mystic may attempt to put aside all other needs in his search for revelations. Moreover, lower-level needs do not disappear. The need for food regularly returns as, on occasion, does the need for freedom from threat. Finally, any given human activity may satisfy several needs at the same time, or perhaps be difficult to relate to any particular need. Nevertheless, across individuals and over time the basic logic of the model seems apparent. Human needs may not be arranged exactly in the manner this model describes, but it seems reasonable to us, as it did to Maslow, that they could be generally depicted in this fashion.

The Expanded Need-Path-Goal Model

Having presented these hopefully adequate explanations and caveats, we can incorporate Maslow's need hierarchy into a fairly detailed need-path-goal model, as shown in Figure 8-2. Rewards on the right are arranged to fall opposite a need which they might be logically expected to help satisfy. Of course, some rewards, such as money, might well be linked to several of the needs. A sizable salary can provide both status

Needs	Paths	Goals
Self–realization (actualization)		Challenging work (job with opportunity for growth, creativity, responsibility)
	Outstanding performance (high commitment, effort, and regular improvement in skill and capability)	
Esteem (ego)		Promotions, recognition from superiors, titles and other marks of status, pay
Social (belonging)	Group norms determine (may emphasize high or low effort–performance)	Recognition from peers Esteem of coworkers Acceptance by group
Safety (security)		Job tenure, seniority, pension plans, etc., avoidance of censure from superiors
	Minimally acceptable performance (meeting at least lower limits of standards— no major violations of rules and regulations)	
Physiological (food, clothing, shelter, etc.)		Regular pay and benefits, working conditions

Figure 8-2   A framework for analyzing motivation

and security, and many of the rewards are highly interrelated (e.g., promotion, pay, challenge, recognition). Nevertheless, the logical linkage between, say, seniority and security seems apparent, as does the linkage between basic pay (or working conditions) and the physiological needs.

How does an organization member with a particular set of needs achieve the rewards he desires? The center section of Figure 8-2 describes alternative paths (i.e., patterns of behavior and performance) which may be seen as leading to different rewards or sets of rewards. As shown, in order to achieve basic pay and benefits, a member must achieve a level of performance which meets at least minimal standards. Further, by maintaining at least minimal performance, he may hope to achieve some measure of security as provided by seniority or other related provisions.

On the other hand, to reap certain other rewards, something more than minimal performance is presumably required. Logically, promotions and related forms of recognition ought to go to those who demonstrate unusual or outstanding competence and commitment.

In the broadest sense, the paths to various rewards are the focal points of the organization's reward system. It is through the manipulation of these requirements that management attempts to extract from employees the behaviors necessary to the achievement of organizational goals. The process of managing the structure of rewards and the paths leading to them is not a simple one, however. First of all, the organization does not have direct control over one of the key rewards shown in the model—peer acceptance. Whether a member is accepted by the other members of his group or department depends in large measure on his willingness to abide by group norms—to stay within the bounds of group expectations concerning behavior. These norms or expectations are, of course, affected by the overall atmosphere of the organization and thus are indirectly manipulatable by management, but in the short run they are not easily changed. Second, management may not have full control over the establishment of paths to rewards other than peer acceptance. Where members are represented by some form of union or other association, minimal standards of performance and their methods of enforcement may be the subject of negotiation. Similarly, members of some professions may expect the right to have their performance evaluated by their peers, using criteria specified by professional societies. Finally, even where management has heavy influence over the establishment of paths leading to various rewards, the process still may not operate as intended. Members tend to behave in line with what they believe is in their best interest, and if they believe, for example, that political maneuvering rather than dedicated performance is the surest route to promotion, this belief is likely to influence their behavior no matter what the stated standards may be. Thus, management must not only create paths, they must maintain them. They must behave consistently in line with the standards they have established, dispensing rewards in a manner which is not only equitable in terms of the standards set but also in a manner which is *perceived* to be equitable.

Considering the characteristics of this model, we can see that whether members of an organization are highly motivated is affected by the nature and juxtaposition of all three of the key variables—needs, paths, and goals. For example, in a situation where many if not most members have high needs for achievement and esteem and where the organization is growing or expanding so that many opportunities for promotion are available, we might expect to find high levels of commitment and dedication—provided that promotions are dispensed in what is perceived to be an equitable manner. On the other hand, in situations where promotional opportunities and other valued rewards are scarce or where they are believed to be allocated inequitably, lower levels of commitment would be expected.

The Expanded Model Applied

Some of the values and shortcomings of our need-path-goal framework can be illustrated by returning to the cases described earlier in this chapter.

Consider the insurance company clerk, Jo Ann Myers, whom we looked in on as she considered her vacation plans. From the description given, we can only draw some very general inferences about her need system. Her thoughts appear to reflect her social or belonging needs, her need for security, and perhaps her need for esteem. She seems most concerned about being able to travel with her roommates, but not so dedicated to this that she is anxious to run the risk of antagonizing her supervisor. She seems quite willing to put forth the effort required to hold her job and receive her regular pay and benefits, and perhaps willing to go beyond this in return for additional rewards. However, the path to recognition and other related rewards is not at all clear. In fact, she is beginning to question whether her supervisor is dispensing rewards in return for dedication and commitment or perhaps on some other basis. It is, of course, not at all certain that Jo Ann's performance would improve measurably if the route to recognition were clarified, but it does seem possible that potential effort and commitment are being dissipated by the absence of well-understood standards.

The need system of Charlie Hutton, the young manufacturing company executive, is somewhat clearer. His esteem needs are highly evident. He wants very much to move up the corporate ladder. And while the path to success may have been somewhat hazy to this point, it is likely to be made quite clear by the recognition that he is about to receive. The concerns his immediate superior raised as to whether Charlie may have been behaving in too brash and unfeeling a manner will likely be put to rest. It seems reasonable that Charlie will perceive his promotion as certain evidence that the organization rewards those who get the job done, even if there is some human cost in the process. Whether this is precisely the path to promotion which the executive team means to define for Charlie is unclear, as are the effects this path will have on Charlie's performance and his contribution to organizational success.

In the final example, the reward system for nonsupervisory, nonmedical staff members at Centerville Community Hospital appears to be aimed at tapping esteem needs with monetary recognition for unusual effort. Moreover, it seems that, in the beginning at least, a number of members of this group accepted this path. They were willing to contribute extra energy and commitment in the expectation that extra pay would be forthcoming. However, this apparently straightforward path had, by the time we viewed the situation, become bent and strewn with uncertainty. Outstanding dedication and commitment, up to and surpassing supervisory expectation, did not appear to guarantee the receipt of merit increases as prescribed in the system. The fact that a clearly prescribed path to certain rewards had not been maintained appeared to be producing a substantial amount of frustration.

At this point, two things seem clear with regard to our understanding of reward systems and their motivational properties. First, it appears that a wide range of reward-system examples can be fitted into our need-path-goal framework and that fitting them in helps to focus our attention on certain key dimensions. At the same time, it also seems clear that this broad framework lacks specificity. It does not detail all the variables at work in determining motivation and performance and it does not describe with much precision how these variables interact. Therefore, it seems worthwhile to spend a few paragraphs examining a model which does detail the motivation-performance process—one which, fortunately, builds on and extends our need-path-goal formulation and thus requires only a short mental leap to grasp.

The Porter-Lawler Model

Figure 8-3 illustrates a process model of motivation in work organizations developed by two psychologists, Lyman W. Porter and Edward E. Lawler, III. A quick glance will indicate that the Porter-Lawler model is not too far removed conceptually from our need-path-goal formulation. Focus your attention on blocks 1, 3, and 7A–B. The variable in block 1, the value attached to rewards, can be related to our list of human needs. Presumably, people value a given reward (or one reward more than another) because of their own pattern of needs, wants, or desires. Further, the variable described in block 3, effort, can be related to the "path" portion of our earlier model—people put out more or less effort as the result of the degree to which they value certain rewards. Finally, the rewards people might be seeking are represented by blocks 7A and 7B. Nevertheless, while these similarities exist, it is also clear that the Porter-Lawler model extends our need-path-goal framework and adds dimensions not included in that formulation. These extensions and additions can best be understood by moving step by step through the model.

     Perceptions concerning Effort and Rewards   Attention is first directed toward those variables which determine or help determine the amount of effort that an organization member expends. As shown in Figure 8-3, the variables in blocks 1 and 2 are viewed as determinants of effort (note the arrows running from blocks 1 and 2 to block 3). The variable in block 1, as indicated above, is the amount of value which the member places on the possible rewards in his environment. Presumably, if there are rewards he values highly, this could lead him to expend high levels of energy in their pursuit. We say *could* rather than *will* lead because the value attached to possible rewards is only one of the variables determining effort. The variable in block 2, the estimated

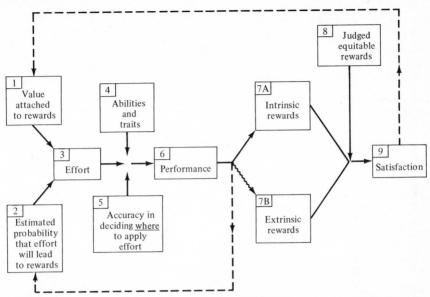

Figure 8-3 A dynamic model of motivation [Adapted from Lyman W. Porter and Edward E. Lawler, III, *Managerial Attitudes and Performance* (Homewood, Ill.: Irwin, 1968)]

probability that effort will lead to reward, is equally important. That is, suppose that an organization member greatly desires some reward, perhaps promotion, but has seen the last three available promotional slots given to newly recruited college graduates. Thus, in this instance, where a high reward evaluation is coupled with a low perceived probability of attainment, even through increased effort, the individual may not be motivated to work particularly hard. Clearly, both variables are essential. If he is to be expected to put forth high levels of effort, the member must both value the available rewards and perceive that dedication and commitment in his work will lead to them.

The Relationship between Effort and Performance   To this point, in both our need-path-goal model and in our discussion of the Porter-Lawler model, we have been focusing primarily on the conditions under which people are motivated to try to do a good job. Unfortunately, however, simply *wanting* to perform well does not guarantee that one *will* perform well. As shown in Figure 8-3, the Porter-Lawler model describes two variables which affect the linkage between effort and performance. In block 4 is a rather obvious variable, the individual's abilities and traits. As their model illustrates, a member must not only have desire, he must have the capability to perform well. For example, an assembly line worker with low finger dexterity might try extremely hard to put together complex electronic devices but still have a high defect rate. Or an individual might want desperately to become a professional football player and be willing to practice for hours each day, but if he is slight of frame and slow of foot, his dreams of gridiron glory are likely to remain just that. Extending these examples, one can create innumerable situations in which physical, mental, or emotional limitations would appear at least to damage, if not sever, the linkage between effort and performance.

While possession of essential traits and abilities is an obvious moderator of the effort-performance linkage, the variable represented in block 5 of the diagram is not. That is, it is easy to assume that if an organization member is willing to put forth effort and has the necessary abilities, good performance will result. As pointed out by the Porter-Lawler model, however, he must also know where and how to use this talent and commitment.

For example, the welder who delays the completion of a project in order to create perfect symmetrical beads on inside (and unseen) joints has, from management's point of view, perhaps misplaced his talent and commitment. Similarly, the office manager who devotes energy and creativity to the task of controlling waste but who fails to allocate work efficiently among the office clerks may be judged a poor performer, much to his or her dismay. Turning back to one of our earlier examples, Charlie Hutton, the young manufacturing executive, has been moved laterally and upward several times in his brief career. He now feels it is important to make his mark early in each new assignment and seems unlikely to give much thought to long-term consequences—those extending beyond his expected tenure. It seems highly possible that this short-time perspective will not serve him well in upper-level managerial positions. While he feels he knows where and how to use his efforts and talents now, the accuracy of his aim may not be good in the future.

Types of Rewards and Perceptions of Equity   Moving on in the model, if an organization member is willing to put forth effort and has both the necessary capability and the knowledge of where to apply these talents, we would expect him to perform well. In return, he would expect to receive rewards appropriate to his performance. The Porter-Lawler model as diagrammed does not describe in detail what the member may receive but does suggest two broad classes of rewards: intrinsic and extrinsic. The terms "intrinsic" and "extrinsic" are used in reference to the work situation in which the member finds himself. Thus, intrinsic rewards would be those flowing from the actual carrying out of his tasks.

For example, feelings of accomplishment, of having important responsibilities, of having used his abilities creatively would fall in the category of intrinsic rewards. Also falling in this category would be the deserved recognition, including bonuses and promotions, which might accompany the successful carrying out of significant, challenging tasks.

On the other hand, extrinsic rewards are those not associated with the actual performance of tasks or assignments. For example, good working conditions, basic pay, and benefits up to or superior to community standards are rewards which may accrue to all members of an organization, whatever the nature of their tasks, simply in return for joining and remaining with the organization.

One might expect a closer linkage between effort and intrinsic rewards, which presumably flow directly from the application of that effort, than between effort and extrinsic rewards, many of which will accrue if the member simply performs well enough to hold his job. Nevertheless, whatever rewards are received (or not received) for a given level of performance provide feedback to the member and thus help determine his perception of the effort-performance-reward linkage. If he has tried hard and received what in his mind are appropriate rewards, the model assumes that his probability estimates of effort leading to other valued rewards will increase. Conversely, if appropriate rewards are not forthcoming, his perceptions of the odds that effort will lead to desired goals will be negatively affected.

Finally, if appropriate rewards are provided—and, more than this, are judged by the member to be equitable (block 8)—the model assumes that his level of satisfaction will increase and that this will in turn feed back and enhance the value attached to, or available from, rewards. That is, a satisfying experience with a reward system may be expected to increase the member's appreciation of what can be obtained through the expenditure of energy and commitment and thus lead to further such investments.

MANAGEMENT THEORY AND REWARD SYSTEMS

Having explored these two somewhat complementary motivational models, we should be equipped with additional tools to aid us in examining the properties of reward systems which we might expect to flow from alternative theories of management. In this section, we will look back across our discussions of the traditional, human relations, and human resources theories of management and attempt to draw out some of the characteristics of the rewards systems which might be advocated by managers holding each of these theories. We will then try to relate these characteristics to the need-path-goal and Porter-Lawler models of motivation.

Reward Systems under the Traditional Model

Viewed broadly, management's key task under traditional theory is to minimize variations in the behavior of organization members. That is, because this model questions the capability of most members to exercise responsible self-direction and self-control, it urges managers to remove all ambiguity from the system through standard operating procedures and, when possible, to build direct control over pace and coordination into the system. Where pace is thus specified and restricted and quality control is built into standard procedures, most members can only be rewarded for conformity. The organization merely buys, on an hourly or daily basis, the willingness to adhere to instructions and avoid deviation.

Thus, for most members, most of the time, the reward system under which they operate is remarkably simple. There is only one fixed path—standard performance—and one fixed reward—the standard wage and benefit package. The prime purpose of the reward system in organizations dominated by traditional theory is to attract and hold a stable, predictable work force. Wages and working conditions up to or exceeding community standards are emphasized in attracting employees, and fringe benefits are designed to hold the employee once he is attracted. Pension benefits are not vested but accrue only if the employee remains with the organization for his full career, and vacations and other benefits are keyed to longevity.

Of course, minor variations around this one path–one reward structure may be attempted, as in our earlier example of the "merit" plan at Centerville Community Hospital. Most such plans, however, are designed to minimize risk to the organization in terms of overall payouts and are constrained with respect to the capacity for drawing forth outstanding performance. This is particularly true over the long run as the narrow limits of the system become visible to its members. Organizations operating under traditional theory are not vitally concerned with these constraints, however, as they are typically not equipped to utilize high levels of commitment and energy across their full memberships. That is, as self-direction and control are suspect, managers must direct and control all behaviors—something which can be done only through standardization. The organization which does not want outstanding performance cannot be expected to be willing to pay for it.

Within a reward system of this type, promotions and other forms of recognition accumulate primarily in return for loyalty and avoidance of mistakes. This may be true even within the managerial hierarchy, where risk avoidance is implied and the "best" managers are those whose decisions are least often clearly in error. What the typical organization member learns under these conditions is to protect himself from blame. He must not only try not to be wrong, but he must have prepared explanations to cover all contingencies. The safest route to possible rewards is to follow only tried and true procedures, those which, even if not successful, can easily be defended.

In addition to the features already described, traditional reward systems are frequently characterized by secrecy with respect to reward allocation and ambiguity concerning the precise routes to such rewards as promotions and pay increases. Secrecy usually results from apprehension over the effects of one organization member knowing what another is receiving. Management is frequently concerned that if one member learns that another, doing a similar task, is receiving more money than he is, feelings of inequity would result. Such feelings could raise tensions, produce frustration, and perhaps even stimulate a messy confrontation. Of course, feelings of inequity ought not to occur in situations in which rewards (say, salaries) have been allocated carefully in accordance with objective, relevant, well-understood, and highly visible criteria. In traditional organizations, however, where both high and low performance are constrained, such objective measures may not be available. Rewards may in fact have been allocated according to factors not directly related to performance and may thus be difficult to defend.

Stated another way, where management is reluctant to define paths to rewards in terms of creative, innovative, self-directed, and self-controlled contributions to organizational objectives, it must fall back on such criteria as loyalty, appearance, attitude, etc. These criteria tend to be abstract, difficult to define and communicate, and subject to a variety of interpretations by both superiors and subordinates. Moreover, by keeping criteria ambiguous, superiors may feel that they have greater control over their subordinates—they do not have to commit their available reward stock in advance and can, if necessary or desired, simply raise the requirements and/or acknowledge unusual acts of personal attention. Finally, ambiguity is pervasive in traditional organizations in part because superiors are seldom given much freedom to allocate any but small rewards within their own units and thus are, quite reasonably, hesitant to spell out paths to rewards which they might not be able to deliver.

Reward Systems under the Human Relations Model

Not surprisingly, reward systems in organizations operated under human relations concepts tend not to be too different from those described under traditional theory. We recall that the human relations manager will retain an essentially machinelike view of organization structure and job design, though he realizes that the human parts in the machine must be regularly lubricated with applications of care, attention, and recognition. Thus, again, outstanding performance is most likely to be defined in terms of loyalty and a compliant attitude. Secrecy will still be prevalent, although perhaps an additional justification will be added—"to prevent hurt feelings"—and paths to rewards will continue to be ambiguously defined.

Symbolic recognition tends to flourish under the human relations model. Five-year pins for loyal service, the twenty-year watch, the "employee of the month" award (complete with dinner for two and twenty dollars cash), the annual award for outstanding civic service, etc., are examples of this type of recognition. Note, however, that most of these are awarded on bases other than that of task performance as such. Dollar awards or other forms of recognition for cost-saving suggestions do tend to acknowledge "creative" contributions, but again these suggestions tend to cover activities which may be only loosely tied to the member's direct task assignment. Moreover, management usually exercises unilateral control over these awards and thus a clear-cut path to them is not prescribed. The member may make what he and his peers are convinced is a solid, worthwhile suggestion only to have it turned down for reasons which do not satisfy him.

In sum, under the human relations as under the traditional model, rewards are used primarily to attract and hold a loyal, compliant work force. Outstanding performance will be ambiguously defined and sporadically and conservatively rewarded—in part at least because the system is not equipped to deal with sizable expenditures of creative energy.

Incentive Plans under the Traditional and Human Relations Models
The reader may well have been troubled to this point by our failure to raise the subject of incentive pay plans, particularly in connection with our discussion of reward systems under traditional theory. This omission was not the result of oversight. Instead, it is our view that incentive pay plans in most instances do not flourish in organizations dominated by traditional management theory. That is, they do not tend to fulfill their presumed objective of stimulating and maintaining outstanding performance.

For such plans to operate as anticipated by Taylor and other pioneers in the scientific management movement, two conditions must prevail. First, obviously, the member must have control over the pace at which he works and must, presumably, be responsible for the quality of his output. Traditional industrial engineering approaches to job design, as noted earlier, have tended to emphasize the desirability of machine pacing wherever possible—both in the interest of efficient materials handling and to assure standard output. However, machine pacing not only brings minimum performance up to standard, it also holds maximum performance to that level. Thus, incentive pay plans have frequently fallen victim to mechanization, or, if retained, only further guarantee a preset level of output.

In addition to the requirement of some control over pace, incentive systems require an operational level of agreement between the organization and its members concerning the legitimacy of output standards or piece rates. Under traditional concepts of management, incentive standards or piece rates are set unilaterally. Management may attempt, as Taylor and his colleagues emphasized, to set these scientifically, but they must still endeavor to convince the membership of their objectivity. In the usual case, management's unilateral control of the rate-setting process is met by covert acts, individually and in concert, to force standards to be set as low as possible. For example, when being observed by a time-study expert, the member may add additional, unnecessary steps, force his machine to operate intermittently, or adopt any other creative ruse to make the task appear more difficult and more time consuming than it actually is. When standards are in fact set which can easily be achieved, members are then careful to produce only enough to guarantee good wages but not so much as to call the easy standards to attention. Management may attempt to adjust standards as new methods are introduced and obviously low requirements are discovered, but these efforts are usually met with stiff resistance—either at the bargaining table for organized employees or through other less-open tactics among the unorganized work force. The incentive system, or at least pieces of it, may thus become "demoralized" and fail to provide appropriate rewards for outstanding performance.

It is possible that agreement concerning standards could be maintained through an approach that allowed members to participate in the setting of the standards. For example, in some clothing manufacturing plants, piece rates are set following joint time study by management and union experts and on-the-spot bargaining. More elaborately, in some (predominantly socialist) societies, work standards may be reviewed, and in some instances revised, by "works committees" partly made up of rank-and-file employees. However, traditional management theory does not provide for experimentation with such arrangements. Instead, unilaterally established standards tend to be met with unilateral efforts to subvert the process, with both sides behaving in what they feel to be a fully justified manner. Members are convinced that, if given free rein, management would raise standards so that nothing more than a decent wage could be earned even when one was working as hard as possible. Management is equally certain that most standards are well below what they might be and that the best that can be hoped for is a reasonable rate of output in return for a wage close to that earned in other plants for related work.

Finally, it must be recognized that for incentive plans to operate effectively, high output must in fact be desired. Where production limits are established, however, high output by all members could lead to at least temporary layoffs. In the absence of guarantees of employment security, members may well restrict output, earning less than is perhaps possible in order to prevent a possible reduction in the work force.

Taking all these factors into account, it is easy to see why output incentive plans have frequently been more successful with sales personnel than with other employees. The salesman does have control over his own pace, and the sales commission is set at a level that guarantees a good return to the organization and thus is not regularly manipulated. Moreover, assuming something less than total market saturation, there are no obvious limits to what the salesman can "produce" and little reason for management to seek to limit high rewards for outstanding performance.

This brief discussion of incentive pay plans will be expanded in the next section as we examine some methods of payment for outstanding performance which do not depend solely on output. In addition, we will look further at conditions such as employment security and the legitimization of standards.

Reward Systems under the Human Resources Model

As stated earlier, the manager's key task under the human resources model is that of facilitating member performance—removing barriers to the application of the full set of mental and physical resources available to the organization. His assumptions direct him toward the promotion of outstanding performance rather than toward the control of substandard effort, and he is concerned, therefore, with the effective utilization of the full range of possible rewards for high levels of commitment and innovative contribution.

Outstanding performance will differ, of course, from one organization to another and from one unit or position to another within the same organization. Similarly, the size and structure of available rewards will differ. In an organization with a highly stable environment and limited opportunity for expansion, outstanding performance may be defined as holding costs down while maintaining high levels of quality and/or customer service. In such situations, certain rewards (e.g., rapid promotions) will also be tightly limited, and the manager's task becomes one of tying the available rewards closely to the types of performance which will contribute most to organizational success (e.g., quality and cost savings). At the other extreme, organizations operating in highly turbulent environments may be less concerned with methods improvement and cost savings and far more interested in product design and marketing innovations which will assist in coping with change. A broader and/or richer set of rewards may be available in such situations, but these too must still be tied closely to behaviors most effective for the organization.

From the comments above, it is clear that a reward system ought to be designed and operated in a manner complementary to the environment which the organization faces. In addition, a reward system structured in line with human resources concepts can be expected to operate most effectively in organizations which attempt to follow the human resources model in other areas: in the way in which jobs are designed, communications and control systems structured and operated, decision making carried out, etc. As our earlier examples suggested, a reward system which attempts to elicit outstanding performance within an organization in which jobs and controls are designed so that members have little control over, or responsibility for, the pace at which they work, or the quality of their output, is not likely to be highly effective. In the following paragraphs, we will describe some reward systems which appear to be both in line with environmental conditions and tied to human resources-type job design and control.

Cost-savings Plan   In situations where markets are stable, or even declining, and expansion opportunities are limited, outstanding performance may well be defined primarily in terms of cost savings—holding quantity and quality constant and trying to reduce production expenses. An appropriate reward system for these conditions would be one which attempts to promote waste reduction, discovery and implementation of changes in procedures to eliminate unnecessary production steps or processes, improvement of reject rates, etc. A key feature of such a system might well be the sharing of cost savings with organization members. That is, members, individually or collectively, might be offered some fraction of the total savings resulting from their efforts or suggestions for change. Under such a plan, sizable dollar rewards might be distributed without any increase in total organization revenues.

From our previous discussion of motivation theory, we would expect that a cost-savings reward system would be expected to be most successful:

1 Where the level of rewards which may accrue is well defined and generally felt to be equitable

2 Where organization members affected by cost-savings changes have some part in the implementation decision process and thus understand rather clearly what is required and why

3 Where basic needs, particularly that of security, are taken into account

One well-known reward system, the Scanlon Plan, was originally designed to at least partially meet these conditions. Born during the depression, this cost-savings reward system was first implemented in a small steel company under the general guidance of Joseph Scanlon, then an official of the Steelworkers' Union. The plan called for a negotiated agreement establishing "normal" or standard labor costs for the plant and a means by which employees as a group gained the benefits of savings beneath the negotiated benchmark. As a result of the adoption of the Scanlon Plan, this marginal plant began to earn profits and its employees earned bonuses even in a period of general economic depression. Labor costs in subsequent applications have been computed as a percentage of various output measures, e.g., a unit of production (or some multiple), dollar value of output, or even operating profits, although many advocates of the plan oppose this last basis for computing labor costs on the grounds that profits are affected by too many variables outside the influence of the typical employee.

In the typical Scanlon Plan application, cost-saving benefits result primarily from employee suggestions and efforts and accrue to the entire work group rather than just to the individual(s) directly involved. This feature, it is argued, tends to reduce friction and develop teamwork. These key aspects of the plan, along with union participation in establishing the labor-cost benchmark and the reward-distribution procedure, have probably helped assure at least some degree of legitimacy for the reward system and thus have helped meet the first condition mentioned above.

The second condition, member understanding of changes and requirements, is addressed in the Scanlon Plan by the establishment of committees whose members represent all levels of the organization hierarchy in each department and which are charged with approving or rejecting all cost-savings changes. These committees attempt to work with members offering cost-savings suggestions until either their suggestions are implemented or until all concerned are convinced that the suggestions are at least temporarily unfeasible.

The third condition, the satisfaction of the need for job security, was met in part by the overall goal of the original Scanlon Plan, which was to keep the organization going and maintain the jobs of all members. More specifically, various versions of the Scanlon Plan have included statements of policy that no present member of the organization would lose his job as the result of any cost-savings innovation.

The involvement of members in the development and implementation of cost-savings plans is, of course, closely in line with human resources concepts. Their involvement is crucial not only in gaining acceptance for the plan (as the human relations model would prescribe) but also in overcoming what may be called the "first slice phenomenon," to which cost-savings rewards systems are particularly vulnerable. That is, initital cost savings may be quite large and rather easily achieved as organization members bring to light or agree to accept changes which many if not most have long recognized as feasible. However, as this easily cut-through fat is removed, further savings become more difficult to achieve. At this point, the full creative capabilities of members at all levels must be brought to bear if gains are to continue. New levels of lateral and vertical cooperation will probably be demanded, and managers and subordinate members will likely be forced to give up or modify favored and familiar processes and procedures. The more managers and members become involved in the design and implementation of the cost-savings reward system, the more likely it will be that their capabilities will be uncovered and utilized. More important, the first-slice phenomenon and other debilitating contingencies can be anticipated in advance by closely involved members, and thus some of their impacts can be minimized. For example, if the process is understood and improved, some portion of first-year savings could be withheld, invested, and then used to supplement possible lean periods later on.

In sum, in situations where organizations face stable or declining output horizons, outstanding performance may well come to be defined in terms of merely doing better what is presently being done. Promotional opportunities and output-related incentive rewards will be limited, and thus cost-savings rewards may become the most viable means of maintaining a healthy reward system. Models of cost-saving plans with close linkages to human resources concepts are available and can be implemented with appropriate modifications in many organizations.

Skill-Reservoir Plans In many heavily mechanized, automated, or near-automated processes, labor costs represent a small proportion of total operating expenses. The key requirement in such situations is to keep the expensive equipment operating with a minimum of down time. Outstanding performance is, therefore, usually expressed in terms of careful monitoring, preventive maintenance, and rapid repair work when something does go wrong. A human resources reward system in this environment might well be aimed at promoting the development of skill and commitment throughout the work force. Consider the following experimental system developed for use in a small, essentially automated special-purpose refinery.

Small crews of workers operate the refinery on three shifts without any direct supervision. They are responsible for monitoring and maintaining the system as it produces to pre-established schedules. Work crews determine their own daily assignments and are expected to monitor the work stations and to cooperate in maintenance activities and repairs.

Members are rewarded in terms of the skills they both possess and acquire. If a team member is judged by his peers and superiors to be qualified to operate—to monitor, maintain, and repair—one work station, he receives the basic or lowest hourly rate, which is itself standard pay for refinery work. If the crew member can operate two stations—supervise and repair two key segments of the system—he receives a bonus for the second station skills. If he can operate three stations, he receives a further bonus, and so on up through the eight or so work stations. Members are thus motivated to learn how to operate all aspects of the refinery in order to qualify for top pay, which is virtually double that received for typical refinery work.

From the organization's point of view, a reward system of this type promotes the development of redundant capability but a redundancy which should provide insurance against mistakes and against costly down time. If repair skills are immediately available in all locations, the total system can be restarted in minimum time, a factor which may more than offset the payment of salaries above those absolutely required. For example, suppose that direct labor costs represent 15 to 20 percent of total costs. If these are increased 50 percent, total costs go up by only 7 to 10 percent. If in the process down time can be reduced by 20 percent or so, substantial cost savings might be achieved.

The absence of direct supervision in this instance is reasonable. With all necessary skills for monitoring and maintaining the process possessed by the crew, and with preset, clear production schedules available, there is no real role to be played by a supervisor; the situation, the needs of the equipment and machinery, dictate requirements to fully knowledgeable personnel. Crew members are trained and paid to behave as professionals, providing preventive care as required and responding appropriately to contingencies. Of course, under the traditional system, members have neither the training nor the information necessary to respond to contingencies, and under the human relations model, members may simply be rotated from job to job to increase interest and variety rather than in-the-pocket pay.

Output-related Reward Systems   In situations where the potential for increasing revenue exists, either through lowering prices as the result of efficient production or through quality improvements with costs and prices held constant, reward systems can be structured around output-related criteria of outstanding performance. Obviously, however, tasks and processes must be designed so that organization members have responsibility for the pace of work and the quality of their output.

An almost classic example of an output-related reward system for lower level organization members is that of the Lincoln Electric Company. Lincoln Electric manufactures welding equipment and supplies and has had an incentive pay plan in operation for over twenty-five years. Members are evaluated in terms of their quantity and quality of output and receive substantial bonuses if their performance warrants. In fact, the typical worker at Lincoln has frequently earned almost double the national average wage in manufacturing.

To keep control over quantity and quality at the level of the individual or small work group, Lincoln has organized its production process to provide room for the storage of parts and equipment as well as in-process goods at the work place. They have constructed what they refer to as a "factory within a warehouse." When a stage of the work is completed and inspected by the responsible member, it is moved along to storage at the next work station. The members at that station draw on the in-process storage at their own pace and, after completing and inspecting their operation, move it along to storage at the next station. Where possible, parts and equipment are also controlled by the operating members at each station. Thus job and process design, in line with human resources concepts, is coupled with a reward system which provides substantial payoffs for individual self-direction and self-control.

Output-based reward systems can, of course, produce harmful consequences unless they are well designed and unless members consider them appropriate and legitimate. Salesmen, for example, can increase "one-time" sales with outlandish claims regarding product or service quality or performance and/or unreasonable delivery or service guarantees. Similarly, operating personnel can sacrifice product quality in an effort to earn quantity bonuses, and line supervisors can sacrifice all but absolutely necessary maintenance in the interest of output bonuses. However, where organization members are involved in establishing and administering rewards for outstanding performance, and where various contingencies are explored and their consequences understood, systems can be constructed and operated which avoid such dysfunctions. Obviously, an output-based reward system, or any other kind for that matter, that is inserted in an environment characterized by mistrust and low commitment is unlikely to cure these conditions—instead, it too will probably be infected. On the other hand, a reward system designed to augment human resources approaches to job design and decision making is less likely to be subverted and more likely to serve its intended function of providing recognition and reward for outstanding performance.

Reward Systems Based on Creativity and Entrepreneurship Historically, organizations have behaved as if they owned the ideas, insights, and ingenuity of their members. If an individual came up with an idea for a new product or service or some important modification of present designs, he might receive nothing more than a letter of commendation or perhaps some small fraction of the ultimate earnings or savings. In many industries characterized by rapid product development, this has led to resignations by members, who then attempt to complete and produce improved designs on their own. The failure rate of such ventures is high, but many are lured by the success of a few who have developed new products and, after selling them in competition with major firms, have sold their manufacturing rights for huge profits.

More recently, some organizations have begun to realize that reward systems can be designed which provide substantial gains both for innovative members and for the organization. Such systems encourage members to approach the organization for financial, administrative, and other types of support in return for a substantial share of expected returns. Price shares depend on the amount of risk assumed by the organization and the costs of support provided. The growing number of such reward systems suggests, however, that organizations are finding it more profitable to generously share the returns from member ingenuity rather than to suppress creativity through restrictive controls and paltry rewards.

It is quite possible to imagine an organization today and in the near future beginning its association with a new member with the following statement:

> Here is your present assignment. We expect you to fulfill it with competence and diligence. Nevertheless, we expect that at some further point this assignment will not tap your full resources. We then expect you to begin to use your free time to pursue things which interest you and to seek out others with similar interests. As ideas for product improvements or new ventures develop, we will be happy to provide you with help in developing and perfecting them. As they reach an appropriate stage of readiness, we hope you will submit them to our review board for funding and assistance. You will have the opportunity to follow your ideas through to implementation,

changing assignments where indicated, receiving not only promotions and salary increases in line with new responsibilities but also an agreed-upon share of the returns directly attributable to your ingenuity.

In the modern, highly diversified organization facing ambiguous and uncertain environments, such a statement, closely in line with human resources concepts, seems highly reasonable.

Intrinsic and Extrinsic Rewards

Our examples in the sections above have all emphasized dollar rewards for outstanding performance. This emphasis appears to move counter to many recent arguments which focus on the value of intrinsic rewards— the feelings of satisfaction and accomplishment flowing directly from carrying out challenging tasks and assignments. Professor Frederick Herzberg is regularly cited as one who minimizes the value of money as a motivating force and focuses on the design of the work itself as the key to drawing out member energy and commitment. In fact, Herzberg argues that pay, benefits, working conditions, and even many aspects of supervisory style serve only as hygiene factors in the work place, not as motivators. That is, these factors are in the environment and are essentially preventive in the sense that if pay, benefits, working conditions, etc., are in line with community standards, they will not generate harmful feelings or attitudes. However, the fact that these conditions are as the member would expect them to be does not turn people on—decent pay, conditions, benefits, even considerate supervision do not, in Herzberg's view, stimulate high levels of performance or commitment, nor produce high levels of satisfaction. On the contrary, Herzberg lists challenging work and recognition received for tasks well done among those factors which produce satisfaction and which are appropriately labeled "motivators."

Herzberg's views have been widely disseminated and appear to have been quite persuasive among managers, despite the fact that research support for his "two-factor" theory of motivation has been less than conclusive. Without attempting to join forces with Herzberg or to ally myself with his critics, let me attempt to place his views in perspective with those expressed here. (The tack chosen here is not to avoid assuming a controversial position, a posture which I rather enjoy, but to avoid joining a debate which I believe is essentially unfruitful.)

To the extent that Herzberg focuses attention on the requirements of good job design (which are, I believe, in line with human resources concepts), his argument is highly useful. Similarly, insofar as his discussion stimulates recognition of the fact that regular pay and benefits, in most organizations, serve primarily to attract and hold members rather than to elicit outstanding performance, it is also useful. However, if Herzberg's views are interpreted as dismissing the possibility of building reward systems which make creative use of money, unnecessary constraints emerge.

Where pay and benefits are used merely to compensate for time served, they probably function much as Herzberg suggests. However, where sizable dollar rewards are linked to outstanding performance in creative reward systems, there is little question that they reinforce other forms of recognition and thus serve as motivating forces. The question is not whether money, as currently used in most organizations, is a motivator; the question is whether it can be. As our examples suggest, dollar rewards can be made a part of an overall approach to management so that they are closely aligned with behaviorally sound approaches to the design of jobs, communications and control systems, and to styles of decision making. Where they are so linked, they can be thought of as virtually intrinsic to the work itself.

CONCLUDING REMARKS

In this chapter, we have attempted to develop some concepts of motivation which are helpful in analyzing the likely effects of various reward systems on the behavior of organization members. We have pointed out that a reward system aimed at generating outstanding performance must provide goals or incentives which are desired by the members of the organization (appropriate to their need structure), and that the organization must allocate these consistently in return for appropriate behavior. Systems collapse when rewards are not available, or when the paths to these are ambiguous or misperceived by members. We have suggested that organizations examine their motivational capital (the rewards actually available) and the extent to which these are in fact linked to desired behaviors. We have tried to demonstrate that creative reward systems can be devised under a variety of environmental conditions. We have not argued for any specific reward-system design. Rather, as has been our aim throughout this book, we have argued that the system ought to be closely aligned with other pieces of the overall management system and must take into account the constraints and opportunities which the organization faces.

Finally, we have called attention to the face that reward systems should not only be designed in line with current organization needs but should also stimulate individual and organizational growth and development. We repeat this requirement here as a fitting bridge to our next topic.

BIBLIOGRAPHY

Herzberg, Frederick, "One More Time: How Do Your Motivate Employees?" *Harvard Business Reviews*, vol. 46, pp. 53–62 (January-February 1968).

Lawler, Edward E., III, *Pay and Organizational Effectiveness: A Psychological View* (New York: McGraw-Hill, 1971).

Lesieur, Frederick G., *The Scanlon Plan: A Frontier in Labor-Management Cooperation* (New York: Technology Press, 1958).

Maslow, Abraham H., "A Theory of Motivation," *Psychological Review*, vol. 50, pp. 370–396 (1943).

Porter, Lyman W. and Edward E. Lawler, III, *Managerial Attitudes and Performance* (Homewood, Ill.: Irwin, 1968), chap. 3.

Schwab, Donald P. and Larry L. Cummings, "Theories of Performance and Satisfaction: A Review," *Industrial Relations*, vol. 9, pp. 408–430 (October 1970).

Whyte, William F. et al., *Money and Motivation* (New York: Harper, 1955), chaps. 2–6.

Chapter 9

Development Concepts
and Procedures:
An Introduction and Overview

In the preceding chapters, we have attempted to portray alternative theories of management and their implications for leadership and decision making, the design of jobs and the manner in which these are linked together into units or departments, the nature of communications and control systems, and the structure and operation of reward systems.

To this point we have dealt with the choices that managers have made or are making on these dimensions—leadership, structure, control, etc.—for a particular collection of organization members in a given setting. In this chapter and those that follow, we will give explicit recognition to the obvious fact that organizations are dynamic rather than static phenomena.

DEVELOPMENT—CHANGE BY DESIGN

Organizations and the people within them are constantly changing. New goals are established or old ones revised, new departments are created and others restructured, people retire or move on to other jobs, some members are promoted and new ones are hired. These changes occur partly by chance and partly by design. The term development is regularly applied when design is intended or attempted. Product development, for example, is presumably a rational process of adjustment to changes in consumer demands and technological capability. Similarly, managerial development is presumably a planned effort to improve the performance of members on their present assignments and to prepare them for more challenging responsibilities. Finally, organization development is presumably a planned program of change aimed at removing present barriers to high performance and enhancing the total system's capacity for adjustment to future demands.

Development can be viewed, in part at least, as a process of renewal. Few managerial policies or practices, few structured relationships between roles or units, few communications or control systems, etc., can be expected to transcend time and circumstance. The vines of precedence and past practice have a tendency to encircle and drain vitality from the organization's sociotechnical system. The system's arteries are hardened by a collection of efficacious solutions to problems which no longer exist, means to ends which have changed, and procedures whose reason for existence cannot be remembered. The renewal requirement intensifies as the rate of environmental change increases. The half-life of most solutions decreases, and the need to constantly hack away at the tentacles of overbureaucratization becomes apparent.

At the same time, development can be seen, in part, as a proactive process. That is, to the extent that the organization can anticipate its future needs, it can and logically should attempt to develop its resources to meet them. Increasingly, development theory, and, to a lesser degree, development practice, have stressed the importance of giving tomorrow's requirements equal if not superior status to those of today.

From a third perspective, renewal and future-oriented development are closely related if not identical. To the extent that development efforts can be aimed at enhancing the organization's capacity for self-renewal—its ability to sense constraints on its processes and to take constructive responses—the present and the future are both well served.

Some General Requirements for Development   Development that is planned change, or change by design, assumes the presence of three factors.

Goal or Target State

First, for development to occur there must be a goal or target state toward which change can be directed. For example, the effort to develop lower-

or middle-level managers for top executive positions presumably requires some knowledge of the skills and capabilities required in those jobs. At the very least, some general image of what an executive is required to do and how he does it, or better still, how he should do it, is necessary. For organization development to take place, some broad model of a desired system of managerial performance is required. That is, top management must have a general notion of the sort of leadership and decision-making style it wants to achieve and some concept of the desired structural characteristics, communications, control, and reward systems it wishes to build. Much of the process of development may focus on the removal of barriers to high performance, but the definition of barriers and the assignment of priorities for their removal demand some image of the conditions which will lead to high performance.

Assessment of Present Conditions   In addition to a defined goal or target state, development requires an assessment or appraisal of present capabilities or conditions. Managerial development requires appraisal of members' current strengths and weaknesses, and organization development requires some assessment of the nature and effects of current systems and behaviors. Of course, the process of establishing future goals and assessing current conditions are closely intertwined. Our notions of what is possible in the future are conditioned by present circumstances, and the simple act of appraising where we are suggests the nature of some desired changes. Nevertheless, although these processes are intertwined, assessment of current conditions is probably most efficiently carried out against the backdrop of previously established "ideal" circumstances. For example, member behavior assessed as troublesome in the context of present systems and procedures might well be viewed as highly desirable as these systems are redesigned.

Change Mechanism   The third factor essential to development is a change mechanism—plans and procedures for moving from the present to the desired state. In the development of an individual member, the change mechanism may consist of training programs, special courses, or even a sequence of new assignments designed to provide needed skills and experience. When the focus of the development effort is an organizational unit, the change mechanism may include individual and group consultation and training in both interpersonal skills and problem-solving abilities. When the organization itself is the development target, the program of planned change obviously becomes lengthy and complex and a host of change devices may be employed.

The entire development process—who or what is to be developed, toward what ends, and through what methods—is shaped and/or influenced by the same set of factors considered in our earlier chapters. Thus, prevailing environmental, organizational and human characteristics, along with the management concepts and theories which rationalize their interaction, are reflected in development goals and approaches. A quick glance over the past seventy years makes this logical linkage apparent.

In the early part of this century, the prime managerial task was to build the organizational "machine" and articulate its parts. Development effort was concentrated on the technical system at the shop-floor level where the need for efficiently designed jobs and procedures was gaining recognition. Management theory supported this focus, emphasizing the lack of member ability for self-direction or self-control and the resulting need for careful training and close supervision and control.

By the twenties, the core technical machinery of many organizations was in place, and the most demanding managerial task had shifted from designing and building the sociotechnical system to operating and maintaining it. Management theory began to focus on people problems resulting from "irrational" but nevertheless understandable human needs for recognition and belonging. To meet these needs and operate the system with minimum friction, it became clear that supervisors needed training in interpersonal skills.

Through the late thirties, the forties, and the fifties, both the organization and its environment became increasingly complex, and coordination emerged as the key managerial concern. New planning and decision-making skills as well as more sophisticated human relations techniques were seen as essential, particularly at the middle and upper levels of management. However, while both the technical and human systems were objects of developmental attention, these problem areas were usually viewed as highly separable.

During the sixties, new perspectives on the organization, its environment, and the role of management emerged, and along with these evolved a new set of development targets and techniques. Environmental requirements were seen as not only complex but increasingly ambiguous and turbulent. The organization could thus no longer be viewed as a special-purpose machine on a fixed course but as an adaptive, coping organism, hopefully responding effectively to changing environmental demands. Similarly, the manager could no longer be viewed as a controller, even a humane controller. Instead, the emerging human resources theory identified his role as that of a facilitator, a developer, and an investor of increasingly abundant resources. Most important, for the first time the development needs of the technical and human systems began to be viewed as complementary rather than competing, and the entire socio-technical system became the focus of development efforts.

Participation in Individual Development

Just as the targets and techniques of development have changed in response to changing environmental conditions and changing concepts of organizations and their management, so too have there been changes in the extent to which organizational members participate in the development process. Reflecting the prevailing managerial models, early development goals and methods were unilaterally conceived and autocratically implemented. Later on it became good management form to at least "talk through" development needs and approaches with affected members, provided that time was available and it was convenient to do so. Only recently has member readiness for and participation in change been systematically considered.

Low Involvement Illustrative of one end of this continuum of involvement in the process of individual development is the case of Charlie Hutton, the young manufacturing executive discussed in Chapter 8. If you recall, decisions related to Charlie's growth and development were made unilaterally by the review board. It was simply assumed that Charlie would accept whatever new assignment they accorded him and would benefit from it in the manner anticipated. Similarly, it is not at all uncommon for top management simply to decide that all supervisors should attend a leadership training course in order to improve their human relations skills. Readiness or motivation for such training may receive no direct attention, and supervisors may be requested to attend solely in accordance with a schedule convenient to the needs of the training section. (You may recall a mention of this type of behavior in one of our examples in Chapter 6.) Here again motivation is ignored, or else simply assumed to exist—an assumption which in many instances is at least marginally accurate. The costs to the member of refusing to accept a short-term assignment or refusing to attend a training program are probably much higher than the costs of acceptance. Most of us, through long periods of schooling, have developed a fairly high tolerance for boredom and apparent irrelevance and have also developed quite a number of techniques for escaping from presumed learning situations with out attitudes and behaviors unscathed.

The allusion to public education programs is intentional. Massive decisions with regard to development are made by various levels of governing groups concerning the education of the young. Through elementary educational programs ideal states are prescribed, assessments made, and change programs initiated with little or no involvement of those affected. Gradually, in secondary educational programs, and then broadly in college and university training, the student is allowed to become involved in his own development—at least to the point of choosing among prescribed curricula. Two factors are involved in this changing pattern of involvement. First, it can be argued that the very young have little capacity for involvement. Their limited experience provides slight basis for sound choices among things to be studied. More important, at least to our later discussions, one outcome of involvement—motivation to learn and develop—can be, or at least frequently is for this group, ignored. As long as compulsory attendance laws are in force and legitimized by parental and social support, an educational program can at least count on the presence of those they are attempting to develop. Of course, many are concerned with motivation early in the educational process, but later on, as coercive mechanisms are diminished and individual freedoms broadened, such concerns cease to be voluntary and at least some attention to motivation becomes a requirement of the educational system. Urging replaces coercion with regard to attendance, and images are created depicting the life-long successes of the trained and educated compared to the inevitable doom of those who opt out of the development process.

In the work organization, as our above examples suggest, a similar pattern of involvement, or lack of it, is frequently apparent. Coercion often tends to give way to persuasion, or even involvement in the development-decision process, only as other forms of leverage are diminished. For example, the unionized member may choose to ignore development efforts not specified in his contract, or the highly mobile scientist or executive may choose to risk sanctions and refuse development attempts he considers onerous.

Member response to unilateral change has seldom been as positive as its advocates anticipate. Frederick Taylor and his colleagues frequently complained about recalcitrance toward new methods and procedures, and industrial engineers have learned to build a "resistance factor" into their predictions of output levels of new systems. Similarly, today operations researchers regularly discuss the "implementation problem." Moreover, members appear to have become sensitized to "sales efforts" and more subtle manipulative approaches.

High Involvement At the other end of the continuum of individual member involvement, we might find a subordinate and his superior engaged in the process of management by objectives. In this process, as discussed briefly in Chapters 6 and 8, performance goals are worked out jointly by both parties and the problems associated with their attainment are carefully considered. It is anticipated that some recognition of attitudes and behaviors which might inhibit goal accomplishment will emerge from the process and that in time new and more effective patterns will be reinforced. The focus on future objectives and the behaviors needed to meet them provides a positive motivational setting and appropriately recognized goal accomplishment helps reinforce these behaviors.

Participation in Organization Change and Development

The extent to which members, individually or collectively, are involved in the development or change process also varies when the target of change becomes the unit, department, or some other substantial segment of the organization itself. Again, at one end of the continuum a sizable portion of the change in structure, practices, and procedures is initiated, planned, and carried out with little, if any, involvement on the part of the segment affected by the change.

Low Involvement (The Syndicate Model)   When substantial changes are made unilaterally, they are frequently made with the help of outside consultants, and the entire process often resembles what I have come to call the syndicate model of planned change. This model operates as follows.

> Someone or some group in the organization becomes concerned about the performance or behavior of some other segment of the organization (such concerns usually do not encompass their own behavior or performance). On their own, if they are high enough in the structure, or with the approval of those in power, a "contract" is let for the "modification" of the segment about which they are concerned. Outside experts arrive from another city carrying black bags which contain the ominous tools of their trade. The "fingered" group or unit—that is, the designated target of concern—is carefully approached and studied. The target group may become aware at this point that its behavior is being "cased" or observed, but its ultimate fate, the what, how, and when of change, is unknown. As the suspense grows, the final act is neared. Pads and pencils are carefully returned to the black cases and the fate of the victim is "sealed" (inside an envelope, in a report detailing what procedures and practices must be modified, and how and what personnel should be moved laterally, vertically, and out). Their task accomplished, the outside experts depart as quietly as they arrived.

High Involvement   Examples of organization change and development approaches that are nearer the other end of the continuum will be described and discussed in detail in later chapters. Such approaches usually call for involvement by groups and units in the study and modification of their own patterns of performance. That is, they attempt to provide some means by which a group or unit can assess its own behavior in an atmosphere conducive to experimentation with new practices and procedures. Further, the more sophisticated of these approaches attempt to build in reinforcement for new behaviors by providing continued feedback on the results of changed behavior.

Although most of the approaches to organization development described in Chapters 11 and 12 attempt to develop maximum participation on the part of all groups and units, we should note here that at their roots all development activities are autocratic. That is, the initial impetus usually comes from some influential member(s) of the organization. Thus, though affected members may quickly be involved in the change, they may well not have been involved in the initial decision to begin such a program. Nevertheless, it seems logical that there should be a close relationship between the process of development and its goal—the ideal state desired. That is, it is highly unlikely that an organization can be moved toward the human resources model through an essentially autocratic program. This intertwining of management theory and development approaches will be explored in more detail in the following chapters.

THE TOTAL PROCESS OF DEVELOPMENT

While the term "development" usually connotes concern with the performance of the existing human organization, the total process extends well over into initial selection and training. At many points in the typical organization, members are selected not only for their ability to perform in some immediate position but also, and perhaps even more, for their long-term growth potential. Similarly, in a thoughtfully designed manpower program, even specific job training is structured to contribute to long-term skill and behavior needs. The interlinkages among selection, training, and long-term growth within the context of an overall manpower development program are illustrated in Figure 9-1. The process model illustrated in Figure 9-1 is obviously simplified and does not include, except perhaps implicitly, the broader focus of organization development.

In Chapter 10 we will follow the logic of the process model illustrated in Figure 9-1. Thus, we will briefly examine selection and performance appraisal, treating these functions primarily as steps in a continuous process of training and development. As we examine and analyze trends in these areas, we will begin to lay the groundwork for an explanation and analysis of current concepts and approaches, such as team training and organization development.

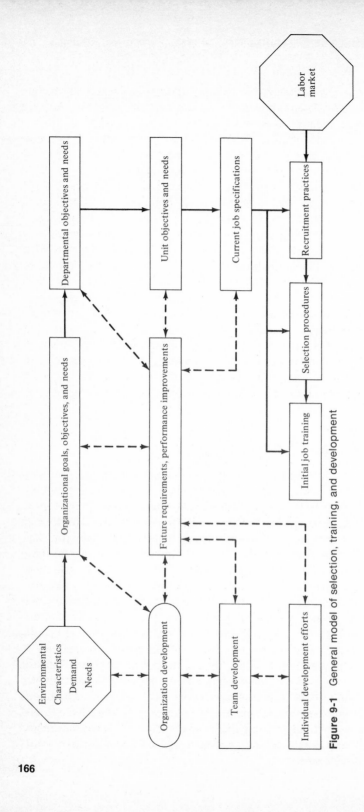

Figure 9-1 General model of selection, training, and development

Chapter 10

Individual Selection, Appraisal, Training, and Development

We suggested in Chapter 9 that organizations, because they are open systems, are constantly being changed, both by chance and by design. More pointedly, we argued that the development process (planned change) reflected environmental demands, prevailing managerial attitudes and theories, and available change models and techniques. Finally, we noted that the process of developing the organization's human resources extended, logically at least, backward to initial recruitment and selection, through current job training, and forward to preparation for future responsibilities.

In this chapter, as we focus more closely on the process of individual selection, appraisal, training, and development, we should again be able to discern the influence of environmental demands and managerial theories. For example, much of modern selection theory and practice has its roots in scientific management, and, despite increasing sophistication in test design and analysis, it has changed little with time. On the other hand, concepts and techniques in the area of performance appraisal have changed substantially, reflecting rather clearly concurrent changes in broader managerial theories and models. Similarly, training techniques, particularly for managers, have undergone major change, partially in response to changing concepts of the manager's role.

A substantial body of literature exists on the topics of selection, training, and performance appraisal. We will make no pretense here of surveying or evaluating that literature. Instead, our comments will be highly selective, giving little space and attention to areas which, in my opinion, are of declining importance, and concentrating instead on more detailed treatment of areas of growing concern, whose implications for management concepts and practice are more pointed.

SELECTION

In the first decades of this century, the selection process was viewed by many as the newly discovered key that would soon unlock the door to something close to an organizational utopia. Taylor argued that selection could be made scientific—that the right type of worker could be found for various types of work. World War I provided psychologists with their first opportunity to move toward Taylor's goal through the development and widespread application of numerous selection devices including skill and aptitude tests. Sizable gains over haphazard selection and placement methods were made, leading some to believe that within a few years organizations would have the mechanisms necessary to choose precisely the members they needed and to place members in jobs entirely suited to their capabilities and personalities.

Unfortunately, over the past fifty years or so a number of things have interfered with this movement toward utopia. First of all, selection theory and techniques have not developed as rapidly as was expected nor have they achieved the predicted levels of efficiency. Logically, a selection device is useful to the extent that it is predictive of some important aspect of job performance or behavior. For example, in an ideal selection process, scores which applicants made on an aptitude test would be closely related to objective measures of job performance. Typically, however, careful analysis indicates that even the best selection devices are only loosely related to job-performance criteria. That is, only a fraction of the variation in behavior on the job appears to be explained by information collected in the selection process.

Second, and much more important, while advances in selection theory and technique may not have met early expectations, they have, nevertheless, moved far ahead of application. Considerably more is known about the selection process than is used in the typical organization.

In fact, few such processes now in use would receive good marks if measured against accepted theory. For example, organizations regularly use untrained interviewers, administer selection tests whose scores have never been validated against performance criteria, and establish arbitrary educational standards whose relationship to job requirements is unknown. Only rarely do organizations go through the detailed process of carefully analyzing jobs to determine the characteristics needed for good performance, which is the logical first step in an effective selection program. Instead, they make guesses concerning requirements, and neither these nor the selection devices are ever evaluated.

Why have many, if not most, organizations failed to keep their selection programs in step with what would generally be considered good practice? There are probably two closely related reasons. First, many organizations use poor practices out of ignorance. Those involved in selection frequently do not have the special skills and knowledge that might help them recognize the shortcomings in their programs and take the necessary steps to improve them. Second, and more basic, organizations have had little incentive to question or upgrade their competence. The costs of poor selection processes are, in the main, either hidden or borne by persons outside the organization, whereas the costs of carrying out the careful analysis and evaluation which experts argue should underlie a good selection program appear high and the returns uncertain. These statements require some elaboration.

The costs of poor selection processes are for the most part hidden because neither the current systems nor their alternatives are ever evaluated. Numerous studies have uncovered procedures which were essentially unrelated to later job performance or, in some instances, even negatively related. Substantial cost savings in these situations could have been realized by dropping or revising the selection procedures. Nevertheless, for the typical unevaluated system, such unnecessary costs and potential savings remain hidden. Similarly, although well-designed selection systems have been shown to shorten training time, reduce turnover, and contribute in many other ways to improved performance, such potential gains are not visible on the present balance sheet. Further, where poor practices reject applicants who in fact could be effective organization members, it is the rejected applicant rather than the organization who bears the cost through missed employment and earnings.

With the costs of present inefficiencies essentially hidden, organizations would be expected to undertake revisions of their selection systems only if the benefits of such changes appeared to be substantial. Selection system returns, however, are greatest when large numbers of applicants are involved, and most entry positions involving large numbers of applicants are near the bottom of the organization. Thus, if as our earlier discussions indicated, lower-level positions in the typical organization have often been purposely structured to require only a minimal set of capabilities, even a crude selection system might be expected to perform reasonably well. In fact, inasmuch as jobs are designed so that the capability to perform effectively on them is widespread in the population, selection processes tend to be keyed not so much toward skills and abilities as toward factors presumed to predict ease of socialization and indoctrination. That is, anyone can do the job or be trained in short order to perform well. The organization is, therefore, most concerned with hiring members who will be accepted by their peers and will in turn accept the job as it is—the ideal employee is one who is willing to follow instructions and who appears regularly at the proper time and place each day.

Of course, in the upper echelons of the organization, managerial, technical, and professional positions are presumed to require specific and frequently sophisticated skills and abilities. Here, organizations frequently delegate or contract out a substantial portion of the selection process. Many, if not most, technical and professional personnel are hired on the basis of credentials acquired from approved institutions, and thus the basic decisions are left to these educational and training establishments. To an increasing extent, managerial personnel are also being selected on the basis of credentials. An MBA from a highly regarded university may be the key to the executive suite. Again, however, selection is essentially left to the business school granting the degree. Near the peak of the organization, positions are increasingly being filled with the assistance of executive recruitment consultants. Although credential-granting institutions and selection consultants may well be doing a good job of screening for organizations, their real effectiveness is seldom evaluated. That is, here, as at the lower level of the structure, positions are being filled by procedures which typically have not been systematically evaluated to determine their relationship to actual job performance.

Organizational ignorance and/or neglect with regard to sound selection theory and technique is currently under attack. Civil rights legislation and recent court decisions have demanded that the procedures be demonstrably related to important aspects of job performance. Thus, presumably, an organization cannot reject applicants on the basis of selection devices unless these have been carefully validated—that is, unless these devices have been shown to systematically predict meaningful variations in job performance. It is too early to evaluate the full impact of these policies on the organizations in question, but it seems clear that a high percentage of currently employed devices and techniques do not meet these requirements. Obviously, some procedures will be evaluated, revised, and presumably improved. In many organizations, however, these legislative acts and judicial decisions may well result in a de-emphasis of selection and an added emphasis on improving the performance of members once they are in the organization—the topic to which we now turn.

PERFORMANCE APPRAISAL

The first step in improving the performance of an organization member is presumably the assessment of his current behavior against some meaningful standard(s). Following this, the organization's task is to recognize areas of excellence and to provide the means and motivation for the member to improve in those areas where deficiencies have been noted. Clear trends are visible, both substantively and procedurally, with regard to the way in which these two steps are accomplished in the typical organization.

First of all, substantively, the focus of assessment or appraisal has tended to change. Early appraisal practices tended to focus closely on personal traits and aptitudes and only loosely on actual aspects of job performance. For example, traits such as neatness, punctuality, loyalty, etc., would be evaluated, along with some general rating of overall job performance. More recent appraisal theory, and in some instances appraisal practice, has moved away from trait evaluation and toward an emphasis on specific aspects of job performance—the extent to which specific job requirements and objectives are being met.

Coupled with this change in the focus of assessment has been a change in appraisal procedures, particularly with regard to the extent to which the member himself is involved in the appraisal of his performance. The trend has been neatly characterized by the psychologist Norman R. F. Maier as the movement from the "tell and sell" (traditional) approach, to the "tell and listen" (human relations) approach, and finally to the goal-setting–"problem-solving" (human resources) approach.

Performance Appraisal under the Traditional Model

Early performance appraisal techniques, in line with the traditional model, emphasized the "tell and sell" approach. That is, members were appraised by their superiors (frequently with regard to personal traits, as suggested above), their deficiencies were reported to them in an interview, and then an effort was made by the superior to sell the member on the need for and means of improvement. Unfortunately, this "revival" tactic frequently failed to meet its objective. With his behavior under indictment, the member regularly used defense mechanisms such as rationalization or projection in order to escape the interview essentially unconvicted (in his own mind) of the various "sins" with which he was charged. With his self-concept under attack, the member was tempted to explain away or blame others (openly or inwardly) for the shortcomings mentioned in the interview. Having noted this response pattern, early appraisal experts urged managers to reduce defensivenes by dwelling first on the member's good points and then bringing up deficiencies. Even with this advanced "sales technique" the appraisal process tended to be one in which superiors remained uncomfortable and member motivation short-lived, if ever existent.

Performance Appraisal under the Human Relations Model

Predictably, given the broader trend in management theory, appraisal concepts moved toward increased member involvement. The "tell and listen" approach appears closely aligned with human relations thinking. That is, under this approach superiors were urged to allow subordinates to talk out their frustrations. It was assumed that once members had the opportunity to express their own feelings concerning the areas in which they had been judged deficient, their defensiveness would be moderated, and they would tend to accept suggestions for improvement. However, even though member involvement was increased under the "tell and listen" approach, it remained rather tightly constrained. The superior continued in his role as initiator and the subordinates' role remained reactive—though not overtly so. Moreover, under the "tell and listen" approach the focus remained on past behaviors—what the subordinate had done or failed to do during the period covered by the appraisal, frequently the previous year. Even when an opportunity is provided for explanation and discussion, it is difficult to remain receptive when actions presumably buried are disinterred and brought forth to confront you.

Performance Appraisal under the Human Relations Model

The most recent trends in performance appraisal are aimed at overcoming some of the motivationally inhibiting factors described above, while at the same time providing more direct means of improving individual and organizational performance. The goal-setting–problem-solving approach attempts to increase member involvement, to emphasize job objectives rather than personal characteristics, and to further increase motivation by focusing on future accomplishments rather than on past deficiencies. In general, the goal-setting–problem-solving approach to performance appraisal follows the format of management by objectives. That is, the process begins with subordinates working with superiors to set their own performance goals and development objectives. When objectives are set on which there is basic agreement, the plan for achieving them is developed. Contingencies are discussed so that both superior and subordinate have as clear a picture as possible of the factors which may inhibit or enhance goal accomplishment. Review points are established to meet the needs of the established objectives. Appraisal is not restricted to traditional calendar periods (e.g., six months, one year) but is carried out at key points highlighted in the agreed-upon plan. Thus, the subordinate might review progress with his superior after two weeks, again after two months, and then not again for full performance appraisal for six months or more—with all appraisal periods reflecting the nature of the specific goals established. The aim of this process is to encourage and assist the subordinate in developing his resources in meeting objectives which he has had a part in setting. Such an approach appears fully in line with human resources theory.

TRAINING

Once needs and deficiencies are assessed, the prime vehicle for development of human resources is training. Training approaches vary from simple on-the-job demonstration, coaching, and counseling to elaborate, lengthy, off-site educational programs usually developed by or in conjunction with a prominent college or university. Just as trends were visible in selection and appraisal, patterns of change are discernible concerning the focus, substance, and methods of training.

With regard to who is trained, the spotlight has shifted from lower-level organizational members to supervisors and thence to middle- and upper-level executives. Simultaneously, the substance of training (what is taught) has moved from an exclusive focus on work skills to the inclusion of supervisor methods and leadership styles and finally to the incorporation of concern for the total life-style of members, units, and the organization itself. Along with these changes, training methods have been the target of innovation. Early efforts relied almost exclusively on demonstrations and lectures, usually on or near the job. Later, educational and training activities began to be held off site, but the lecture method remained central, perhaps augmented by case discussion and other exercises. In the fifties a new approach emerged—sensitivity, or laboratory, training. This approach emphasizes interpersonal interaction and feedback in an essentially unstructured atmosphere and was initially centered almost exclusively in remote, off-site training locations. Most recently, sensitivity, or laboratory, methods have begun to be applied inside the organization, with the focus shifting from the individual to the work team. These overlapping trends in training substance, focus, and methods require some discussion.

Focus and Content

Scientific management focused attention on the training needs of lower-level organization members. Frederick Taylor's assistant provided Schmidt, the pig-iron handler, with detailed instructions on how to lift, carry, and even how to rest—all with rather astounding results in terms of increased output. Taylor envisioned that training, or more aptly retraining, was crucial to the implementation of new and improved methods, tools, and techniques, and advocated the establishment of the role of training supervisor (one of his eight functional foremen) in each department. Similarly, the Gilbreths felt that even skilled craftsmen could and should be taught how to arrange their materials and how to move their hands and manipulate their tools for maximum efficiency. Although most training never reached the heights of precision and detail prescribed by Taylor, the Gilbreths, and others, its focus for twenty or more years remained almost exclusively on lower-level members and their work methods. Training (exclusive of apprenticeship programs) was usually brief and was most often done on the job or in "vestibule" locations off the main production floor but using similar or related tools and equipment. Training for the higher skills was usually through formal or informal apprenticeship programs of two to six years, in which the trainee worked with senior craftsmen, learning his skills by observation and coaching, generally augmented by some classroom instruction.

In the twenties, and then with growing intensity through the thirties, forties, and fifties, training interest shifted upward from work skills at the lowest levels to the methods of supervision and leadership employed by foremen and supervisors. Two of the reasons underlying this shift deserve attention here. First, training was still required and carried out for lower-level members, but this effort had begun to lose some of its challenge. Simplified, routinized, and increasingly mechanized tasks required little in the way of training, and although efforts were continuously made to improve methods and procedures, much of whatever variance existed appeared to be attributable to the interpersonal and communications skills of the trainer—usually the superior. Second, human relations criticisms of organization practices were beginning to grow. Much of this criticism focused on leadership style, particularly on the failure of supervisors to give appropriate attention to the "human needs" of their subordinates. To meet this growing criticism, training programs were begun for foremen and supervisors, emphasizing human relations skills—how to listen (with interest), give recognition, administer humane discipline, etc.

Management and executive education followed close on the heels of supervisory training and moved clearly into the spotlight in the late forties and through the fifties. To this point, managerial and administrative personnel had increased greatly as a proportion of total organization membership, and the art, or if you will the science, of management was receiving increased attention. College and university business education began to shift attention upward from the shop floor to decision- and policy-making practices in the middle and upper regions of the organization hierarchy. This growing attention to the managerial process suggested the need not only for training new entrants but also for refurbishing older members of the team.

Numerous university "executive development programs" emerged during this period with their typical target being the fortyish executive who was expected to move to senior responsibilities within the next few years. Most programs attempted coverage of then current concepts and theories of leadership and decision making, coupled with some attention to developments in technology, marketing, and finance. Similarly, most tried to avoid specific "how to do it" prescriptions and, instead, tried to give new perspectives and understandings which the manager could use to improve his performance in his own environment. Perhaps the most unusual of these programs with the broadest educational focus was billed as a several months' liberal arts education for the executive and his wife. Special courses were designed in art, music, and literature, among other topics, with the end goal being the enhancement of the executive's total life-style. It was reasoned that the broadly educated man with numerous interests was most likely to approach major decisions from the most advantageous perspective—moving calmly through the exploration of facts and alternatives and being keyed to the consideration of all sides of complex issues. Although this particular program was short-lived, its less-exotic counterparts have continued to flourish.

Laboratory, or sensitivity, training emerged as a training vehicle for organization members during roughly this same period. Its focus, too, was broad, encompassing the total interpersonal life-style of the trainee, and its targets, initially at least, were similar—the middle- and upper-level manager. The substance of sensitivity or laboratory training is so closely intertwined with its method that we might well be advised to consider it at greater length and depth in the following section.

Training Methods

The basic format for skill training has remained roughly constant—learning through doing, augmented by coaching and classroom instruction. The most significant changes have been in the area of training aids and equipment. Charts, diagrams, and instruction manuals, though much improved, remain as mainstay teaching aids, but these have been augmented by increasingly sophisticated mechanical and electronic devices which allow simulation of the operation of processes and equipment. Heavy-equipment operators, pilots, and, most recently, astronauts learn their needed skills by manipulating the controls of mock-up equipment whose characteristics are carefully designed to approximate those of the actual equipment they will be operating. In addition to these developments, programmed instruction, usually most effectively employed in conjunction with lectures and demonstrations, is gaining increased attention as a means of acquiring or upgrading specific skills. Programmed instruction is built around the concept of rapid and repeated reinforcement. Trainees read a section of new material and then are immediately quizzed on what they have read. They must respond correctly or return to the material for additional study. Programmed instruction can use a computer console, a visual-display screen, or specially designed textbooks to present its material, to evaluate and correct test responses, and to give instructions as to whether the trainee should proceed or reread the portions already covered. A major advantage of both simulators and programmed learning is the opportunity for trainees to move at their own pace and to practice to the limits of their individual needs.

Although the basic approach to skill training has remained essentially the same, there have been major innovations in leadership training and development. Early methods of training relied heavily on classroom teaching—lectures designed to tell supervisors how to behave effectively with their subordinates. Occasionally these were augmented with films and devices, some of which now appear incredibly naïve. For example, one widely marketed "human relations" packet included reading material and a packet of cards. Each of the cards carried a prescription for "effective" leadership behavior, e.g., "Smile" or "Give Recognition." The supervisor was expected to shuffle the cards at the beginning of each month and then to draw the top card each day and follow its prescription. One can imagine subordinate reaction to a once-a-month smile from a normally dour supervisor.

Somewhat more penetrating and lasting techniques such as case studies and role playing also came into widespread use in management training during the thirties, forties, and fifties. The case study method of instruction was borrowed from legal training and adapted for use in business school programs by some of our leading universities. Cases describe presumably real organizational settings and the behaviors of superiors and subordinates within these. Trainees read the cases and, with the aid of the instructor, attempt to analyze and evaluate what occurred and why and how dysfunctional occurrences might have been avoided. Role playing attempts to move beyond rational analysis to emotional involvement by asking trainees to assume the identity of characters involved in realistic interaction. Through case-study analysis, and to a much greater extent in well-designed role-playing sessions, trainees have the opportunity to learn "experientially"—to feel as well as to merely think about concepts and behaviors. Such experiential learning opportunities become increasingly important as the substance of training turns to attitude and behavior modifications—where, for example, the focus is on an effort to help managers examine and modify the ways in which they interact with peers and subordinates. Thus, logically, as the trend in training efforts moved from operatives to managers, and as the trend in subject matter shifted from work skills to leadership and life-styles, the quest for deeper and more meaningful training experiences intensified. The sensitivity, or laboratory, approach was a key product of this search.

The basic sensitivity, or laboratory, methodology emerged from experiments aimed at helping counselors, therapists, and others in related roles develop heightened awareness of group processes and particularly of the impact of their own behavior on others. This approach rests heavily on the change model advocated by the late psychologist Kurt Lewin. According to Lewin, change in human attitudes or behaviors is a three-step process. First, current attitudes and behaviors must become "unfrozen." This unfreezing step usually occurs when and if an individual receives disconfirming evidence with regard to his current attitudes or behaviors—when his image of himself and how he is perceived by others is somehow shaken. This discordant feedback presumably provides the motivation for the second step, the attempt to change—experimentation with new attitudes or behaviors in an environment structured to provide for such an opportunity. The third step, reinforcement or "refreezing," occurs as the new behaviors or attitudes receive support—as positive feedback is achieved.

The format which was developed for the application of this model appears, in comparison to traditional training methods, almost embarrassingly simple. A group of training subjects (usually ten or twelve) were brought together with a "trainer" in a comfortable, informal setting. No formal agenda was presented. Instead, the trainer, by example and guidance, attempted to lead the group to explore whatever interpersonal dynamics emerged within the group. The basic guidelines the trainer sought to impart were: (1) a focus on the "here and now"—the attitudes and behaviors emerging at the moment within the group, and the feelings and response behaviors which these aroused—and a conscious avoidance of attempts to analyze the perhaps deeply rooted "whys" of these behaviors and attitudes; and (2) a norm of open and direct expression of feelings, particularly those occurring in response to the behavior of other members of the group ("leveling"). Thus, a member of the group who attempted to "take charge" (perhaps his usual behavior in unstructured situations) might receive fairly widespread feedback from the other members that his behavior was arousing major resentment. For many members of such groups feedback of this sort produced an eye-opening experience, something their subordinates or associates had been hesitant to provide. Such feedback, the opportunity to see oneself through others' eyes, could thus result in unfreezing old attitudes and behaviors. As the one-to-two-week training session continued, members had the opportunity to experiment with new behaviors, frequently using the trainer's behavior—direct, nonevaluative, supportive—as a model. Positive feedback from other members could then provide reinforcement for these new attitudes and behaviors.

As this new methodology proved successful, at least in the eyes of its developers and many, if not most, of its training subjects, it seemed logical to expand its application to other populations, particularly to those where interpersonal competence appeared to be a crucial factor in successful behavior. Managers and administrators seemed logical targets for this opportunity, and organizations soon began to send middle- and upper-level managers to such sessions. Initially, most groups were made up of subjects all of whom came from different organizations—sessions which have come to be called "stranger labs." Later experiments were begun with "cousin labs," made up of members of the same organization carefully drawn from various levels and departments so that no two subjects were in a direct authority relationship. Finally, experiments were begun with so-called family labs, made up of subjects with a direct superior-subordinate relationship in a given organization.

As suggested, these early applications of the sensitivity, or laboratory, approach were typically held at remote locations well away from familiar organization settings. This, along with the practice of putting together trainees from a wide variety of backgrounds, roles, and organizations, was considered useful in promoting openness and the willingness to experiment with new behaviors. The most recent trend, however, has been toward "in house" (at the organization) application of modified laboratory training methods with a superior-subordinate work team as the subjects of the training effort. This trend toward "team training" is a logical step toward the broader concept of organization development. In the following chapter we will analyze in greater detail the trends in assessment and training described here, with particular emphasis on the most recent developments. In addition, we will attempt to illustrate by case example the interlinkages among selection, training, and development efforts under changing internal and external environmental conditions (e.g., markets, organization size, and complexity) and modifications in basic managerial philosophies.

BIBLIOGRAPHY

Bass, Bernard M. and James A. Vaughn, *Training in Industry: The Management of Learning* (Belmont, Calif.: Wadsworth, 1966).

Campbell, John P., Marvin D. Dunnette, Edward E. Lawler, III, and Karl E. Weick, *Managerial Behavior, Performance and Effectiveness* (New York: McGraw-Hill, 1970), chaps. 6–13.

Dunnette, Marvin D., *Personnel Selection and Placement* (London: Tavistock Publications, 1966).

Ghiselli, Edwin E., *The Validity of Occupational Aptitude Tests* (New York: Wiley, 1966).

Maier, Norman R. F., *The Appraisal Interview* (New York: Wiley, 1958).

McGehee, William and Paul W. Thayer, *Training in Business and Industry* (New York: Wiley, 1961).

Schein, Edgar H., *Organizational Psychology* (Englewood Cliffs, N.J.: Prentice-Hall, 1965), chap. 3.

Chapter 11

Emerging Concepts of Individual and Organization Development

As is often the case, hindsight provides a clarifying perspective for the events which have occurred in the areas of assessment and training. The trends described in Chapter 10, particularly those with regard to training, seem to have come about as logical responses to the application of three criteria of success—relevance, transferability, and systemic alignment—against a backdrop of changing environmental conditions and new requirements for organizational survival and growth. These factors have all combined to produce a movement toward what has been termed organization development. We will attempt here to describe briefly these factors and then to apply them in an analysis of the trends already observed. In so doing, we should create an understanding of some of the foundations of organization development.

DEVELOPMENT CRITERIA AND ENVIRONMENTAL DEMANDS

The criterion of relevance, as applied to training and development efforts, is straightforward; it simply questions whether these efforts are being

180

directed at the most important topics and targets. For example, training in mechanical skills might be judged less relevant for the manager than development efforts aimed at increasing his planning and communicating competence. Similarly, the criterion of transferability is basically clear and direct. This criterion simply measures the extent to which skills and behaviors acquired in learning situations are actually carried over into the work situation. If, for example, a manager learns new behaviors which are in conflict with the expectations of his superior, peers, or subordinates, there may be little transfer of these behaviors from the training session to the work place.

The final criterion, systemic alignment, is somewhat less obvious in content and application than either relevance or transferability. Systemic alignment refers to the extent to which behaviors learned and applied in one portion of the organization blend or fit neatly with those in other portions of the system. For example, a work unit might, as the result of intensive development activities, discover new patterns of behavior which substantially increase their potential contribution to the organization. This potential contribution will only be realized, however, to the extent that adjacent portions of the system are equipped to accommodate it. To be more pointed, changed attitudes and behaviors among nurses in a hospital may not be effective without complementary changes in physician attitudes and behaviors, or the assumption of quality responsibility by a work team may require adjustments in attitudes and behaviors among inspectors and other control personnel.

These criteria of training and development effectiveness take on added meaning when considered in conjunction with changes in organizational environments and requirements. For example, what is relevant in training topics and targets when an organization is small and its systems relatively simple may be quite irrelevant as its size and complexity increase. Similarly, issues related to transferability and systemic alignment will change, rather obviously, as changes are made in who is trained in what. To extend and clarify this point, we have noted that the typical organization has become much more complex than it used to be. Complexity requires coordination, which shifts the training focus upward from operatives to managers and shifts the substance of training from job skills to planning, communications, and interpersonal competence. New job skills learned on a simulator may be quickly and easily transferred to the shop floor and possibly require only minimal adjustments in the overall system. On the other hand, substantial changes in managerial practices or behavior may be quite difficult to transfer—to implement within the ongoing system. Further, not only have organizations become more complex, but the environments within which they operate have become far more dynamic, increasingly turbulent, and unpredictable. Typically, such environmental conditions place heavy demands on the organization's ability to cope or adjust to change and to coordinate these adjustments across units and departments—requirements which produce new training needs and new problems of transferability and systemic alignment.

The interaction among these criteria and with system and environmental changes can perhaps only be clearly understood if we examine them within a specific organizational context. In the following pages we will trace through the changes in selection, training, and development in a hypothetical organization—an organization whose experiences and behaviors are a composite of actual events across numerous organizations. The case should illustrate how development objectives and procedures flow from organizational and environmental needs and prevailing managerial theories.

TURNER INDUSTRIES: A CASE HISTORY ILLUSTRATING TRENDS IN SELECTION, TRAINING, AND DEVELOPMENT

Turner Industries is a medium-sized organization whose primary activity is the manufacture of valves and mechanical and electrical metering devices. In addition, Turner Industries includes Turner Engineering, a small but highly competent organization which provides a host of services in conjunction with the design, manufacture, and implementation of complex systems involving transfer of liquids and gases under high pressure. Finally, Turner Industries operates Turner Aerospace Equipment, which builds special valves and metering equipment on contract from firms and agencies in the aerospace industry.

Turner Industries traces its origins back to T. J. Turner's Pipe and Machine Works, founded in 1897. T. J. Turner had immigrated to the United States from England where he had been trained as a machinist and toolmaker. He worked for almost ten years in the main plant of the largest locomotive manufacturer, finally quitting in disgust over the failure of the organization to implement some of the new valve equipment he had designed. Turner lived frugally for a year and a half while he perfected and patented four innovative designs and then was fortunate to get financial backing for the manufacture of these devices from a member of his wife's family. Sales were quite slow initially and the shop sustained itself by doing custom pipe and machine work for other individuals and organizations. By 1905, however, the value of the Turner designs was gaining wide recognition, and contract work gave way to the manufacture of standard designs.

T. J. Turner had built his initial work force by hiring only skilled machinists and pipe fitters. Three experienced machinists came to Turner from the locomotive firm he had worked for and four more (two of these distant relatives) came over from England. Apprentices and helpers were hired locally, with each at least nominally agreeing to accept the "Turner Pledge"—abstinence from tobacco and alcohol (other than beer) and saving of 10 percent of his wages each month. Turner helped make this pledge palatable by paying wages equal to community standards and agreeing to match employee savings up to the 10 percent of monthly wage.

By 1912 the work force at Turner Valve, Inc. (the name and financial structure were changed in 1908), had grown to over 100, with about 40 percent of these skilled craftsmen and apprentices and the remaining forge and foundry "hands" and operators of special-purpose machines designed by Turner and his highly skilled toolmakers. In addition, the office force had grown to ten and the "contract and service" group, headed by Turner's eldest son John, who had recently completed study at an Eastern law school, numbered seven. All training at Turner, up to this point, was done "on the job" under the direction of the senior craftsmen and the four department foremen, all but one of whom were members of the initial work force. The "Turner Pledge" had been dropped as the work force expanded, though Turner still sought to hire only clean-cut young men. He was able to be quite selective given that pay and working conditions at Turner remained ahead of local standards and the personal saving-matching incentive plan was still in force.

Business grew rapidly at Turner during World War I and the product line expanded greatly as Turner and his designers produced innovations to meet military needs. In addition, the nucleus of Turner Engineering was formed around a group engaged in consulting and design work on government contracts. By the midtwenties Turner Valve employed almost 3,000 management, office, and plant personnel. Almost 100 of these were in the newly formed "field force." This group, made up of some fifty, generally young, civil and mechanical engineers, metallurgists, and electrical specialists, along with thirty-plus highly skilled mechanics, pipe fitters, and electricians and a small office force, was under the direction of Richard (Dick) Turner, T. J.'s youngest son. Dick Turner had received a degree in mechanical engineering in 1914 and had joined the family firm immediately thereafter. With his father's concurrence, he spent the first two years working with the senior craftsmen in all areas of the plant and had just taken over direction of the gauge shop when he left the firm to join the Army Air Corps with two college classmates. Dick served with distinction in France (six medals, T. J. would note) and returned in 1919 to join the emerging engineering group. By the midtwenties, Dick's engineering skill and leadership talents were widely recognized, and he had personally helped the engineering group secure numerous contracts for work related to the growing aircraft industry. John Turner, the eldest son, had by this time moved up from the contract section to become executive vice-president, and John and T. J. agreed to give Dick free rein (within reason) to take the engineering group wherever he felt it should go. They did so by agreeing to Dick's request in 1927 to give it separate identity as Turner Engineering. Both John and Dick Turner were respected throughout the company and were especially well liked by the older employees, many of whom felt they had helped raise them. (Understandably, there was much speculation but no open discussion concerning Albert Turner, T. J.'s middle son. It was known that he had dropped out of medical school, over T. J.'s objections, to join the ambulance corps in Europe, and it was rumored that he had decided to remain in France "to paint, or write, or something.")

In the middle and late twenties, Turner Valve began to experience its first serious employee-relations problems. During the war years, T. J. and John had cooperated with the employees in the formation of an in-house union and had worked with its representatives in developing a pension plan and other employee benefits. Nevertheless, in the twenties difficulties began to mount, particularly in the foundry and in the gauge-assembly section. The recently hired personnel manager, Tim O'Donovan, felt that the main problem was that the new supervisors in those sections (and even some of the old ones) simply didn't know how to get along with their men. O'Donovan, who had been a high school football coach before the war and a training officer during the war years, felt strongly that "you get from your men what you deserve—if you take an interest in them, listen to their problems, show them that you care, they'll stick by you when it counts."

With the approval of John and T. J., O'Donovan set up the firm's first supervisory training program—a series of five after-work lectures (the supervisors received extra pay for staying over), four given by O'Donovan and the final lecture given by T. J. himself, describing how the company had begun and giving his philosophy of business and management. Despite O'Donovan's enthusiasm for the training program, business was booming at the time and scheduling difficulties prevented the program from reaching the bulk of the supervisory force. Nevertheless, O'Donovan felt that a good start had been made and was busy preparing a long-range program of training, not only for present supervisors but also for those most likely to be promoted to foremen. As he pointed out, "Teaching a guy to be a good machinist doesn't teach him to manage men." Moreover, he argued, within three years after the training was begun, most of the shop-floor problems and grievances had disappeared. John Turner, while acknowledging the usefulness of training, was not quite so willing to attribute shop-floor peace wholly to supervisory training. In fact, he felt that economic conditions and the threat of layoffs had "helped smooth some troubled waters."

John Turner had become president of Turner Valve in 1929 when his father had resigned, partly as the result of age (T. J. was sixty-nine) and partly as the result of John's superior expertise in financial matters (T. J. retained his position as chairman of the board). During the early depression years, John attempted to hold layoffs to a minimum through careful cost control and aggressive market-development efforts. His cost-cutting efforts delayed the full resumption of the supervisory training efforts until the late thirties. In addition to cost savings, John had a second reason for holding back approval on the full-scale supervisory training program which O'Donovan continued to advocate. In John's view, the long-term future of the organization would depend on its middle- and upper-level managerial personnel, most of whom, he felt, could not be developed out of the ranks of current supervisors. In line with this thinking, John began in the middle and late thirties to hire a number of young graduates of the best-known law programs and business schools, one of whom was his own son Woodrow, who had received his MBA in 1937. With Woodrow's help (significantly, O'Donovan was effectively bypassed on this decision), John set up a program whereby these young men would rotate through departments throughout the organization before being placed in their first major position. In addition, John toyed with the idea of sending some of his established managers "back to school," but the advent of World War II interrupted his plans.

During World War II, Turner Valve, Inc., grew rapidly, particularly in the newly formed aeronautics and marine division (later to become Turner Aerospace). Woodrow, who held a reserve commission in the army, was quickly activated but, unfortunately (from his point of view), never saw combat. Instead, he was assigned a number of increasingly important staff posts in Washington and later in Europe and achieved the rank of colonel. T. J.'s only other grandson, Eddie, followed in his father's (Richard's) footsteps and joined the Army Air Corps. The Turner family and firm were shocked and saddened in 1943, for in December of that year old T. J. was rushed to the hospital where he succumbed to pneumonia. Some attributed the old man's death (he was eighty-three) to the fact that he continued to come to the plant each day in all types of weather and would sit in his favorite, poorly heated office near the toolmaking department going over designs and quality reports. Others noted, however, that the old man had "begun to fail around Thanksgiving, right after they got the word that young Eddie had been killed in combat."

By the end of World War II, Turner Valve had grown to over 15,000 employees. Woodrow returned to the firm as vice-president for planning and employment services. He was urged to take charge of the aeronautics division but declined; many felt he did so because "that job would have been Eddie's." The new corporate structure of Turner Industries emerged under John and Woodrow's guidance and expansion continued, despite what, to the Turners, was an alarming growth in labor-relations problems and "bureaucratic" inefficiency.

In the early fifties the firm suffered its first strike (the company union had given way in the thirties to an international union affiliated with the AFL), and though the strike was short, it highlighted a dramatic growth in grievances. Woodrow, who was now executive vice-president, felt the strike, the growth of grievances, and the mounting inefficiencies and problems with the management structure were clearly related. He had continued to hire the best young business-school graduates (with an increasing number of MBAs) and had given the training department a sizable budget to send other promising middle managers to various executive-development programs. Nevertheless, he felt that much of what was being learned in the executive programs and in the now-firmly-established in-house supervisory training program was not being applied in the plant. Major supporting evidence for this feeling was provided by research done by two university professors who, with Woodrow's support, studied the effects of the supervisory training programs on supervisors' attitudes and behavior. Their research indicated that although supervisors appeared to acquire new attitudes and insights concerning leadership during the training program, they were as likely as not to revert to their previous views once they had been back on the job for awhile. Woodrow, along with the chief of the training group and the researchers, agreed that what was happening was logical, if not desirable. The supervisors were returning from the program to work under middle managers who frequently did not share the values presented in the program, whose behavior, which the supervisors either emulated or conformed to, was not good "human relations practice." These problems seemed to occur even though many of the middle managers had themselves been through some form of management training.

Searching for a means of "shaking those guys out of their ruts," Woodrow approved a training-group recommendation in the late fifties which suggested sending a steady stream of managers to sensitivity, or laboratory, programs in the East. Woodrow himself had visited the training laboratory site in 1956 shortly after he became president and chairman of the board of Turner Industries. (His father, John, resigned both posts in 1955 and his Uncle Richard resigned at the same time to clear the way for the succession. Woodrow had urged his uncle, who was only fifty-eight, to take the chairmanship, but he declined, arguing that he never had been anything but an engineer. Some observers outside the firm felt that Richard and Woodrow did not get along, but insiders knew that Richard and his nephew were quite close and that Richard had simply never really gotten over Eddie's death.)

Woodrow had visited the laboratory training facilities at the urging of a consultant to his firm, a behavioral scientist affiliated with the faculty of the business school where Woodrow had received his MBA back in the thirties. Woodrow took part in an abbreviated "lab" run by a colleague of the consultant and was impressed by the experience. Some of Woodrow's subordinates were rather surprised by his behavior after he returned from the lab. He seemed to listen with greater intensity and to express his own views more directly than he had. The slight though visible discomfort of his subordinates was apparent to Woodrow and was discussed with the consultant. The consultant pointed out that Woodrow's staff, only two of whom had been through a training lab experience, were simply not prepared for his changed behavior and would not be until they too had undergone a similar experience. It seemed apparent to Woodrow and the consultant that a similar pattern of frustration or discomfort might be occurring throughout the organization as individual managers returned to superior, subordinate, and peer roles with others who had not had the experience.

The consultant, at Woodrow's urging, began to work with the training group to set up laboratory training programs at facilities near the plant. The training design, finally implemented in 1960, was built around a three-day, intensive program which utilized a number of questionnaires, exercises, and other devices aimed at aiding managers to gain insight into their own attitudes and behavior. Managers from different levels, but not from the same departments, were to participate in the program as rapidly as reasonable scheduling would allow.

In 1964, Woodrow and the consultant reviewed the results of their training program. Testimony from most managers who had attended the program indicated that they felt it had been worthwhile, but many felt that they had not been able to fully relate the training to their work environment. Interviews throughout the plant produced comments such as:

"I know how I ought to be behaving, but how do I do it when the guys I work with don't level with me?"

"I noticed some changes in my boss's behavior following the program, but it's going to take more than good intentions to clear up this mess."

Sifting through numerous comments such as these, Woodrow and the consultant agreed that the training in interpersonal skills had to link somehow directly to job-related problems. The outcome of their discussion was a commitment to attempt a program of "team training," following the model of successful application of this technique in other organizations. The consultant and two of his colleagues, later to be assisted by members of the Turner training staff, would begin to work with key units in the structure. The consultants would interview members of these groups in an effort to uncover matters of major concern with regard to policies, practices, and behaviors which they felt were impeding their performance. The consultant would attempt to get the group, the superior and his several subordinates, to address these and any other issues which might be brought up while the consultant sat in on these problem-solving meetings. The consultant's task would be to try to help the group create an atmosphere in which it could confront its problems, pointing out, when he felt it worthwhile, aspects of the dynamics of the group which might be inhibiting progress.

In 1967, Woodrow and the consultant reviewed the successes and failures of the team-training approach. Several outstanding examples of progress were visible. In Turner Aerospace the electronics unit had ironed out a long-standing struggle between quality control and purchasing and was enthusiastic enough about the experience to request aid from the corporate training group in setting up further team-training efforts downward in their structure. In Turner Engineering the metals group had arrived at an entirely new structure as the result of the problem-solving efforts begun with the consultant (a structure closely resembling the matrix organization described in Chapter 5). Moreover, the corporate controller's office had established several new policies highly applauded by controller groups in the several affiliated organizations—policies which resulted, in part at least, from team-training sessions.

Finally, Woodrow was concerned because much of the attention appeared to be aimed at removing currently visible obstacles and solving long-standing problems. Although the gains were real enough, he was concerned about the longer-term needs of the organization. Woodrow felt that technological and market changes would place major pressures on the total organization system within the next five to ten years and was not at all convinced that the organization was prepared to cope with these demands.

ANALYSIS OF THE TURNER INDUSTRIES EXPERIENCE

With the expression of these concerns, it is appropriate for us to abandon our somewhat lengthy association with Turner Industries. We should do so for at least two reasons. First, hindsight is easier than foresight. It is one thing to understand and illustrate rather clearly what has happened in an organization and why, and quite another and far more difficult thing to prescribe for the present or forecast for the future. Second, we should step back from the Turner Industries case in order to structure and comment on the insights it offers. The Turner case has taken us near the leading edge of modern development theory and practice and has posed for us some of the more crucial, only partially resolved problems currently facing the field.

What can we learn from the experiences of T. J., John, Richard, Woodrow, and others at Turner Industries? Most clearly illustrated, I think, is that changes in training and development methods and targets have occurred in response to changes in organizational needs and in response to changing concepts of management. The shift upward in training focus, first to supervisors and then to managers, occurred as procedures at the shop-floor level were rationalized and simplified and problems of facilitation and coordination increased. Human relations concepts were clearly visible in the early efforts as solutions to organizational problems were sought exclusively in the domain of improvements in interpersonal competence. In fact, human relations concepts remain dominant even through the shift to sensitivity, or laboratory, methods— the focus remained on changing attitudes and behaviors, frequently accepting or ignoring the work context in which these occurred. Finally, the movement toward team training acknowledges, in line with the human resources model, the indivisibility of social and technical systems in organizations. Team training attempts to deal with interpersonal issues but recognizes that these arise not only from the personalities of individuals but also from the ways in which their jobs and roles are structured and from the demands placed on them by organizational policies and procedures.

Illustrated only slightly less clearly in this case are the issues of relevance, transferability, and systemic alignment. The movement upward to supervisory and management training, and toward training methods aimed at producing deeper, more pervasive changes, reflected the search for relevance in training substance and focus. Similarly, the movement from "stranger labs" to team training within the organization reflects recognition of both the criterion of relevance and that of transferability. With the development of the team-training approach, the problem of transfer of learning appeared in large measure solved. That is, as actual problems facing an ongoing unit become the training vehicle, a short-run payoff is anticipated in the form of improved immediate solutions. Moreover, the process of working together to solve problems with the trainer's inputs helps build increased competence for future problem solving—competence which is in part generalizable but which is also in part rooted in improved understanding of, and adjustment to, the factors determining behavior and performance within the unit or team.

Nevertheless, while the team-training approach appears to meet the criteria of relevance and transferability, it too may fall short when measured against the criterion of systemic alignment. At Turner Industries, even the successful applications of autonomous team-training efforts served to highlight the interdependencies among the various segments of the total organizational system. Attempting to adjust one portion of the system without full consideration of the impact of these adjustments on other segments of it or on the total system appeared to be at best of limited benefit to organizational performance and at worst damaging to the overall system. What appeared to be needed at Turner to meet simultaneously the criteria of relevance, transferability, and systemic alignment was a coordinated development program aimed at the total organization—organization development, the topic to which we turn in the next chapter.

BIBLIOGRAPHY

Fleishman, E. A., "Leadership Climate, Human Relations Training, and Supervisory Behavior," *Personnel Psychology*, vol. 6, pp. 205–222 (Summer 1953).

Organization Development: The State of the Art

The Turner case and its discussion in the previous chapter have, as suggested, brought us to the doorstep of a loose collection of values, concepts, and techniques regularly referred to as organizaton development (OD).

In theory OD is a coordinated effort by organization members (usually with the aid of outside consultants) to uncover and remove attitudinal, behavioral, procedural, policy, and structural barriers to effective performance across the entire sociotechnical system, gaining in the process increased awareness of the system's internal and external dynamics so that future adaptations are enhanced. In practice, OD turns out to be whatever people are doing under that title. That is, empirically, we find the tag OD attached to leadership courses in traditional classroom settings, weekend retreats for superior-subordinate work groups, executive groups discussing their day-to-day decision-making processes with an outside consultant-observer, the collection, analysis, and feedback of perceptual and attitudinal data across an entire system, etc.

The low correlation between OD theory and practice described here (and illustrated in our later examples) handicaps description and analysis and provides a ready target for the critics' barbs. Nevertheless, despite its fragmented appearance, there is an underlying commonality in OD efforts, and, in its more advanced forms, OD represents the zenith of applied behavioral science in organizations today. It thus deserves our close, if labored, attention.

UNDERLYING VALUES AND CONCEPTS

The basic values stated or implied in OD theory and practice include:

1   A concern for human feelings and human needs for support, dignity, and fulfillment in work.
2   The endorsement of open expression of perceptions, attitudes, and feelings within work groups and between superiors and subordinates.
3   A belief in the efficacy of confronting interpersonal and interdepartmental issues, rather than smoothing them over or forcing solutions.
4   A general predilection toward participative decision making and individual and work-group self-direction and self-control.

The key concepts expressed or implied in OD theory and practice include:

1   Basic attitudes and behavioral change are most effectively accomplished through experiential learning opportunities structured around the Lewinian change model—(a) unfreezing (through feedback concerning existing attitudes and behaviors), (b) change (through experimentation with new behaviors in supportive settings), and (c) refreezing (through positive feedback concerning new attitudes and behaviors).
2   Learning is most effective when it occurs within the natural work group and is related to existing conditions and requirements.
3   Changed behaviors (policies, procedures, roles) require coordination across work groups and thus the focus of development must extend beyond the individual and the work group to the entire interdependent sociotechnical system.
4   The role of the OD consultant is not to diagnose process barriers and prescribe alternatives but to facilitate the acquisition of process awareness and problem-solving skills within the work group.
5   As process-learning occurs, work groups become more capable of adjusting to changing requirements and of working out relationships with other organizational units and with their external environments.
6   As process skills are acquired across the organization, the total

system becomes more adept at devising and implementing policies, procedures, and structures which more closely match internal and external requirements.

7   Organization development is not programmatic but continuous, and constant monitoring of the sociotechnical system's processes is required.

SOURCES OF VALUES AND CONCEPTS

These values and concepts flow from three sources: (1) the development and exposition of the human resources model of management, (2) the natural trial-and-error evolution of training concepts and techniques, and (3) the emergence of systems theory and the growing recognition of interdependencies within the organization and between the organization and its environment.

The value placed on human worth and capability and the creation of opportunities for fulfillment through self-directed, self-controlled work accomplishment is clearly related to the shift in emphasis from the human relations to the human resources model, as is the emphasis on open, confronting, participative, problem-solving behavior.

If you recall, whereas the Hawthorne experimenters had pointed out the crucial role of feelings and attitudes as determinants of performance, the managerial solution to this "problem" at Hawthorne was the establishment of a nondirective counseling service, located away from the work place, where organization members could presumably go to dissipate their negative emotions. For most managers, even into the fifties, the office was a place devoted to work, and feelings and emotions were ideally to be checked at the door, or less ideally to be dealt with through covert methods, that is, through a variety of morale-building, friction-removing mechanisms such as employee committees, suggestion systems, company teams, etc. At the very worst, the manager might be forced on occasion to close his office doors and hear out an aggrieved member.

Similarly, a good group meeting, according to the human relations standards of the forties and fifties, was one in which harmony prevailed as the members came to apparent rapid agreement on some issue. Disagreements were "smoothed" over through such mechanisms as a quick joke to relieve tension or a promise to "talk that over when we get this issue settled," with group pressure (evidenced by obvious member discomfort) suppressing all but the most obtuse or obstreperous dissidents. Even the behavioral research of the day appeared to lend support to these values and behaviors. Early research on task groups had identified numerous acts contributing to group performance. Almost from the beginning it became common practice to refer to those actions related to the task itself—formulating it, shaping it, and pushing it toward completion—as part of the "father" role in the group, while acts made by members to relieve tension, provide support for group members, renew morale, etc., were considered part of the "mother" role. In the male-oriented world of the thirties, forties, and fifties, this terminology clearly demonstrated the secondary importance accorded to attitudes, sentiments, and group process as opposed to task behavior and apparent substantive accomplishments.

In a related fashion, the emphasis on experiential learning within the actual organization is clearly linked to the evolution of training requirements and techniques described in Chapter 10 and illustrated in the Turner case. The conflict between the values and behaviors emanating from innovative individual and group-development efforts and the organizational environments in which these were to be put to use was clearly one of the factors leading to the concept of the organization itself, rather than the individual manager or the work group, as the target of change. If the convert to openness, trust, confrontation, and process awareness was to practice his new beliefs and behaviors, he needed support from his superiors. More important, if work groups were to improve their performance through the removal of process barriers, they required both the permission to change some policies and procedures established above and the cooperation of lateral units who were the ultimate source of many of their concerns. If these conditions were to occur, it seemed likely that development activities would have to occur simultaneously or, more likely, in planned sequence throughout the system. Thus, by the late fifties and early sixties, a number of pioneering scholar-consultants were beginning to structure large-scale, sustained efforts across total organizations or their major components, and the training and development path to organization development was near its destination.

While the linkage between evolution in managerial philosophies, training theory, techniques, and the underlying values and concepts of OD seems clear, the contribution of systems theory has not yet been covered here and deserves some attention.

THE "SYSTEMS" ROUTE TO ORGANIZATION DEVELOPMENT

Managers and students of organizations have always been aware that organizations are products of their environment and depend on it for their survival. Adam Smith's allusion to the "natural" tendency of businessmen to collude in restraint of competition is an early testimony to environmental awareness. The rapid growth of advertising and public relations activities in the first half of this century is more recent evidence of this recognition. Nevertheless, many members of organizations and some management theorists have at times tended to behave as if organizations were relatively static, closed systems. Moreover, in particular periods and under certain circumstances, such a view is not entirely inappropriate. During, for example, the halcyon days of American manufacturing supremacy, it must have appeared to many of our leading organizations as if their environments could be influenced if not directly controlled to meet their needs. Compliant members were generally available, raw materials appeared to be abundant, the buying public was moderately gullible and apparently insatiable, regulatory agencies were generally permissive, and competitors were reduced to a precious, peaceful few. Further, short-term fluctuations could be handled by inventories at both ends of the process, employees could be tied to the organization through nonvesting fringe benefits, and competitors would remain pacific as long as pricing policies moved in precise parallel and market shares remained roughly undisturbed. Under these circumstances, firms might not be maximizing profits nor public agencies developing enthusiastic support, but the future was secure and the present moderately rewarding.

Though such circumstances probably still exist for some organizations today, there is strong feeling (though little empirical evidence) that conditions have changed and are changing rather dramatically for most organizations. As early as the fifties, the seminal writings of Peter Drucker were calling managers' attention to the need to be responsive to the several "publics" on whom they were dependent and were pointing out the constant need to ask and answer the question, "What is our business?"—i.e., what is the best investment of our resources? By the late fifties and early sixties, a growing body of research in the United States and abroad appeared to point to the fact that while traditional "mechanistic" organizations might still be highly useful under stable environmental conditions, more fluid, less-bureaucratized "organic" organizations seemed better suited to rapidly changing conditions. The writings of this period began to be heavily sprinkled with "systems" concepts and terminology developed in the physical and biological sciences, and few scholars would dare fail to pay at least perfunctory homage to the gods of instability and uncertainty.

Warren Bennis was an early and eloquent spokesman for the more dramatic position that increased complexity and uncertainty would ultimately doom *all* traditional bureaucratic organizational forms. Bennis and other spokesmen called for "planned change" toward more adaptive structures and processes and saw changed managerial attitudes and behaviors as prerequisites to organizational change. While authorship of specific terminology is obscure, the jump from planned change of the total organization system (precursed by major shifts in managerial attitudes and behaviors) to the inclusive concept of organization development is not a large one.

Two key contributions are apparent along this "systems route" toward organization development. First, the application of systems concepts, particularly those from the biological sciences, to formal organizations provided the beginnings of an alternative to the bureaucratic model of organizational structure and process. The imagery of organisms developing adaptive skills in the face of changing environmental conditions could be laid out beside the bureaucratic model of a special-purpose machine with carefully articulated parts producing to predictable environmental demands. Although this "organic versus mechanistic" dichotomy has been subjected to heroic overuse almost from the beginning, it prompted the search for, and specification of, the conditions and mechanisms necessary for adaptiveness. Rapid, unfiltered feedback emerged as a clear requirement, as did response mechanisms unencumbered by extensive procedural requirements or the constraints of officialism. These conditions are rather closely aligned with the norms of open, direct, confronting behavior which were associated with sensitivity, or laboratory, training and which carried over into other experiential development approaches in organizations. The linkage of these behavioral norms directly to requirements for organizational effectiveness provided an important rationale for the expansion of managerial and team training and development efforts aimed at enhancing these behaviors throughout the "system."

Second, and perhaps more important, the application of systems concepts to organizations, particularly the notions of organic, adaptive behavior, emphasized the need for a continuous "learning" effort throughout the system. If systems were to be adaptive, they would have to learn more about their own internal processes, for it would be process skills rather than substantive expertise which would transcend changing situations. That is, if the organization or its units were "taught" or had prescribed for it (them) a new structure or process, instant obsolescence could occur in the face of rapidly changing environmental conditions. On the other hand, if the organization learned how to monitor its own processes, to surface inhibiting forces (e.g., attitudes, behaviors, role relationships), and to confront these in a manner conducive to positive change, rapid adjustments to new situations and demands could occur. It will be argued below that organization development efforts tend to be successful to the degree that they are built on and hold to an appropriate "learning model."

SOME EXAMPLES OF OD TODAY

The paths toward organization development described above converge, as suggested earlier, on a rather messy, poorly defined destination— current organization development theory and practice. In the following pages, several recent examples of "organization development" (the term, as will be seen, seems to be frequently misapplied) are presented. (These are composites of real experiences, with changes made to preserve anonymity.) Three points (and their definitions) are worth comparing across these cases: (1) entry—how the OD effort was begun, with particular attention to the conditions under which outside consultants are brought in and allowed to operate; (2) change techniques—the actual technique(s) used to influence member attitudes and behaviors, e.g., team training, data feedback, the grid; and (3) the sustaining mechanisms (if any)—procedures, devices, systems, etc., instituted during the OD effort and aimed at focusing and maintaining attention on process learning and development over time, e.g., the decision to collect and feed back attitudinal data on a continuing basis.

ORGANIZATION A—(A Limited Effort)   Organization A is a regional subsystem of a nationwide firm which has the reputation of being well managed and innovative with regard to behavioral science concepts and research. An organization development unit was formed at the firm's headquarters in the midsixties. To a large extent, the members of this newly formed unit were recruited from the firm's extensive management-development activities and were primarily skilled in the design of training programs and techniques. As a corporate-level staff group, the OD unit had no prescribed route of entry into the various regional organizations. As a starting point, the OD unit devised a three-day "learning laboratory" to which regional organizations could send members of their managerial teams. The three-day program was designed around a number of instruments— attitude questionnaires, group problem solving tasks, etc., which participants completed, analyzed, and discussed with the aid of the OD-unit staff members. In postsession critiques, most participants rated the training program as worthwhile (though a few considered it "childish" and a "waste of time") and many felt it should be followed up by extended efforts in their own regional organizations.

These attitudes were reinforced by the strong verbal support given the OD unit's effort by top corporate officers, and two of the regions moved quickly to "invite" the OD staff into their areas to run a modified version of the three-day program for operating teams throughout their hierarchies. The invitation was particularly swift and strong in one of the regions (not organization A), where the regional manager urged that he and his entire managerial staff be involved in the effort as quickly as possible. The OD staff responded to this request (which was viewed by some of this regional manager's peers as a rather clever political expedient, given corporate management's support of the OD unit) and moved the majority of their most highly qualified staff into the effort.

Over a two-month period, approximately sixty managers from ten operating groups within the region attended the three-day program, with the regional manager and his five subordinates serving as the pilot group. In these sessions, a number of procedural- and policy-related barriers to effective performance were uncovered and discussed, and members of the OD staff held follow-up sessions with many groups in which changes in these areas were considered and implementation planned. The OD unit's efforts received considerable praise from many members of the region, and a glowing write-up of the entire program appeared in the corporate magazine. (Within a year, however, there was little visible evidence of continued developmental efforts in that region.)

Organization A, along with several other regional subsystems, had little contact with the OD unit during its first few years of operation, though a few younger members of the staff did go to corporate headquarters to attend the standard three-day program. By the late sixties, organization A had received several queries from corporate headquarters regarding its "readiness" for an OD effort, and many members of the top staff of the organization had expressed the opinion that "we really had better get on with it." At the request of organization A, a member of the OD staff visited with their top staff, and, after several delays, a time for a three-day training program for the regional manager and his immediate subordinates was set. As organization A was geographically far removed from headquarters, a consultant affiliated with a university in the organization's area was drawn into the effort "to provide continuity." The three-day session was dutifully attended by the top regional team (a highly competent group by most standards), and the general feeling at the end of the program was one of relief that the session was over and "nothing painful had happened." The outside consultant who had attended part of the program was invited to meet with the top-management group for a "follow-up session" during which the group skillfully "solved" a number of problems occurring at lower levels in the organization. His comments concerning whether lower-level management might be "by-passed" by their decisions were pushed aside politely by the group, as were his suggestions that an attitude survey conducted the year before which showed considerable discontent within the region might be examined. The consultant was not invited back by the group, and there was little further contact between the group and the corporate OD unit.

Analysis of the OD Effort in Organization A

Entry There is no evidence that the top-management team of organization A (with the possible exception of the assistant personnel manager) recognized any real need for a developmental effort in their system. No major crises were visible, they were staying within their general budget guidelines, and operating performance, if not exceptional, was at least not causing major customer complaints or drawing the attention of top management. Moreover, the top team functioned quite smoothly and most looked upon their present assignments as leading to advancements (or at least lateral moves) within the next three years. Under these conditions, most members of the team were quite willing to suppress a number of concerns as long as they posed no personal threats, and none wanted to do anything to really "rock the boat." Most looked upon the OD program as something which corporate headquarters expected them to do (the phrase "get our ticket punched" was frequently used) and which, while probably unnecessary, could be reasonably easily endured. The relationship with the corporate OD man posed no problem. He was anxious to gain acceptance and as long as they cooperated with him (on the surface at least), he would be forced to give them a good report.

The "professor" posed another problem. He represented much more of a potential, though undefinable, threat; not because they felt he would report on their activities to upper management but simply because he would be looking at their actual job behaviors. Thus, while any troublesome moments in the training session with the OD staff member could be dealt with by a joke or two and a comment that "that deserves further attention," the session with the professor produced some feelings of defensiveness. As it turned out, the professor was personable enough, and even seemed pleased with the openness with which they responded to one another (of course, they were aware of his presence and were taking special care to be frank and at the same time supportive). His questions about why they were dealing with certain issues at the shop level were a bit troublesome, but it was clear that he really did not understand their need to "stay on top of the situation at all levels." Particularly unsettling were his questions concerning what the group felt his role with them should be, if in fact there was to be a role. Given that they really had no answer to his question and that he did not seem eager to "sell himself to them," they were quite relieved when circumstances over the next two months made it impossible to get together again. When neither the professor nor corporate OD raised the issue of resuming his "process consultation," the issue was quietly allowed to die.

It is clear in this instance that there was no real readiness in organization A for any sort of change effort. Motivation, to the extent it existed at all, was mildly negative—"get this over with, with as little bother as possible." Given this lack of readiness, no real entry into the system was possible. There simply was no meaningful, surface-penetrating role for either the OD staff man nor the professor.

Change Techniques   The three-day "learning laboratory" which had proved to be a thought-provoking device in its earlier application, seemed to present the top team of organization A with little challenge. The mild "unfreezing" exercises provoked little introspection, and the experiential atmosphere of the learning lab gradually gave away completely to a traditional classroom lecture-discussion situation. Present behaviors and attitudes were not subjected to any meaningful analysis (the feedback instruments produced almost nothing in the way of criticism or concern about the group's processes), no new behaviors were explored, and thus no visible changes were induced.

Sustaining Mechanisms   The availability of the professor provided a possible means of developing a long-term OD effort, but the unwilling-ness/inability of the group to consider and agree upon a meaningful role for him negated this potential sustaining mechanism. Even the OD staff was left with little basis for attempting to "re-enter" the system, at least until time brought about a reconstitution of the top team.

Given the negative flavor of this analysis, the question, "Why present this example?" is appropriate. The answer is twofold. First, the example is presented because it is perhaps all too typical of many development efforts operating under the heading of OD. At best, perhaps the seed of an idea or two was planted—much as would be the case if the managers had attended any three-day "management development" program (which this effort essentially turned out to be). Second, while no obvious harm was done, there is inherent in this type of effort a hidden damage in the form of what I call an "innoculation effect." If anything, this effort convinced the top team of organization A that behavioral science in general and OD in particular had little to offer. The program was no more hurtful than a smallpox vaccination, and it served to "protect" them against any serious effort at examining their own managerial processes. More will be said on this point later.

ORGANIZATION B—(A Sustained, Low-Intensity Effort)   Organization B is a medical school (part of a major university), whose internal and external environments became increasingly turbulent during the mid and late sixties.

The student body became embroiled in antiwar protests and many coaligned with community action groups demanding that the medical school expand and improve its services to medically deprived citizens. In the midst of these activities a unionization drive occurred among the nonmedical staff and then spread over to the interns and residents in the city hospital operated by the medical school. A new president was appointed during the early stage of this period of turmoil—a highly respected MD with a reputation for creative ideas concerning health-care delivery.

From the beginning, the new president set out to create a "new climate of openness and innovation," and he was joined in this effort by the director of nonmedical personnel, who was generally considered to be fair and thoughtful even by those leading the drive for unionization. They both recognized the need for improved communication and planning and felt that major benefits would accrue from management and supervisory training throughout the system (many of the department heads were trained in medical specialties but had had no administrative training). Following up on this reasoning, they appointed a psychologist as advisor to the personnel director and the president and pulled together, under him, the available training personnel. The psychologist in turn brought in two professors from another part of the university who were active in OD work and had had experience in health organizations. Over a series of meetings it was decided to move simultaneously along two lines: (1) design some means of "unfreezing" the entire system—to break through the crust of established role relationships and communications patterns, and (2) design a long-term management-training effort which would eventually impact all departments in both classroom and team-training formats.

As a step toward implementing the first of these strategies, a representative (student, faculty, staff, etc.) planning-and-development committee was formed. The initial meetings of the committee were not particularly fruitful. Most members adopted a wait-and-see posture, while some student and staff members used the forum to air established grievances. Nevertheless, the committee did plan and coordinate one "town meeting" on the school's role in community service which was generally credited with relieving some tensions and reactivating machinery for further talks. Despite this success, many committee members sensed a lack of direction and felt no real progress was being made in establishing any real community of interests. Responding to these feelings, the psychologist and two of his consultants planned a two-day, off-campus retreat for the committee and members of their constituencies. In the informal atmosphere of the retreat, communications improved significantly. The planned format had participants moving back and forth between small, heterogeneous task groups, which generated lists of concerns and priorities, to general sessions in which these lists were examined and discussed. In the final sessions, self-selected groups worked to achieve consensus regarding goals in several key areas.

Most of the participants judged the retreat "very worthwhile." However, the atmosphere of cooperation and achievement was difficult to transfer back to the campus, and within a few weeks the planning-and-development committee members were again discouraged and disgruntled. As one member put it, "We meet and talk and plan and nothing happens." However, as another member noted, "We're actually accomplishing far more now than before, but the problem is now we can see how much more really could be done."

Shortly after the retreat, the second of the two strategies was implemented as department heads were invited to attend the first of the planned management-development courses. The course was designed to cover such topics as leadership style and subordinate responses, motivation, performance appraisal, joint goal setting, etc., in twice-a-week sessions (during working hours) over a period of six weeks. While the format was essentially classroom lecture and discussion, the materials were well designed and the instructors, drawn from local campuses and consulting organizations, were well above average for courses of this type in terms of subject-matter knowledge and classroom capability. Attendance at this opening session for upper-level administrators and department heads was encouragingly high (over half of the target group attended six or more of the sessions) and was attributed to the carry-over of enthusiasm generated by the retreat. Subsequent sessions of the course moved ahead as planned, and within fifteen months over two hundred administrators and supervisors had attended from all areas of the medical school. Moreover, a number of department heads and supervisors had requested follow-up, team-training activity in their own units (more, in fact, than the newly structured OD unit's staff—the psychologist and several former members of the training department—were able to handle).

Appraising the situation two years after the beginning of the OD effort in organization B, the psychologist who now headed the OD unit wrote:

We are not as far along as I hoped we would be, but perhaps further than I had any right to expect in such a complex situation. The development course has been a success, judged by the number of archaic work policies which have been revised and the fact that "managing" in general is now getting some attention. Moreover, in a few areas we have had some rather dramatic results—one whole department, for example, has "turned around" following a series of team-training meetings requested by the department head. (He had attended the opening session of the course and became concerned about his own leadership style. After several of his subordinates attended, he reluctantly raised several issues with them and got some pretty direct feedback. He asked if we could help, and I think we did. The atmosphere over there has clearly improved, and we are getting almost no complaints from inside or outside of the unit now. Of course, I don't know how long it will last and a couple of members have suggested we run some more sessions.)

On the other hand, outside the course itself, I'm not sure where we are. A number of integrative committees have been formed to focus on minority issues, community action, and student relations, and we seem to be doing more talking than demonstrating, which I think is good (although the demonstrations did keep the pressure on for change). Still, at the top, I don't see much real movement. The top administrators have cooperated by sending people to our courses and approving team-training sessions, but they've not really gotten involved themselves. Particularly since X left [the "new" president had left the post three months earlier] there seems to be little happening up there. I supposed we will have to bide our time until something comes along to get their attention. Meanwhile, there is plenty for us to do in the general training area and with specific units.

Analysis of the OD Effort in Organization B

Entry Conditions in organization B were favorable for the beginnings of some change and development effort. The strife in the internal and external environments provided a great deal of "disconfirming evidence" concerning the efficacy of continuing "business as usual" and energized the system (or some parts of it, at least) to search for alternatives. At the same time, the multiple-crisis situation appeared to call for a more rapid set of responses than the status-constrained, ritual-encrusted system was likely to be able to deliver. The external consultants regularly cautioned against hasty moves and inflated expectations. They were occasionally joined in these entreaties by the in-house change agents (including the newly hired psychologist), but the development group (later the OD unit) also felt a strong need to "get things moving while the time was ripe." Thus, while the retreat generated a great deal of enthusiasm, disappointment had to follow as it was discovered that most of the structural, policy, and procedural problems taken to the retreat had been brought back intact, and no real machinery had been devised to deal with them. Expectations were much more effectively managed regarding the training program. The sessions were presented as "introductory" and the need for follow-up clearly stressed. Even here, however, some administrators and supervisors had ideas for changes which proved difficult if not impossible to implement. The role of the OD unit has been legitimated, but its mandate seems clearly limited to the lower reaches of the organization.

Change Techniques A wide range of change efforts have been attempted in organization B. The outside consultants interviewed members of the top team and made an effort to get the group to confront its own attitudes, perceptions, and priorities at the beginning of the program. By and large these efforts were unsuccessful. Although there was some increased awareness of basic barriers to improved performance, the pressure to move ahead was strong and the team members never confronted most of these concerns. At the retreat, data on attitudes and perceptions were collected and discussed enthusiastically, but no machinery was put in place to pursue and implement points of possible agreement. The development program itself was viewed as a long-term change mechanism, and it too included some experiential sessions (data feedback on participants' leadership attitudes, role-play sessions on joint goal setting and appraisal, etc.). In the team-training sessions requested by various units, the OD staff members and outside consultants have used a variety of techniques to help these groups gain awareness of their own processes and to confront and remove barriers to effective performance. Most of these efforts have been fairly low key and overtly noncoercive, which is probably appropriate given the nature of the system and its state of readiness for change.

Sustaining Mechanisms   As the external and internal strife have subsided, the OD unit has found itself increasingly alone in the effort to muster and channel energy for change. The management-development course has sustained some interest in improved administrative practices (as evidenced by continuing requests for team-training sessions) but, as noted by the OD unit head, the top of the system has gradually withdrawn from the change effort. Thus it has become increasingly difficult to get approval for policy and practice changes initiated at the lower levels.

ORGANIZATION C—(A Small-Scale Success)   Organization C is a small (150-member) manufacturer of electronic components. The founder, now president and major stockholder, has purposely kept the organization small by avoiding opportunities to pursue major contracts which, in his words, would "have changed the whole character of the firm and made us vulnerable to major swings in employment and profits." Most of the firm's employees are engineers and technicians, with only thirty to forty production employees (about half of whom are women). The president is an electrical engineer who considers himself a progressive manager and has attended a number of executive-development programs and seminars at nearby universities. Two years ago at one of these programs he became intrigued with a discussion of OD approaches and invited the discussion leader, a professor at his own alma mater, to have lunch with him and his top-management group. At the lunch, the president asked the consultant how he would "go about developing organization C" and was a bit dismayed with the reply, "I'm not sure, what would you do?" Over coffee, the president grasped the intent of the question and began to mention a number of problems that concerned him. As he mentioned these, several other members of his group voiced similar concerns. The professor noticed two of the members were rather silent during the discussion and asked them for their views. Reluctantly, they indicated some areas of disagreement. The president again picked up the professor's intent and commented to the group, "I guess we have just had lesson 1."

The luncheon was followed by an invitation to "join us on a regular basis and see what we can do." The professor agreed, if the group would promise to read a number of both critical and supportive selections on OD and then set aside half a day to discuss whether and how they should continue.

Most of the group members did the suggested reading, and the opening session operated like a seminar with informed questions concerning change techniques, conditions for effective change, how to keep a program going, etc. The professor pointed out numerous "failures" in OD and helped the group analyze why these occurred. Finally, the group moved to the question of how these "failure scenarios" could be avoided. A number of key "sign posts" were identified and discussed. At the end of the meeting, the motivation to proceed was high, and the group agreed to meet again the following week. It was also agreed that the consultant would meet with the several members individually between these sessions to get acquainted, get their views, and answer further questions.

In the following session, one of the group members immediately launched into an elaborate plan for an attitude survey throughout the firm and was interrupted by the president who had suggestions for modifying the plan. Several other group members said nothing but looked toward the consultant who walked over to the board and wrote out an anonymous quote from one of his interviews: "This group is bright as hell, but half the time you can't get a word in edgewise and when you leave the room you may be more confused than when you came in."

The president shook his head and said, "Lesson 2!" "No," replied another member, "Lesson 1 repeated." For the next hour the group discussed with the consultant how they could get around their tendency to rush ahead without stifling creativity. They finally agreed to ask one of the members at each meeting to play the role of process consultant—to stop the group when he sensed they were moving faster than consensus allowed and to implement any of several techniques they had been reading about to improve group process. The professor agreed to play that role for the remainder of the first meeting and the next one and then to pass it along to another member. It was agreed that for the time being the professor would meet with their team every two weeks and that starting the following month he and two of his colleagues would begin meeting with the work groups below each of the top-team members. They discussed how these sessions would be implemented and agreed that the same general entry format used with their group would be followed. They also agreed that the basic goal of each "intervention" would be to surface and deal with the issues confronting each group while working toward a development program for the entire system.

The work with the top team moved ahead smoothly, with noticeable improvements in the willingness to both express and hear out dissident views. By the end of the sixth meeting, the group agreed that each member should be a process consultant, rather than having only one appointed member. By this time, the group was regularly using such devices as listing alternatives without evaluation and pausing in the midst of discussions to write out feelings and opinions individually and then collecting and posting these for evaluation.

At the lower levels, entry was smooth in four of the six groups, and marginally effective in accounting and marketing. The problem in the accounting group was centered on the issue of a new cost-control procedure which was "getting absolutely no cooperation." This problem was taken back to the top team and became the focus of discussion there and subsequently in several of the other groups. An interdepartmental task force was formed to go over the new procedures (they had gotten only surface attention before) and to determine what accounting's real needs were for reporting purposes and what the various departments actually needed to guide their operations ("Lesson 3," someone announced when the task group was formed). In marketing, a major morale problem surfaced over the role of marketing-group members in the design and pricing of special-product orders. Again, a joint engineering-marketing committee was formed to work on these problems, and the president agreed to abide by a request that he "keep his damn hands off" minor customer-relations issues, for the time being at least.

The only major disagreement during the next year, as the process unfolded down the organization, occurred in production. The director of production and his supervisory group wanted to move rapidly into job enrichment and work-team control over training, rating, job assignments, and even selection (the desired program looked remarkably like that in a new plant which the consultant had visited and had discussed casually with the director of the production unit). The consultant found himself in the position of arguing against something he had praised, on the grounds that the move was too much too fast and would overtax both the available consultation resources and the system's ability to adjust. The consultant argued that such an effort needed a year or more of careful groundwork in the department, working through all contingencies with those involved (e.g., the work team's responsibility to avoid discrimination in selection and job assignments) and tracing out the implications of these moves for other units. The consultant's view was upheld, and the development effort is proceeding, but at a slower pace than the production-unit manager would like, and his relationship with the consultant and several members of the top team is still undergoing repair.

At the most recent meeting of the group, the president and the top-team members shared generally positive feelings about the OD effort and the president turned to the consultant and said, "OK, what do we do next?" The consultant's reply, "That's a good question, what do you think you should do?" brought a general laugh from the group.

Analysis of the OD Effort in Organization C

Entry Entry conditions in organization C seem almost ideal, but they did not occur simply by chance. The consultant, from the beginning, helped the group by example, by assignments, and by open, nonselling discussions to become informed consumers of his services. Note that the group and its individual members would have moved much more rapidly than he allowed them to do. His constant reminders of the dangers of "innoculation" and falling into the "syndicate model" were heeded and most major mistakes were avoided. Note that a ready-made "curriculum" was available in organization C, in the form of the issues in accounting and marketing. These provided a chance for the top-team members to learn with real problems and to test out their learning.

Change Techniques The consultant and his colleagues relied here primarily on process observation and feedback while the groups read about, discussed, and used a number of process conventions. In the main, the consultant's real role here was helping groups to surface problems and then guiding them through the system for solution, using these problems and the problem-solving processes as learning devices at each stage.

Sustaining Mechanisms At the time the case closed, no formal sustaining mechanisms had been developed. The issue had been raised with the consultant by several members of the top team, who were concerned when he announced that he felt he should meet with the group only "three or four times a year." The accounting group was discussing the feasibility of some form of human asset accounting (an approach to the measurement of the accumulated investment in organization members, primarily through training and development activities, developed at the University of Michigan and referenced at the end of this chapter) but no plan had yet been formulated. Similarly, the personnel department was considering semiannual surveys of member attitudes and perceptions throughout the system. The consultant's view was that either or both of these techniques might prove useful but only if the system was prepared to really make use of the data generated.

ORGANIZATION D—(A Limited Application of the Managerial Grid)
Organization D is a small- to medium-sized agency of the federal government, with members located throughout the fifty states. In recent years the
agency has been attempting to make the transition from a regulatory-
controlling function to a more service-oriented role. The change in mission
has caused some strain within its ranks and has forced some re-evaluation of
the previous quasi-military training-and-development focus which gave little
attention to modern concepts of administration. Three years ago, the training
director of the agency and two of his regional subordinates attended a public
session on the managerial grid. They were enthusiastic about the grid
approach to OD (see Figure 12-1), feeling that it combined training in
managerial concepts with the machinery for policy and practice review and
change. Approval was obtained to try out the approach in two regions, and
the regional training staffs were instructed to attend grid training sessions
and to arrange for grid consultants to assist them in implementing the
program. The consultants ran the introductory (phase I) sessions of the grid
with the top administrative group in each of the two regions, with the agency
training-staff members sitting in as either participants or observers. The
opening sessions were a bit stiff, but the participants began to unfreeze a bit
as they discovered that the learning exercises were less threatening than they
had feared. By the end of the phase I session, most of the participants were
"talking the language," i.e., joking with one another about 1,9 and 9,1

Communication	**Planning**
1. Grid seminar Organization members learn theories of behavior on a one-by-one basis.	4. Developing an ideal strategic model Executive leaders specify in terms of business logic the intellectual foundations of the firm.
2. Teamwork development Work teams apply grid theories to increase individual, interpersonal, and team effectiveness.	5. Planning and implementation Line management planning teams use management science and technology to redesign each business segment and thereafter to change its operations according to the ideal strategic model.
3. Intergroup development Organized units that must cooperate to achieve results apply grid theories to increase effectiveness with which they coordinate effort.	6. Systematic critique The corporate excellence rubric is used on pre, intermediate, and post bases to review, consolidate, and evaluate progress made and to plan next steps of operational improvement.

Figure 12-1 The six phases of Grid® organization development and corporate excellence. The management grid® is a descriptive graph illustrating variations in management styles depending on the amount of concern shown for people and for performance. For example, a 1,9 manager has high concern for people but gives little attention to output, while a 9,1 manager is just the opposite. [From Robert Blake and Jane Mouton, *Corporate Excellence Through Grid Organization Development* (Houston: Gulf, 1968), p. 9]

behaviors and considering the impacts of such styles on their subordinates and the agencies with whom they interacted. Clear approval was given to the training group to begin phase I sessions with teams in the field "at a pace commensurate with scheduling needs and available resources." In fact, the training director of one of the regions got "more support than he wanted" in the form of a memo from the regional managers to field units *requesting* that they give "immediate, full, and complete cooperation to this important training effort." Upon hearing about that memo, the training director in the other region worked with his top official to word a somewhat more diplomatic and informative request.

In both regions, the training effort has proceeded more slowly than was hoped. Peak service periods had to be avoided in order to have the training teams intact, and vacations and transfers inhibited scheduling in other periods. Nevertheless, within two years about 80 percent of the field units had been through phase I of the grid and about 20 percent had begun phase II. In the meantime, however, the agency training director had retired and his replacement, while willing to continue the grid effort in the experimental regions, did not share his predecessor's enthusiasm for the program. Thus, promised increases in funding for the efforts were not forthcoming and new programs were begun which competed with the grid for attention. The programs are continuing in both regions, but the training directors anticipate that it may now take as much as two more years for the bulk of the groups to get through phase II, and by then "many field units will have had so many transfers that most of the continuity in the program will have been lost."

Analysis of the OD Effort in Organization D

Entry   The beginnings of the grid OD effort in organization D do not show ideal entry conditions. The participants were given little choice concerning their involvement, and the field units in particular tended to receive fairly abrupt notice of this training requirement. Nevertheless, given that the basic atmosphere of the agency was autocratic, the entry procedure was not viewed as anything out of the ordinary. Moreover, the heavily instrumented, highly structured format of the grid program allowed the extensive use of in-house training personnel and apparently was well suited to the expectations of most participants. Note, however, that the upper reaches of the organization (above the regional level) approved of but were not involved in the program.

Change Techniques   As noted earlier, the grid program begins with a phase which, in many respects, approximates an instrumented family laboratory-training session. Participants give and receive feedback on their leadership styles and managerial attitudes. The conceptual framework of the grid provides both a means of describing existing attitudes and styles and an implicit prescription concerning the most desirable approach to management, i.e., the 9,9 style. In subsequent phases, participants examine and develop a plan for improvement of their own operation and their interactions with other units, culminating in an organizationwide plan for improvement. To the extent that groups follow the planned and instrumented format in these phases, they test their plans and planning process against the grid concepts and thus receive reinforcements for positive changes. Again, however, with most groups in organization D moving only through phase I, substantial changes in behaviors, policies, and practices could not be predicted.

Sustaining Mechanisms There were no formal sustaining mechanisms (other than the continuity in the grid program itself) built into the OD effort in organization D. In fact, the program, as later events indicated, was heavily dependent on the support of one individual in agency headquarters. His departure left the regional training managers as the primary support for the effort. It now seems highly unlikely that the program will ever reach a stage of development large enough to have substantial impact on agency policies and practices, particularly since there are no forces in place at headquarters level to support and approve change growing out of the grid OD effort.

ORGANIZATION E—(Success and "Failure" with the Data Feedback Approach) Organization E is a large, nationwide manufacturer and distributor of consumer goods. About six years ago, several members of the top-management group became interested in a survey-feedback approach to OD. Among the pioneers in this approach were members of the Institute for Social Research at the University of Michigan. Extensive work with numerous organizations using the data-feedback approach has been carried out there, much of it through the Institute's Center for Research in the Utilization of Scientific Knowledge, under the direction of Floyd Mann, an early advocate of the feedback approach. From discussions with Professor Mann and his colleagues and from involvement with them in some of their activities, I can describe a typical survey-feedback operation and its key steps* as follows:

1   Extensive discussions are held with top management to explain the survey-feedback approach and establish the conditions (timing, location,

*These steps are described in more detail in Floyd C. Mann, "Studying and Creating Change," in W. G. Bennis, K. D. Benne, and R. Chin, *The Planning of Change* (New York: Holt, Rinehart, and Winston, 1961), pp. 605-613.

etc.) under which it will be carried out and to obtain their approval to begin the process.

2 Key members of the top-management team and specialists from other levels (e.g., members of the personnel department, in-house behavioral scientists, etc.) are involved in the planning of the initial survey covering all members of the organization or units involved.

3 Rosters are prepared so that data collected from a work team or unit can be reassembled, aggregated, and fed back directly to that group.

4 Questionnaires are administered to all organization members. This is frequently done through group administration during work hours.

5 Aggregate data for the entire organization (not identifying specific members of work teams) is fed back to the top-management team and is discussed with the aid of the researchers.

6 At each subsequent level, work teams or units (the superior and his immediate subordinates) examine the data supplied by their own members and discuss the implications of their own (aggregated—not individual) responses and the action steps which might be taken in line with these implications. A member of the research-consulting team usually helps the superior prepare for the meeting with his subordinates and facilitates their analysis of the data and their movement toward action steps.

Approval was achieved at corporate headquarters for an experimental OD effort in one of the sales and distribution regions of the firm. Corporate officials explained to the regional managers their interest in and enthusiasm for the program and all indicated their willingness to have the experimental effort in their area. The region chosen for the initial effort was one in which the regional manager appeared highly receptive and cooperative.

The effort began in the region with a two-day training program for the top regional team in which concepts of organizational behavior and leadership were illustrated and analyzed through lectures, case discussions, and role-play exercises. In addition, the basic OD approach, involving a systemwide survey of member attitudes and perceptions concerning current operations, and data feedback sessions in which each work team would examine its own views, was discussed in detail. The facts that all data would remain anonymous and that no one but the work team itself would have access to its own data were stressed. It was pointed out that work teams would probably not only make changes in their own behaviors as the result of this instrumented introspection but would likely have suggestions for changes in policies and practices outside their units. The top team agreed that it would be essential that these suggestions be given full hearing and that every effort be made to comply with them and/or to work out acceptable alternatives. In subsequent sessions, the top team worked with the consultant to plan for the initial systemwide survey and gained additional insights into the OD program goals and techniques in the process, particularly as they worked through how best to present and introduce the effort at lower levels. The need for initial training sessions similar to their own at each level was acknowledged and sufficient time and funds were budgeted for this activity.

The survey was carried out and the data processed to provide an overview of responses from the entire system and separate data packages for each work team. Training sessions were held at each level, as planned, while the data were being processed. Beginning with the top groups, each manager had a prefeedback planning session with a member of the consulting team and then ran his own feedback session for his subordinates, with a consultant present to aid with the process. In the typical group, participants were initially reluctant to comment on and discuss the data before them, but with appropriate interventions from the consultants and the well-coached supportiveness of the superior, most groups moved along rapidly in the latter stages of the day-long session. Perceptions were discussed and clarified and the action plan developed to remove barriers to effective group performance. Many suggestions for changes in systemwide policies and practices were uncovered and brought to the attention of appropriate groups at higher levels. Most of these were responded to quickly and this immediately reinforced the positive attitudes generated in the feedback sessions— something was actually being done. In many groups positive performance effects were quickly visible, and many members began to talk about the "improvements which would be shown on the next survey," even though it was as yet unscheduled and certainly was many months away.

Given the extensive attention to training, planning, and preparation at each level, the initial survey and feedback effort took over three months to complete throughout the system. However, within a year from the beginning of the program, the actual dollar performance of the region had improved significantly. Some portion of the improvement was clearly attributable simply to increased motivation, but many linkages could be drawn directly to actual changes in policies and practices at all levels.

Corporate headquarters was delighted with these results and immediately approved additional funds for continued survey feedback efforts in the experimental region. Moreover, strong pressure was mounting to extend the program to all regions of the organization as rapidly as possbile, including corporate-level personnel. The consultant was pleased with the response but cautioned against moving so rapidly that resources might be overextended and prefeedback training and planning curtailed. He argued for a repetition of the "experimental" effort in a second region and reluctantly agreed to a slightly scaled-down time frame. Pressures to "move ahead" were also felt by the regional manager chosen for this second effort, and the training and planning sessions carried a bit of a "yes, yes, we know all that, let's get going" atmosphere. Even so, the effort proceeded generally as scheduled, although one level had a foreshortened training effort, the feedback sessions were planned so that the outside consultants could not be present at as many sessions as they had hoped, and greater reliance was placed on members of the in-house training group.

Dollar performance gains also were achieved in the second region, but they were not as great as those in the original system. Further, the number of suggestions for policy and practice changes was diminished and fewer were actually implemented. The overall program was still judged by corporate headquarters to be highly successful, and pressures for rapid implementation in other areas were now very high. These pressures were increased by the fact that, despite the gains made in the experimental regions, overall system performance was not up to expectations, and there was a general feeling of "a need for something to give us a real competitive boost."

By this point, the consultant was aware that top management's time perspective toward the program was changing and that the original discussions of a sustained effort over a several-year period were competing with desires for immediate implementation "to complete the program" and move on to something else.

By now, implementation in a third region was planned by corporate officials but with a much-reduced budget and time frame. Training sessions were reduced or eliminated, and feedback was planned in conjunction with scheduled work meetings over the space of two weeks. Training and feedback sessions thus were frequently hastily prepared and run, and much less attention was given to follow-up activities concerning policy and practice changes at all levels.

Dollar results from this latter effort were not significant, but this remained difficult to interpret, given that the entire system continued to lag behind expectations (with the exception of the original experimental region). The consultant was concerned about the lack of impact in this last region and about his inability to move ahead as planned at the corporate level.

Analysis of the OD Effort in Organization E

Entry   The initial conditions in organization E were quite supportive for a positive change effort. The corporate level, while not actually involved in change itself, was supportive and recognized the need to allow experimentation in the regions. In the original experimental region, the rapport between the consultant and the regional executives was excellent, and the level of understanding concerning what the program could and could not be expected to achieve was high. Moreover, the top group recognized the crucial role their behavior would play in the effort and was actively engaged in planning for the entire effort. In the subsequent applications, entry conditions deteriorated, and the OD effort in some instances began to take on the appearance of a one-shot, "sales-promotional" activity. The consultant's resources were overtaxed and both training and follow-up activity was minimal.

Change Techniques   The survey-feedback approach, as indicated, relies on the data-discussion sessions to "unfreeze" current attitudes and behaviors and to provide the initial format for a continuing team-training effort. The initial training and coaching sessions are essential in providing a supportive atmosphere for feedback and also in the supplying of the conceptual framework within which action programs can be evaluated.

Sustaining Mechanisms   The data-feedback approach has a built-in sustaining mechanism in the form of continued annual surveys. However, these may be reduced to the level of perfunctory exercises unless actual changes result from the initial efforts. In the absence of sufficient training, coaching, and follow up, action programs are likely to be shallow and perhaps ineffective (as seemed to be the case in some of the efforts in the second and third regions described here). Further, support at the corporate level, which had sustained the initial efforts, began to change in nature and intensity. Support was still there, but it was not sufficient to lead to major changes in total system performance.

A CRITIQUE OF OD TODAY

The five cases presented above give, I believe, a realistic picture of organization development as it exists today, illustrating both the accomplishments and shortcomings associated with various efforts to apply behavioral science concepts in organizations. In the following paragraphs we will move back from these case studies and attempt a broader appraisal, considering both objective and subjective criteria and evidence.

Objective Evidence

To this point, no definitive appraisal of the effectiveness of organization development can be made using objective data. Success stories abound concerning each of the approaches described above—the grid, the survey-feedback approach, systemwide team training, etc.—but these in no way constitute scientific proof. Most of the documentation, where it exists, concerns single case studies, frequently carried out by or through those involved in the change efforts. Case studies provide little opportunity for effective control of factors which may be as important to the outcome as the OD effort itself, and the regular charge that OD successes are nothing more than "Hawthorne effects" can seldom be refuted. Moreover, with much of the data reported by participants in or advocates of OD programs, failures probably tend to be forgotten or rationalized and truly experimental designs are avoided as being possibly detrimental to the organization involved. Finally, even longitudinal studies of the sort attempted at Michigan have difficulty in establishing cause-effect relationships in the face of the complexity and dynamism inherent in any system (further accentuated by change programs) and the frequent shifts in development timing and strategy necessitated by real-world contingencies.

Given these problems, the comparative, at least partially controlled research which has been done has tended to focus not on total OD efforts but on the efficacy of specific-change techniques. By far the bulk of this research has focused on the T-group, which is not surprising since that was one of the earliest and perhaps the most dramatic approach to organizational change. Here the evidence, or the lack of it, clearly lies with the critics. That is, there are few undisputed findings illustrating a clear linkage between traditional T-group training and changes in managerial practice and organizational performance. Although the extreme claims of damage to individuals and to organizations as the result of T-groups are also exaggerated and largely unsubstantiated, the less-dramatic charge of "no visible impact" seems to have been upheld. The proponents of T-groups respond by acknowledging the lack of "hard" data but point out that much of the direct change expected from a T-group session is in the attitudes and perceptions of the participants, and self-reported changes in these variables is disallowed by many critics. Moreover, the proponents continue, changed attitudes and behaviors require reinforcement in the "home" environment and unless the organization follows through by sending most of its members to training sessions, it cannot expect major impacts. Finally, many early proponents of T-groups now acknowledge that, in the face of these barriers to transfer and reinforcement, team training with actual work groups may be preferable.

The lack of "scientific proof" that OD efforts lead to positive changes in organizational performance does not imply that we conclude the converse—that OD efforts do not lead to improved performance. There is, in fact, more than enough "anecdotal" evidence to warrant the *belief* that such efforts may, under favorable circumstances, result in major benefits. Moreover, the difficulties involved in "proving" cause-effect linkages in this area do not imply that such efforts should be abandoned. Such research, even with inconclusive results, is beneficial in that it (1) keeps attention focused on key variables and the mechanisms by which they are or may be related, and (2) provides the impetus for practitioners to improve their concepts and techniques and for theorists to expand and improve their models. This last point is extremely important because current decisions on complex behavioral issues are more often guided by beliefs (theories, models, etc.) than by empirical evidence.

A "Subjective" Appraisal of OD

If OD efforts are difficult, if not impossible, to evaluate "objectively," we can at least hold current practices up against the theoretical framework from which they are presumably drawn. To do this we must first synthesize from various sources and summarize the crucial elements of this framework.

In a sentence, OD theory holds that organizations (members, particularly managers) must learn to be aware of their processes and to use this awareness to constantly improve the alignment of their sociotechnical systems with the requirements and opportunities inherent in their internal and external environments. That is, OD is not designed to develop business but to develop the organization to do business (or to provide a service, to govern, etc.). In a limited sense, this premise is not unlike that of scientific management, which sought to develop technical competence, or of human relations, which sought to develop responsiveness to social and egoistic needs in order to enhance member cooperativeness with technical requirements. In fact, early OD concepts and practices have been criticized, probably appropriately, as being little more than "advanced human relations." In a broader sense, OD goes well beyond these earlier efforts in scope (focusing on the entire sociotechnical system rather than on limited aspects of either one or the other), sophistication (rejecting simplistic notions of "one best way" and "happiness leads to performance"), and, most important, in its prime change mechanism (development occurs as members learn experientially rather than by following the dictums of engineers or personnel specialists).

It is this last point that gives us the clearest conceptual clue concerning the differences between OD and earlier development approaches. If OD is truly to be built on an experiential learning model, then the role of the OD consultant (either an "outsider" or a member of some internal OD group or unit) is definable. His task is neither to "teach" behavioral concepts nor to prescribe behavioral or attitudinal changes. Rather, his role is that of managing learning opportunities—creating and capturing situations in which organization members can examine the implications of their actions and experiment with changed behaviors.

This learning model carries at least three important implications beyond those concerning the role of the consultant.

First, *learning requires readiness—motivation to learn and some prior base to which the new awareness can be attached.* Note that this requirement was clearly not met in the case of organization A, where the participants went through the three-day program to "get their card punched," nor in the limited success regions of organization E, where time pressures and budget constraints limited member involvement in planning and foreshortened the data-feedback sessions. Only in organization C and in the first, "experimental" region in organization E do we see sufficient attention given to the requirement of readiness for learning.

Second, *learning requires sequencing—a series of appropriately sized opportunities to explore and experiment with new concepts and behaviors.* Again, the three-day learning lab attended by the top team of organization A probably contained more new concepts than they were able to handle, even if they had been motivated, and, as pointed out, follow-up sessions which might have given meaning to some of the concepts were aborted. Similarly, the training director in organization D recognized that the lack of resources and support to move field units through the latter phases of the grid OD program was probably resulting in much of the phase I learning fading away from lack of reinforcement. Finally, the requirement of sequencing was largely ignored in the last region scheduled for survey feedback in organization E, where hurried coverage and lack of follow-up precluded any real impact.

Third, *learning requires resources—substantial investments of time and money and continued evidence of high priorities for process evaluation and change.* Most of the case experiences described earlier illustrated the lack of adequate time and resources for meaningful development activities. They were evident only in the experimental region of organization E, where both the field resources and top-level attention in the form of rapid response to change suggestions demonstrated high priority for the OD effort, and in organization C, where the president's continued involvement in the program guaranteed the presence of resources and priority.

The fact that only one of the five OD efforts described here (and part of one other) appeared to meet the requirements of current OD theory is not, in my view, a distortion, proportionally, of what is happening generally today. Moreover, these proportions should not be at all surprising. Our discussion in earlier chapters indicated that most managers evidenced *traditional* or *human relations* views, and, as suggested, the targets of OD efforts seem much more closely aligned with the *human resources* model. To the extent that managers' views are reflected in the character of their organizations, powerful forces are at work to prevent the application of the OD model described here. For example, many organizations, in line with human relations prescriptions, have a history of repeated but minimal investments in development "programs" designed to improve cooperation and reduce resistance without tampering with existing structure or process. Organization-development efforts in these environments carry a heavy burden of suspicion that they are simply "this year's model" of what has come and gone many times in the past. Such suspicions are quickly made credible by top-management lip service without involvement and by "sales effort promotion" which quickly fades as the realities of change are surfaced.

Moreover, OD practitioners, particularly internal consultants, are, under these circumstances, frequently seduced by "programmatic" pressures into violations of their own model. Requirements of readiness and sequencing are only partially met in order to "get the effort rolling while the time is ripe." Flushed with success from an OD effort in one unit (where resources were adequate and learning groundwork was laid), the OD department too often attempts to routinize its approach and apply it rapidly and broadly across the system. The results are predictably limited and the scar tissue from one more glancing jab of applied behavioral science is thickened. As one internal consultant remarked at an OD workshop, "I have just realized that the most successful move I've made in the past year is the prevention of expansion of our OD effort." This tendency toward seduction provides a good argument for having an outside consultant to the OD unit charged with the task of constantly holding the requirements of the learning model up against the unit's efforts.

The Role of Top Management in OD Programs

The lack of congruence between the requirements of the learning model presumably underlying OD efforts and OD in practice is frequently attributed to "the absence of top-management support." Clearly, as our cases illustrated, top management's role is substantial, and it has become axiomatic in many OD circles to note that "of course, any effort must begin at the top." Despite the apparent logic and clarity of this axiom, much misunderstanding exists concerning the relationship of top management to OD. One interpretation of this axiom pictures top management's role as that of giving initial approval to the effort and then continuing to supply it with funds. Another interpretation pictures the consultant working with top management until it is fully developed and then moving down to the next level of the hierarchy. There are serious shortcomings in both these views.

First of all, if an OD program is at all successful, top management cannot merely supply funds. A successful OD program will quickly generate requests for changes in policies and practices which demand top-level approval, and failure to respond thoughtfully and quickly can immediately doom the effort. Under experimental conditions, top management can give prior, blanket approval to changes resulting from an OD effort in a limited area of the organization. However, changes are difficult to contain within a given subsystem, and any reversion to old policies at the end of the "experiment" brings long-lasting damage.

Second, top management cannot be developed in a vacuum. A creative OD consultant can use top management's own decision-making behavior to generate limited learning, but the real curriculum for top management is the system below them. As illustrated in the case of organization C, top management got the chance to test its understanding of new concepts and behaviors when issues in the various subsystems were surfaced. The consultant had created a readiness on their part to learn, but they needed his help most in examining the processes by which they would solve these problems generated by OD efforts at lower levels.

What is suggested here is that top management ideally should be directly involved in the OD process from the beginning but that its learning will be sequential. The effort does not proceed in lock step down the system but flows down into the system and then up again, with top-management members learning not only from their own internal processes but also from being confronted with the impact of their behaviors on those below them.

A Final Criticism of OD

Our objective and subjective appraisals of OD theory and practice have not dealt directly with one important and frequently raised criticism. Moving away from its somewhat less-ambitious beginnings, OD has more and more billed itself as a "total systems approach dealing with all facets of the system and creating an improved responsiveness to environmental demands." To many, this claim is rather grandly overstated. Such critics point out that many OD efforts result in only a few policy and role changes and in only a few instances are major structural changes or redesigns of technical systems associated with an OD effort. Moreover, this criticism continues, the most crucial decisions in an organization's life may have little or nothing to do with its internal processes but may concern its relationship with other organizations in its environment. Here, they claim, the linkage between OD efforts and crucial issues of growth and survival are quite obscure. This criticism is not trivial and deserves detailed attention. We will meet this need in the next chapter where we explore a general model of organizational adjustment to environmental demands.

BIBLIOGRAPHY

Argyris, Chris, *Management and Organizational Development* (New York: McGraw-Hill, 1971).

Beckhard, Richard, *Organization Development: Strategies and Models* (Reading, Mass.: Addison-Wesley, 1969).

Blake, Robert and Jane Mouton, *Building a Dynamic Corporation through Grid Organization Development* (Reading, Mass.: Addison-Wesley, 1969).

French, Wendell L. and Cecil H. Bell, *Organization Development* (Englewood Cliffs, N.J.: Prentice-Hall, 1973).

Friedlander, Frank and L. David Brown, "Organization Development," *Annual Review of Psychology*, vol. 25, pp. 313–341 (1974).

Harrison, Roger, "Some Criteria for Choosing the Depth of Organizational Intervention Strategy," paper delivered at the Fourth International Congress of Group Psychotherapy; in David A. Kolb, Irwin M. Rubin, and James McIntyre, *Organizational Psychology* (Englewood Cliffs, N.J.: Prentice-Hall, 1971), pp. 355–368.

Marrow, Alfred J., David G. Bowers, and Stanley E. Seashore, *Management by Participation: Creating a Climate for Personal and Organizational Development* (New York: Harper & Row, 1967).

Schein, Edgar, *Process Consultation: Its Role in Organization Development* (Reading, Mass.: Addison-Wesley, 1969).

Walton, Richard E., *Interpersonal Peacemaking: Confrontations and Third Party Consultation* (Reading, Mass.: Addison-Wesley, 1969).

Chapter 13

Organizational Adjustments to Environmental Demands

Chapter 12 closed with the unanswered criticism that organization development, despite its proponents' claims, seldom deals directly with the total system—that is, that the bulk of OD concepts and techniques focus on superior-subordinate and peer relationships and ignore or provide little guidance for changes in the basic structure and process of organizations or their relationships with their external environments. Moreover, with minor changes in wording, this indictment is frequently drawn to include the whole body of behavioral science, management theory, and concepts which have given birth to OD.

On the surface, at least, this charge is difficult to refute. Much of the literature of management and organizational behavior, particularly that born in the human relations era, deals with the removal of interpersonal barriers to effective performance in existing structures. Moreover, few modern management theorists are as specific in their structural and procedural prescriptions as were Weber, Taylor, and the early developers of "management principles." Finally, it is clearly part of the stated OD ethic that the consultant neither evaluate nor define changes for the existing system but rather aid it in freeing up and developing its own ability to guide its destiny.

It is easy enough, of course, to respond to this criticism in kind by pointing out that the Weberian bureaucratic model, scientific management, and human relations theories were all similarly guilty of focusing on *how a given* set of goals should be accomplished and ignoring, for the most part, the processes by which the organization was/is aligned or realigned with its environment. Similarly, it can be argued that these early approaches were pointed in their prescriptions simply because they frequently avoided explicit recognition of situational contingencies and inter- and intrapersonal variability. Nevertheless, responses of this sort serve primarily to stimulate a burst of countering fire which further impedes careful analysis. What is needed is a conceptual framework into which these changes and responses can be fitted and evaluated. An effort to construct the beginning of such a framework follows.

AN ILLUSTRATIVE MODEL OF ORGANIZATIONAL ADJUSTMENT

Two initial, not particularly demanding, assumptions are essential to this attempt to place in perspective organizational adjustment to environmental demands. First, we assume that most organizations are forced to meet the test of some economic and/or social criteria in order to survive. Clearly, depending on size and other determinants of vulnerability, some may elude evaluation or ignore demands longer than others (and a few, the cynic notes, seem to have escaped entirely). Nevertheless, it seems reasonable to imagine that organizations (their managers) will attempt to monitor and respond to their environments in order to survive and, hopefully, to flourish. Second, we assume that, given options, organizations (their managers) will choose the least demanding or costly adjustment appropriate to the demands of their environment. Both of these assumptions, particularly the second, will prove troublesome to make operational and maintain, but they do provide a beginning rationale for the model illustrated in Figure 13-1.

As shown in Figure 13-1, we are associating stable-accepting environmental conditions with relatively minor procedural adjustments, while major shifts in goals and structure are linked with uncertain, demanding, or threatening conditions in the environment. In between, we assume that changes become more demanding-costly as they involve larger and more concretely defined segments of the total system—e.g., that a shift from functional to product-line organization is more demand-

Types or classes of adjustments

(1)	(2)	(3)	(4)	(5)
Procedural adjustments	Managerial policy and process adjustments	Intra–departmental structure and process adjustments	Inter–departmental (major) structure and process adjustments	Supra or extra organizational adjustments
Management determined changes in work procedures, information flow, scheduling, routing, etc.	Changes in the amount or type of participation in decision making, goal setting, e.g., MBO, quality responsibility, etc.	Changes in job design, e.g., job enrichment, work role and work flow, work group involvement in scheduling and quality control, role relationships, etc.	Changes in degree of centralization of major decisions, functional vs. product arrangements, mechanisms for interdepartmental coordination, relations of subsystems to various aspects of the environment, etc.	Changes in basic product or service offered or clientele, type of ownership, merger, dissolution, etc.

Perceived environmental conditions

Clientele, resources, regulatory agencies, competitiors, etc.

Stable	Somewhat unsettled	Turbulent
Known or predictable demands, acceptable environmental responses to product or service offered, low perceived threat to survival, etc.	Indications of some shifts in demand or acceptance, perception of possible distant threats to survival, etc.	Unclear or uncertain demands, lack of acceptance of product or services, high perceived threat to survival, etc.

Figure 13-1 Organizational adjustments to environmental demands

ing-costly than the redesign of some jobs within a single department and that such redesign is in turn more demanding-costly than some forms of increased subordinate participation in unit decision making. Concurrently, we portray the more demanding-costly adjustments as being triggered by increasingly turbulent (demanding) environmental circumstances. Stated another way, we imagine managers as being relatively unexcited about undertaking anything beyond minor tinkering with a system which appears to be running well but becoming increasingly willing to undertake preventive maintenance or corrective action if symptoms of real or potential danger are perceived. Conversely, we would imagine that managers would be ill-disposed to consider a tune-up as an appropriate adjustment to the discovery that the system is on the wrong side of the freeway.

We should quickly note here that our environmental conditions and adjustment mechanisms continua probably aren't really continuous or unidimensional. Some process or policy adjustments may be (or may be perceived to be) far more demanding-costly than some major structural changes, and turbulence in one portion of the environment may be far less of a real or perceived threat than turbulence in another portion. Nevertheless, admitting these frailties, it is fairly easy to illustrate some fits between this framework and real-world situations. For example, the recent rash of mergers and changes in ownership structure among brokerage houses can be viewed as responses to rapidly deteriorating environmental conditions. In a somewhat less-dramatic fashion, many textbook publishing firms, in the face of increasingly fragmented and uncertain markets, have made major structural changes in an effort to increase adaptability, and some international labor unions appear to be reversing the trend toward centralization in an effort to become more responsive to needs and demands at the local level. Nearer the stable end of the continuum, a number of universities which remained relatively untouched by the major student disorders of the 1960s nevertheless responded to portents of potential turbulence by increasing the amount and kind of student participation in campus decision making.

OD EFFORTS AND THE ADJUSTMENT MODEL

Linking back to our examples in Chapter 11, none of the organizations engaged in OD, or what were called OD efforts, were faced with major environmental turbulence. Their environmental conditions could be described as ranging from relatively stable to somewhat unsettled but not severely threatening. Risking valid criticism, we can argue that these organizations can be arrayed much as they appeared (in alphabetical order, A to E) from stability toward turbulence. Recall that organization A (the region of the nationwide service organization) was performing adequately on all measures and its top-management group saw little reason, other than mild corporate-level pressure, for undertaking the three-day "OD" program. Organization B, the university medical school, was feeling pressure from some elements of its environment, but its basic purpose and structure had remained relatively free from direct attack. Organization C (the small manufacturer of electronics components) was doing well in the marketplace and began their OD effort as an attempt to become even more adaptive. Organization D (the federal agency) was undergoing at least a nominal shift in its basic role, but the pace of this transition was largely under the agency's control. The training director who began the grid effort there saw it as essential to the change, but his successor appeared to give both the goal change and the development effort lower priorities. The original experimental region of organization E (the nationwide manufacturing-distribution firm) faced a relatively stable environment both within the corporation and without. However, the later regions faced a more unsettled internal and external environment, as corporate pressure for rapid implementation increased and market performance on the whole failed to meet expectations.

A somewhat obvious but nevertheless important notion begins to emerge from this brief analysis of OD efforts and environmental turbulence. It appears that some amount of real or potential environmental concern is necessary to provide energy for an OD effort but that the likelihood of maintaining an effective OD atmosphere decreases substantially as environmental conditions move toward severe turbulence. Risking even more criticism, we can argue that the OD effort in organization A was simply "underenergized"—that the mild pressure at the corporate level provided only enough fuel to get the top group through the three-day program. There was more than enough present and potential turbulence in organization A's internal and external environments to stimulate a major development effort, but the nature of the organization's sensing devices (the measures of performance applied), and the short-term role perspectives of the management group, allowed these environmental conditions to be kept out of sight. At the other end, the later OD efforts in organization E can be viewed as "overenergized" in terms of top-management pressure for rapid implementation, while at the same time underfueled in terms of supporting resources and a willingness to confront and follow up on suggested changes. Only in Organization C (the electronics firm) was the consultant able to "manage" the energy level—sustaining development efforts and accomplishments without allowing the system (or part of it, the production department in that case) to "run away."

On closer analysis, this notion of the need to energize without "flooding" an OD effort fits neatly with the basic learning concepts associated with T-group efforts and carried over into the general OD learning model. If you recall, the Lewinian change model called for unfreezing, changing, and refreezing attitudes and behaviors. Unfreezing, the provision of disconfirming evidence, can be related to perceptions that there are environmental demands for changes in the organization. Thus, *unfreezing* in the T-group energizes the individual to experiment with new behaviors, just as some environmental turbulence may energize the management of an organization to experiment with changes. At the same time, T-group advocates recognized the need for change to occur in a generally *supportive* atmosphere. They were aware that overwhelming amounts of harsh, disconfirming evidence could produce dysfunctional reactions which would minimize learning or even result in undesirable changes. Thus, an effective T-group leader has the task of maintaining the energy for change within the group, while preventing it from running away—the same task successfully accomplished by the OD consultant in organization C.

OD EFFORTS, MAJOR STRUCTURAL CHANGE, AND GOAL REALIGNMENTS

Several reasons why OD efforts are not typically associated with rapid, major structural changes or shifts in goals, domains, markets, etc., are apparent from our discussion thus far. Our adjustment model suggests that these changes are most likely to be made under conditions of *reasonably* severe environmental turbulence. Crisis conditions appear to require immediate, dramatic response, thus working against the needs of the OD learning model. Further, rapid responses of this magnitude tend to use up the energy which might be available for a sustained development effort. (Recall our earlier examples, such as the Turner case, which saw supervisory training and management-development efforts submerged or abandoned during real or presumed crisis.) Certainly, if the threats *are in fact* immediate and severe, it is easy to argue that it is entirely appropriate to temporarily abandon or delay development efforts (just as I suspect it would generally be.considered good medical practice to repair severed arteries before beginning physical therapy). On the other hand, from the OD consultant's point of view, major structural and goal changes provide excellent opportunities for learning, for experimenting with new behaviors and approaches. However, if changes are large and the demand for rapid implementation excessive, the curriculum becomes impossible to manage and most learning opportunities are lost.

Major changes in process, structure, and goals can result from (or be associated with) OD efforts, but these are neither the targets of a successful effort nor its first products. Note that in organization C a number of process and interdepartmental role-relationship changes were being explored in the later stages of the effort, explorations which might well lead to major departmental and/or goal realignments. Through the efforts of the consultant, the management team was learning about the impacts of various actions on the entire sociotechnical system and was beginning to make behaviorally sound adjustments. The management-theory base for OD which they were exploring contained alternative structural and control mechanisms (see Chapters 5 and 6), and some members (the production supervisor in particular) were anxious to implement a number of these options which appeared to fit the needs of their internal and external environments. The consultant, however, was most concerned that the members of the organization explore fully the implications of any changes and that any changes be made with the full participation of all affected members. He was aware that no structural or goal changes could be expected to be permanent solutions and thus was more concerned that organization members learn about the *process* of change than with the adoption of some immediate alternative.

This analysis leads to a second, as yet unsupported, claim regarding the relationship between OD efforts and major revisions of structure and goals. A well-managed OD effort could lead to both an improved readiness for such revisions and an improved set of sensing mechanisms to determine the need for them. Readiness is enhanced by increased knowledge about the behavioral processes involved in the organization's sociotechnical system and the development of new skills in the application of participative approaches to planning and implementing changes. Perhaps equally important, process awareness leads to improved ability to identify the need for change. We have seen earlier that traditional structures and practices, because of their emphasis on stability and efficiency, tend to "deny" the existence of such demands until they reach crisis proportions. The development of process awareness, perhaps aided by formalized measurement and feedback devices, plus the general attitude that demands for change can be viewed as opportunities rather than threats, are possible outcomes of a successful OD program. Perhaps most important, an OD program which moves an organization toward a human resources concept of management's role tends to minimize routine supervisorial activities and to increase the search for "investment opportunities" for the organization's resources. For upper management, particularly, and for increasing numbers of lower-level members, this search is extended outward to the external environment.

THE "ULTIMATE" ORGANIZATIONAL ADJUSTMENT

If we follow the predictions and prescriptions of Bennis and others, the organization of the future will frequently be a temporary device designed to accomplish a limited objective and then to have its resources reassigned (reinvested) to other, more pressing environmental demands. One legitimate argument against OD (and human resources management approaches in general) is that organization members tend to become "attached" to the system. A well-managed organization may well fulfill more needs than the nonwork experiences of many members and may thus make them reluctant to give up any aspect of their organizational situation. This has already proved something of a problem in some

organizations where temporary project groups frequently try to perpetu-
ate their existence beyond the life of the project. This concern is both a
testimony to the efficacy of these concepts and a warning against
half-hearted application—the creation of pocket utopias which will be the
basis for invidious comparison!

Two needs must be met if organizational members are to be willing to
"self-destruct" satisfying work arrangements in the face of shifting task
requirements. First, members must have been fully involved in the
planning of the work arrangements and thereby be aware of process
requirements and task commitments. Second, and probably more important, members must have assurance that their resources will be
reinvested in another rewarding work arrangement. A successful OD
effort could build the sort of mutual confidence, and awareness of process
needs, necessary to allow the voluntary abandonment of satisfying
temporary structures. This places a heavy burden on management to
continually monitor the environment for investment opportunities for the
organization's human resources and to be adept at creating, or facilitating
the creation of, a variety of challenging work arrangements—but that is in
fact management's designated role in the human resources approach.

A related concern is that OD concepts, by emphasizing a nonevaluative role for the consultant, may lead to development attempts in systems
which might actually be better off if they were simply allowed to die.
What this concern appears to imply is that some sort of organizational
euthanasia may be desirable. A logical argument can be built for this
notion. Certainly most of us are aware of some systems which appear to
be good candidates for a "mercy killing," or which at least do not appear
to warrant further investment of resources to maintain their marginal
existence. However, both the morality of this suggestion and its practical
implications are questionable. Who is to make the decision, and on what
basis, that a given organization is not worth "saving"—that its human
resources are beyond reinvestment? It seems unlikely that "dying"
systems will have either the insight or the resources to employ development aid, but if they should, is it the consultant's role to evaluate the
organization's chances and refuse to work with it? Resurrection, as
Herzberg is fond of noting, is more difficult than giving birth, but there are
too many notable instances of amazing recovery to flippantly argue that
rational decisions of this sort can and should be made.

CONCLUDING REMARKS

The model developed here suggests some logical linkages between
environmental conditions and types of organizational adjustment. It
seems highly logical that organizations whose goals, products, services,

etc., are out of line with their environment's needs will give this issue first priority. At the same time, most of us have anecdotal evidence of situations in which management appeared to be giving its time and attention to minor procedural and policy issues while ignoring imminent disaster. Similarly, our model portrays major structural changes as appropriate adjustments to severe misalignments with environmental conditions. Again, however, anecdotal evidence abounds of organizations clinging to antiquated structures long beyond their usefulness or making frequent major structural adjustments on what appear to be whimsical bases. We have implied that it is one of the main goals of OD to help managers become more aware of the impact of their decisions and behaviors on the performance of the total system and thus to become less-likely victims of over- or underreaction.

We have noted that OD efforts usually do not begin with or lead immediately to major structural or goal realignments. This is not because current OD concepts are opposed to structural adjustments or unconcerned about financial needs or changes in product or service requirements. Rather, this occurs (1) because OD efforts are usually not undertaken by organizations with immediate needs for radical therapy, and (2) because OD concepts view major structural and goal decisions as being best made when the system is capable of analyzing and considering their full implications—and willing to do so.

It can be and is argued that structural changes will by themselves induce changed behaviors and that therefore these should receive first attention in research and practice. I think they do deserve high priority, and, as we have noted, some OD efforts can be appropriately criticized for focusing on interpersonal problems which may well be inevitable consequences of existing structures and role relationships. Nevertheless, these do not seem to be sufficient arguments to justify reliance on traditional "syndicate model" consultation or applications of behavioral science findings—where "experts" analyze and prescribe structural changes. Instead, it seems more in keeping with modern concepts to develop the system's (its members') own capacities to identify needs and make appropriate changes.

BIBLIOGRAPHY

Bennis, Warren, *Beyond Bureaucracy* (New York: McGraw-Hill, 1966), chaps. 1 and 2.

Lawrence, Paul R. and Jay W. Lorsch, *Organization and Environment* (Homewood, Ill.: Irwin, 1969).

McWhinney, William H., "Organizational Form, Decision Modalities and the Environment," *Human Relations*, vol. 21, pp. 269–281 (August 1968).

Chapter 14

Some Concluding Comments and Speculations

Authors are wont at the end of a book to return to the beginning. Conscience dictates that the god of continuity, so frequently and joyfully abandoned in middle chapters, must be ceremoniously reinstated. Bowing to this need, I recall for your attention and mine the general conceptual model we constructed and discussed in Chapter 2.

THE GENERAL FRAMEWORK

We have attempted, more or less successfully, to operate within the framework illustrated in Figure 14-1. We began by noting that one way of conceptualizing the managerial function was by creating an effective and efficient integration of organizational and human characteristics. We pointed out that both organizational variables (goals, technology, structure, etc.) and human variables (capabilities, attitudes, needs, etc.) were linked directly to the organization's environment and thus were constantly vulnerable to change. Effective and efficient management, therefore, is

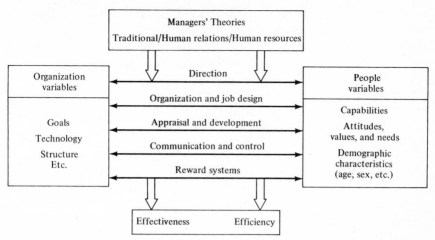

Figure 14-1 Managers' theories as a factor influencing choice of integrative mechanisms

necessarily adaptive—creating, revising, and modifying integrative arrangements in response to changes in organizational and human characteristics. Further, we argued that managerial decisions with regard to job and system design, the structure and function of information and control systems, the nature of rewards and their distribution, the kind and amount of participation in decision making, etc., were among the more crucial factors involved in arriving at integrative (or, perhaps, disintegrative) arrangements of human and organizational variables. Rather obviously, as illustrated in the shape of the model (and our discussion), managers' choices of behaviors and mechanisms along these dimensions, i.e., job and control design, decision-making style, etc., ought to be responsive to human and organizational characteristics. Not so obvious, perhaps even after our discussion, is that choices along these several dimensions are interrelated—e.g., the decision-making style adopted ought to be complemented by the design of the control and reward systems. Our final introductory observation concerned the important role which managers' own theories and philosophies played, both in filtering their perceptions of environmental demands and response options and in shaping their choices among the perceived alternative behaviors and mechanisms.

Managers' Theories

Moving from introduction to analysis, in Chapter 3 we examined the evolution of managerial theories and philosophies. We discovered that, viewed through the wide-range lens of historical hindsight, managerial thought did in fact appear to reflect environmental demands and, to some extent at least, organizational and human characteristics. In the early part of the century, as our private and public organizational complex was being constructed and set in full motion, the manager's role was viewed as that of a controller and rationalizer of a sizable machine whose task was clear and whose prime need was the careful articulation of its physical resources.

A modification of the manager's role was born in the second quarter of the century and reached maturity at its midpoint, parented by the growth of turbulence in the organization's internal environment. The organizational machine was constructed and now required maintenance in the form of some minor, belated form of recognition of member needs for belonging. The manager was still viewed as a controller, and whereas the goals of the machine remained clear, its complex demands for coordination and nurture were recognized—the manager must not only guide the machine but must use participative devices and interpersonal skills to control friction among its parts.

Finally, we saw that in the last decade or so, a third conceptualization has emerged. This view began with the argument that most organizations, even those employing good human relations practices, were wasteful of both the capabilities and commitments of many of their members and that these wasted resources were also frequent sources of *internal* problems. This argument was subsequently linked to the recognition of growing turbulence in the external environments of many organizations which demanded the full and creative use of their human resources. This conceptualization required a major rethinking of the manager's role. Now his function was viewed not so much as that of a controller (no matter how warm and humane his approach) as it was that of a facilitator—a developer of human resources and creator of opportunities in which these resources could be invested.

Implications of Roles

In Chapters 4 through 8, we explored the operation of these three conceptualizations of the basic role of management under varying environmental conditions—the implications of each for organization and job design, communications and control systems, leadership practices, and rewards. With frequent references to constructed case examples based on real situations, we traced out the impact of choices among alternative mechanisms and behaviors on these dimensions both on the sociotechnical system of the organization and on its relationship with its external environment.

From Theory to Practice

Finally, in the last few chapters, we have examined past and present approaches to the development of organizational members and the sociotechnical systems which, and in which, they operate. We discovered, not surprisingly, that the focus of training and development efforts, the techniques employed, and their explicit and/or implied objectives, are reflections of existing organizational and human characteristics, available behavioral science–management concepts and techniques, and environmental demands. Thus we argued that the current thrust—organization development—is responsive to the recognition that complex interdependencies within organizations require that the sociotechnical system as such must be the focus of development efforts; that development theory and techniques rest heavily on relatively modern experiential learning models; and that the (not always stated) objective of these efforts is the creation of adaptive, self-renewing systems capable of confronting performance barriers and applying their full resources to dynamic environmental demands.

SOME KEY POINTS REVISITED AND EXPANDED
Human Relations Is Alive and Well and Living in Most Organizations

Of key importance is the recognition that the "share of the market" held by each of our alternative managerial models is quite uneven. The overwhelming majority of American managers, my continuing survey research indicates, hold attitudes most closely aligned with human relations theory. Not surprisingly, then, my anecdotal evidence, drawn from extensive contact with a wide range of organizations each year, suggests that most sociotechnical systems operate with traditional structures, policies, and practices, laid over with a thin veneer of human relations modifications. Moreover, for a variety of reasons, this situation is entirely understandable.

First, as we have suggested, human relations has been broadly advocated in the managerial press for the past three decades and widely taught in college and university classrooms and in management and supervisory training programs. The human resources model, on the other hand, is of much more recent vintage and has really only been identified as a clearly separable model within the past ten years.

Second, the human relations model, we have argued, is a comfortable and comforting collection of concepts and prescriptions, promising to allow the manager to retain his role as controller of the system while minimizing conflict and gaining the compliance of a loyal, perhaps devoted group of subordinates. Put beside this, the human resources model, where it has been explicitly formulated, appears to demand continuous risk taking and even to promote confrontation and dissent.

Third, for many organizations in many areas, there are no clear-cut clues in their external environments that changes are required. Performance goals are either being met or else "lowered to conform with more reasonable expectations, given current conditions." These organizations are, by their own standards, effective, and their level of efficiency—the opportunity costs of alternative approaches—untested. Under these circumstances, the human resources model's call for the development and investment of the creative, adaptive, self-controlling capabilities of organizational members at all levels is rather easily ignored. No machinery exists for the utilization of these resources and the risk-taking necessary for their profitable investment is unappealing. Some of the organizations in this category are beginning to recognize growing internal dissension, but their concern then is simply to return to an earlier level of compliance, which seems to dictate additional applications of human relations techniques.

Fourth, human relations concepts and practices tend to prevail because many alternatives are underdeveloped and misunderstood. Traditional structures and processes, appended by human relations accessories, have enjoyed decades of development and refinement. Contrarily, the full implications of the human resources model in many areas, e.g., the design of control and reward systems, remain hazy and in large part untested. Even in the more developed areas, such as that of job design, human resources implications frequently appear to lack the concreteness and specificity of familiar industrial-engineering approaches.

An Unrecognized Complementarity

We suggested earlier that for many organizations clear-cut environmental evidence of a need for change is not apparent, at least to their controlling factions. What happens, however, when and if these demands are perceived? Their human relations orientation then tends to dictate responses that treat their social and technical systems as entirely divisible. Management's task, this approach holds, is to respond first to the problem of realigning technical processes to meet environmental demands and then to redesign roles and relationships, hopefully obtaining compliance with these changes from their membership. As the required changes become more frequent, however, management finds itself in a continuing process of retraining, reassigning, and redirecting, with growing levels of resistance. Further, while many organizations complain, probably legitimately, about the lack of system-specific skills, the overall capability of their human resources has probably increased as new, better educated, more sophisticated members have been added. However, new technical system designs, developed with little attention to available human needs and resources, may even reduce existing levels of autonomy and responsibility, with possible further increases in internal turmoil.

Thus, to many managers the problems created by growing turbulence in the external environment—the demand for higher standards, lower costs, adaptability, and flexibility—are simply compounded by what appear to be increasing demands for more responsible, meaningful, challenging work assignments, particularly among the younger members of their work force. However, while to the manager external and internal demands and dissensions appear to be simply additive, and, therefore, almost overwhelming, a logical, less-involved analyst might well see these "problems" as complementary. That is, he might view the current untapped human resources of the organization as the means of responding to the demands of the external environment, rather than as barriers to efficient responses. If the external environment is demanding more rapid, creative, and adaptive responses from the organization, it would seem logical to design sociotechnical systems which maximize rather than minimize opportunities for responsible, flexible behavior. It is not entirely Pollyanna-ish to imagine a joint solution to internal and external problems and demands. It is one thing, however, to imagine such a solution and quite another to accomplish it.

Managers, by and large, do not acknowledge the feasibility of "complementary" solutions. Where they respond to internal dissension with job and system redesign, they tend to do so out of respect (perhaps heartfelt) for the needs for "dignity from and satisfaction in work," not in the name of improved organizational responsiveness to external needs. It is more often than not implied that management is sacrificing preferred (and, thus, presumably more efficient) solutions to members' human needs. This is, of course, the sort of well-intentioned, unrecognized patronization that many women and minority-group members have found most galling and which may well exacerbate dissension among growing numbers of organizational members.

Managers, we have suggested, tend to respond as they do because they have been given a limited concept of the role of management and a limited repertoire of job and system designs. It is less easy to explain the response of many behavioral scientists to this dilemma. Among those interested in organizational behavior, low priority is frequently given to applied research (and low status to applied researchers), and this is then justified by the assertion that the sole task of behavioral science is that of understanding organizational processes rather than of devising improved mechanisms or working toward their implementation. Thus, managers tend to get the bulk of their advice from traditional consulting firms, which, by and large, have not yet stocked their solution kits with a full range of behaviorally sound structure, process, control, and reward-system designs. On the other hand, many behavioral scientists feel obligated to display for managers an eclectic array of concepts from which they (the managers) can choose their solutions. I have argued that this is a bit analogous to the doctor pointing to the medicine shelves and, after a confusing discussion of the efficacies and liabilities of each of the compounds, leaving the patient to select his remedy. It seems to me that the behavioral scientist does not have to choose between description and prescription, that the OD model provides a joint learning opportunity for both the behavioral scientist and the organization members while new approaches, appropriate to that situation, are being discovered and implemented. The half-life of edge-of-the-art knowledge in many fields is decreasing, and thus the defense that behavioral scientists must "wait until they know enough" (in an area where very little is ever known for sure) appears somewhat incongruous. The pace of change is such that the task of applying behavioral-science concepts to organizations may be a bit like that of painting a mural on the side of a charging elephant—it is hard to be precise, but unless the challenge is accepted quickly, no mark at all is made.

CONTINGENCY VERSUS UNIVERSALISM

With the above comments as backdrop, it is suitable here to consider directly the most recent thrust of conceptualization in the area of organizational behavior. The last several years have seen an intensified search for and glorification of "contingency" models, with corresponding indictments of "universalistic" prescriptions. A contingency model argues basically that "it depends." For example, advocates of this view might point to the finding that mechanistic structures appeared to operate effectively in stable environments, whereas more organic systems appeared to be warranted under turbulent conditions, as support for the contention that a contingency theory of organization design is essential. At the same time, contingency-model advocates might, for example, contend that descriptions of the requirements for effective leadership (such as group-oriented, participative decision making) fail to take into account individual and situational differences. There are actually few current examples of "universalistic" concepts, as most theorists give at least passing recognition to the need for situational modifications of whatever models they are advocating. Nevertheless, a few notions, such as the virtues of openness and confrontation as opposed to forcing or smoothing solutions to problem solving, are frequently advocated as applicable in virtually all organizational situations.

There is, of course, no doubt that the basic contingency model premise is correct—"it depends" *is* always an appropriate answer to any query about organizational behavior, and naïve universalistic prescriptions that do not provide for individual and situational differences deserve indictment. Despite basic soundness, however, contingency theories have two important real, or potential, limitations. First, contingency models, unless carefully constructed, tend not to have major impact on behavior. Practitioners tend to greedily accept the notion that every situation is different as justification for current practices. Second, to be operational, contingency models require certain core concepts and prescriptions which are then amenable to modification according to situational demands. In the absence of these, a separate model must be constructed for each different set of conditions (a limitless task). If the search for contingency models submerges the continuing search for synthesis and agreement on core concepts and directions, then behavioral-science theories of management and organizational behavior run the risk of becoming even more fragmented and impotent than they are at present.

To illustrate both of these limitations, consider the following two models of superior-subordinate relationships.

Contingency Model A

This model argues that, under certain conditions, autocratic decision making (the "tell and sell" approach) is appropriate and that, under other conditions, joint decision making (something akin to MBO) is appropriate. The manager is urged to evaluate his situation (time pressures, cost of mistakes, etc.) and the "readiness" of his subordinates (the way they view their jobs, their willingness to become involved, etc.) and then determine which approach to use.

Contingency Model B

This model argues that joint decision making tends to offer the best chance of tapping the full range of possible solutions and of maintaining informed member commitment. Joint decision making is thus the preferred model under all conditions, and the manager's task is that of creating a relationship with his subordinates which will endorse unilateral decision making on (1) routine issues of little concern to members, and (2) "real" crises which demand instant response (there are expected to be few, as most contingencies of this sort will have been covered in joint discussion). The manager is charged to work with each individual group member, and to move him or her to the highest level of joint planning (and subsequent self-control) of which that member is capable and which he or she desires.

Both these models are based on contingency concepts. The difference is that the second is built around a basic, unifying premise (prescription). Neither of these models is now, or ever can be, supported by uncontestable empirical evidence. Yet, in my judgment, the second model reflects far more accurately than the first the full range of modern behavioral-science knowledge and, because it establishes a preferred direction, has far better chance of actually influencing managerial behavior.

Expanding this example, it is obvious that I take the weight of all available evidence to be supportive of the human resources model, not as a universal solution to be immediately force-fit to all situations but as a basic conceptualization of the managerial role which provides a main thrust to be modified according to situational demands.

THE FUTURE: PROBLEMS AND PROMISES

Recent survey evidence suggests that managers in increasing numbers are beginning to give verbal support to human resources assumptions and concepts. This does not necessarily portend dramatic changes in their behavior or in the structure and process of organizations. If you recall, currently accepted human relations concepts took two decades or more to gain widespread acceptance as expected practice. And, as frequently suggested, actual practice of human resources concepts is far more demanding than their human relations counterparts. Moreover, shallow OD efforts have spread so rapidly that the dangers of an "innoculation" effect may be growing.

On the other side, a number of organizations which have moved fairly far into human resources practices are beginning to have problems, or at least are beginning to admit they are having problems. This, I think, is a most encouraging sign. The human resources model is fraught with problems, as is any other managerial approach. Human capabilities must be integrated with organizational characteristics, and whether this is unilaterally decided or jointly planned, mistakes will be made and changes demanded. The choice is never between structured versus nonstructured situations. The human resources model demands a structure clearly understood and contributed to by all members, a demand which is never fully or permanently met. Control is demanded under any approach—though it differs in both kind and degree under the human resources model—and control must always expect errors. Similarly, rewards must be constructed and dispensed, whether traditional, human relations, or human resources prescriptions are being followed, and this is never an easy task.

Thus, to imagine or imply that adopting the human resources approach provides a "solution" to continuing managerial problems is nonsensical and would be the best argument against its adoption. As suggested, the manager who begins to develop and invest his human resources is likely to find himself with a continuing and increasing set of demands for opportunities to use those resources. Similarly, the organization which structures self-controlling systems must be prepared for those systems to make mistakes. Organizational members at every level are vulnerable to planning errors, prejudice, and perverseness. Increasing evidence suggests the widespread ability to learn and develop in these areas, but first the opportunity to learn—and to make mistakes—must be available.

I have argued that many of our organizations are affluent enough in physical and capital resources to take some reasoned risks in experimentation with human resources concepts and practices. They are not yet at a point where dramatic realignments or adjustments are immediately demanded and prudent investments in development and restructure now could preclude or ease later crises. On a broader scale, I would argue that our society itself is at a similar point. We are affluent and moderately disturbed but not, as doomsayers cry, at cliff's edge. Again, the choice appears to be between continuing past and present practices (institutions, laws, procedures, etc.) and hoping that they will be adequate to deal with future crises, or else beginning now to experiment with well-paced redevelopment. At the societal level as well as at the organizational level, it seems clear that the mainstream demand is for changes which minimize repression and broaden opportunities for rewarding contribution.

Which direction are we taking—will we take? Both the societal- and organizational-level trends, if they exist, are difficult to interpret. At the organizational level, it does seem clear that our once-vast lead in managerial skill and system design is now being challenged. Twenty years ago, there was little to learn abroad. Today, human resources–oriented innovations in organizational practice in such places as Japan and Scandinavia, for example, are clearly worthy of study. Similarly, at the societal level there does appear to be a growing willingness to discount challenge and "enjoy what we've got." Certainly the ecologists' indictment of unlimited growth is sound and it may well be that our system is not and cannot operate at a level which would use our full human resources. Nevertheless, as minority groups are ready to testify, a no-growth policy may result in greater enjoyment for the haves, but it may also result in lessened opportunities for the have-nots. Again, we may be pressing against the limits of today's systems. If you recall, we discussed the dilemma of the organizational unit whose development efforts produced more capability and commitment than its task demanded. There the solution was for development of the total system. At the societal level, the solution may be analogous. There seem to be enough problems—challenges—throughout the world to go around. Thus, the managerial function at the societal level may also be that of creating, or capturing, challenging opportunities for the investment of our society's human resources in the solution of mankind's problems.

To avoid the risk of closing on a note which sounds as if I'm under thirty (I've characterized that age group as having an underdeveloped sense of humor and an overdeveloped sense of destiny), let me quickly state that I have no worldwide-systems' prescriptions at the ready. I do not believe, however, that they are beyond man's combined capabilities. My views are captured in a bit of recent statement-response graffiti adorning a Berkeley wall:

Mother Nature has to pick up after utopians.
True, but no trail at all is left by the tidy.